Rapid growth of selected Asian economies

Lessons and implications for
agriculture and food security

China and India

D1378210

REGIONAL OFFICE FOR ASIA AND THE PACIFIC

FOOD AND AGRICULTURE ORGANIZATION OF THE UNITED NATIONS

Bangkok, 2006

© FAO 2006

ISBN 92-5-105508-4
ISSN 1819-4591

For copies write to: Purushottam K. Mudbhary
                              Senior Policy Officer
                              Policy Assistance Branch
                              FAO Regional Office for Asia and the Pacific
                              Maliwan Mansion, 39 Phra Atit Road
                              Bangkok 10200
                              THAILAND
                              Tel: (+66) 2 697 4236
                              Fax: (+66) 2 697 4445
                              E-mail: Purushottam.Mudbhary@fao.org

Contents

PART I:

China's rapid economic growth and its implications for agriculture and food security in China and the rest of the world

PART II:

Indian agriculture and scenario for 2020

Contents

Foreword

Asia and the Pacific region is the most economically vibrant region in the world today, having achieved and maintained accelerated economic growth in recent decades. As a result, within one generation, many people in this region have escaped from the poverty trap. Ensuring an enabling policy and economic environment, supported by adequate investment and strengthened human and institutional capacities have fuelled this growth; advances in the agriculture and rural sectors have played their part and, in turn, they have benefited from good overall economic performance. Among recent trends, growth in China and India is noteworthy in terms of its sheer scale and the degree of regional and global impact that is being manifested at an increasing rate. In these two major countries, as in other Asian economies, the agriculture sector continues to play a pivotal role in almost all stages of development; smaller vibrant economies in the region, such as Thailand and Viet Nam have demonstrated how effectively they have made agricultural growth and trade contribute to reduction of poverty and food insecurity. Even in the Republic of Korea — regarded as a paragon of manufacturing-based export-led growth — agriculture has nevertheless played a crucial role in the initial stages of development.

Despite Asia still having the largest number of food-insecure people, the current trends of economic growth and agricultural performance indicate that the region stands a good chance of reaching the first Millennium Development Goal (MDG1) — halving the proportion of hungry people by 2015. However, achieving the World Food Summit (WFS) goal of halving the number of undernourished will require significant acceleration of hunger reduction efforts in the next ten years. Achievement of MDG1 and the WFS goal could be accelerated if the positive impacts of rapid growth in the larger economies are captured by other countries in the region, including in their own agriculture and rural development sectors. These sectors are an essential conduit for the benefits of economic growth to reach the less favourably placed segments of the population.

As a part of their mandate to analyse the driving forces of change in the region and the emerging policy assistance needs of member countries, the Regional Office for Asia and Pacific and the Policy Assistance Division of the Food and Agriculture Organization of the United Nations (FAO) launched a study to improve understanding of these major developments and their implications. In this context, they conceived and carried out a diagnostic study on *China, India and selected Asian economies: implications of rapid economic growth for agriculture and food security in Asia and Pacific Rim countries.* The study has been elaborated by national experts and covers the experience of five selected Asian countries — China, India, Republic of Korea, Thailand and Viet Nam. In the case of China and India, the study analyses their recent phenomenal growth and the implications for their own agriculture sectors and those of other countries, particularly in the region but also further afield. For the Republic of Korea, Thailand and Viet Nam, the study covers similar ground but draws particular attention to the lessons of experience from policies, institutional reforms and programmes implemented in these countries which might be of value to a wider regional audience.

Considering the recent volumes of literature on the strides made by China and India, the FAO case studies have not sought to duplicate the work of others but instead have drawn on them where appropriate, building further analysis and interpretation on existing knowledge. The studies help to gauge the existing and emerging impacts on countries in the region; in addition, the Chinese and Indian experience gives important insights into the major factors driving economic growth, highlights being the roles of the agriculture and non-agricultural sectors and the major policy and institutional changes that have facilitated agricultural growth, poverty reduction and food security. They also draw attention to crucial challenges to surmount if growth is to be sustained in these two countries.

The experiences of the Republic of Korea, Thailand and Viet Nam provide interesting examples of major success in economic transition and the accompanying evolution of agricultural development and food security. Although the countries differ in stages of development and in their historical contexts, initial conditions and economic systems, each has made significant strides in addressing poverty and food security by adopting policy and institutional measures tailored to specific contexts. Documentation of their experience is expected to provide relevant lessons to a number of countries that are presently grappling with similar issues, including the reduction of inter-sectoral disparity, adjustment of domestic policies in tune with the new rules of international trade and sustaining agricultural growth and rural development to eradicate poverty and hunger.

The results of the diagnostic study are presented in a set of three volumes. This second volume presents the country studies on China and India, which discuss agricultural development and economic growth and the implications of rapid growth in these countries for their own economies and those of other countries in the region and beyond. Volume 1 presented a synthesis of the experiences, lessons and implication derived from the five country studies supplemented by additional information from various published sources. Volume 3 presents the country studies on experiences and lessons from Republic of Korea, Thailand and Viet Nam.

We hope that readers, particularly those concerned with agricultural development policy, will find the diagnostic study interesting and useful in their work. This work needs to be addressed further and FAO invites other national and regional institutions that are active in analytical and policy fields to join forces for future endeavours.

He Changchui
Assistant Director-General and
Regional Representative for Asia and the Pacific
FAO

Mafa Chipeta
Director
Policy Assistance Division
FAO

Acknowledgements

The Regional Office for Asia and the Pacific and the Policy Assistance Division are pleased to express on behalf of FAO profound gratitude to the many senior officials of governments who collaborated with us in this work; to the authors of the national country studies and the resource persons and referees. We also take this opportunity to express our gratitude to the Government of Republic of Korea which funded the Seoul Workshop. Among its own staff, FAO acknowledges the leading role played by the Policy Assistance Branch for Asia and the Pacific in Bangkok, in particular Purushottam Mudbhary who organized and coordinated the preparation of country studies by the authors and inputs of resource persons and the workshop in Seoul, and Saifullah Syed, who launched the study and organized the first review workshop in Bangkok. Effective contributions from FAO headquarters involved many officers, and in particular Neela Gangadharan and Carlos Santana of the Policy Assistance Division.

The country studies in this volume are principally the work of national experts and their collaborators. The study for China was prepared by Jikun Huang, Director, and Jun Yang, Research Fellow, of the Center for Chinese Agricultural Policy, Chinese Academy of Sciences, and Scott Rozelle, Professor, Department of Agricultural and Resource Economics, University of California at Davis. The India study was prepared by Bibek Debroy, Secretary-General, PHD Chamber of Commerce and Industry, and Laveesh Bhandari, Director, Indicus Analytics.

Individual country studies benefited from the comments and suggestions received from senior government officials and resource persons who participated in the workshops in Bangkok (June 2005) and Seoul (December 2005), as listed in Appendices 1 and 2 of Volume 1, and referees who reviewed the draft country studies. This distinguished group included Ammar Siamwalla (Thailand); Arsenio Balisacan (Philippines); V.S. Vyas, Y.K. Alagh, S.S. Acharya and Rajiv Mehta (India); Debapriya Bhattacharya (Bangladesh); and Hari K. Upadhyaya (Nepal). The FAO team in Rome (Neela Gangadharan and Carlos Santana) and Bangkok (Purushottam Mudbhary) and Randy Barker, consultant, provided comments and suggestions on various drafts. Robin Leslie provided editorial assistance in the preparation of this volume.

PART I

China's rapid economic growth and
Its implications for agriculture and food security
in China and the rest of the world

Jikun Huang and Jun Yang
Center for Chinese Agricultural Policy
Chinese Academy of Sciences

Scott Rozelle
The University of California, Davis

Contents

Contents (*continued*)

Contents *(continued)*

Abbreviations and acronyms

ATC	Agreement on Textiles and Clothing
CAPSiM	Chinese Agricultural Policy Simulation Model
CBE	Commune and brigade enterprises
CCAP	Center for Chinese Agricultural Policy
CEEC	Central and Eastern European Countries
CGE	Computable general equilibrium
DRC	Development Research Center of State Council
Efta	European Free Trade Association
FAO	Food and Agriculture Organization of the United Nations
FBD	Five Balanced (or integrated) Developments
FDI	foreign direct investment
GATT	General Agreement on Tariffs and Trade
GDP	gross domestic product
GTAP	The Global Trade Analysis Project
HRS	Household responsibility system
IFPRI	International Food Policy Research Institute
IIASA	International Institute of Applied Systems Analysis
LEI	Agricultural Economics Research Institute of Northland
MDGs	Millennium Development Goals
MOFTEC	The Ministry of Foreign Trade and Cooperation
NAFTA	North American Free Trade Area
NDRC	National Development and Reform Commission
nec	not else classified
NSBC	National Statistical Bureau of China
OECD	Organisation for Economic Co-operation and Development
PPP	Purchasing price parity
R&D	Research and Development
RE	Rural enterprises
ROW	Rest of world
Sacu	Southern African Customs Union
SOE	State-owned enterprises
TFP	Total factor productivity
TRQ	Tariff-rate quotas
TVEs	Township and village enterprises
WFP	World Food Program
WHO	World Health Organization
WTO	World Trade Organization

Executive summary

A. Introduction

China's economy has experienced remarkable growth since economic reform initiated in 1979. The rapid economic growth has been associated with unprecedented progress in poverty alleviation. Based on China's official poverty line, the absolute level of poverty incidence fell from 33 percent in 1978 to less than 3 percent in 2004. Even based on World Bank's US$1/day (in PPP terms) poverty line, rural poverty incidence also fell from more than 30 percent in the early 1990s to about 8 percent in 2004.

While past accomplishments are impressive, there are still great challenges ahead. Income disparity rose with economic growth. There is also growing concern regarding the implications of China's rapid growth upon the rest of the world. The overall goals of this study are three-fold: 1) outline the main changes in agriculture, food security and rural development and policies that have been associated with overall economic growth; 2) extrapolate these trends in the future and assess the implications for internal food security; and 3) assess the implications of the overall rapid economic growth of China for sustainable food security and agricultural development in other countries, particularly in Asia with significant attention to the greater Pacific Rim.

B. China's economic growth and agricultural and rural development

Overall economic growth

Average annual growth rates of the GDP have reached nearly 10 percent in the past 25 years. In the early reform period (1979–1984), the household responsibility system (HRS) significantly increased agricultural productivity. Growth in agriculture provided a crucial foundation for the successful transformation of China's reform economy. Since the mid-1980s, rural township and village enterprises' (TVEs) development, measures to provide a better market environment through domestic market reform, fiscal and financial expansion, the devaluation of the exchange rate, trade liberalization, the expansion of special economic zones to attract foreign direct investment (FDI), state-owned enterprise (SOE) reform, higher agricultural prices and many other factors all have contributed to China's economic growth.

Rapid economic growth has been accompanied with significant structural changes in China's economy. Whereas agriculture accounted for more than 40 percent of the GDP in 1970, it fell to 15 percent in 2004. China's export (import) to the GDP ratio increased from less than 6 percent in 1980 to 36 percent (34 percent) in 2004. China also became the world's largest recipient of FDI in 2004.

Agricultural and rural development and food security

Average annual growth rates of agricultural GDP reached 4.5 percent from 1979 to 2004. In the meantime, China's agriculture has also undergone significant structural changes. The share of cropping in total agricultural output fell from 82 percent in 1970 to 51 percent in 2004. Within the crop sector, production has been shifting to more labour-intensive and higher-value crops.

A number of factors have simultaneously contributed to agricultural and rural development. These include the HRS that transferred the collective agricultural production system to individual farms by contracting land-use rights to individual rural households, technological change, price and marketing reforms, trade liberalization, irrigation expansion and creation of off-farm employment. By 2003 about half of China's rural labour force earned at least part of its income from off-farm jobs. Non-agricultural income has exceeded agricultural income since 2000.

1

Growth in production has substantially increased per capita food consumption in China. Per capita food availability per day rose from 1 717 kcal in the early 1960s to more than 3 000 kcal by the late 1990s. Access to food in rural China has also improved over time primarily through land that was equitably allocated to farmers, market infrastructure development and government disaster relief programmes as well as non-farm employment.

Impacts on poverty reduction

Overall economic growth has contributed to most of rural poverty reduction in China. During the past 20 years, a 1 percent increase in per capita GDP led on average to a 0.7 percent decline in rural poverty incidence. However, economic growth is an essential but not sufficient condition for nationwide poverty reduction. Given the same growth of GDP, a 1 percent increase of agricultural share in the GDP will lead to a nearly 1 percent drop of poverty incidence. Off-farm employment is also critically important for poverty reduction in China. Government investment in agriculture, rural infrastructure and rural TVE development is also important in this respect.

Challenges

While progress in agricultural and rural development has been notable, there are also many lessons to be learned and great challenges ahead. China's rapid economic growth has been accompanied by widening income inequality. In the agriculture sector, China may face major challenges in its war against water scarcity and increasing labour productivity. Trends in environmental degradation suggest that there may be considerable stress on the agricultural land base. Other environmental stresses are soil erosion, salinization, the loss of cultivated land and decline in land quality.

C. Prospects for China's economic growth in the future

China's growth environment is strongly conducive for its development despite the fact that there are some associated risks. The key forces that will favour China's economic growth in the future include macroeconomic stabilization, high domestic savings, an abundant and enormous pool of rural labour, increased spending in research and development (R&D), a rising trend in human capital, an improving market environment and governance, smooth urbanization, trade liberalization, a rising FDI and a national strategy to pursue "Five Balanced Development". There are also a number of factors that may limit China's economic growth over time. These include unexpected internal and external macroeconomic instability, a declining growth rate for the labour force, an increasing ageing population, a likely decline of the domestic saving rates in the long run, a diminishing natural resource base for rapid economic growth and intensification and sustainability of agricultural production in the coming decades.

Based on the overall evaluation of China's growth environment in the next two decades, our baseline scenario projects that the average annual growth of China's GDP will be about 8.9 percent from 2001 to 2005, 8 percent from 2006 to 2010 and 6 to 7 percent in the following decade. With these growth rates, by 2020 China's per capita GDP (about US$3 400) will approach the average income of the high-to-middle income countries (in 2000). Total GDP in 2020 will be 4.3 times as large as that in 2000, making China the third largest economy in the world (just behind the United States and Japan).

D. Domestic implications of China's rapid economic growth

The five major domestic implications of China's rapid economic growth are summarized here. 1) China will play an even greater role in the global economy. By 2020, China will emerge as the second largest importer and exporter in world. Continuously seeking a favourable external trade and political environment is one of the most important factors for China's sustainable economic growth. 2) Given China's commitments to agricultural and rural development it is likely that China's rapid economic growth will threaten neither its own food security nor food security in the rest of the world; instead it may enhance both China's and the world's food supply. 3) China needs to continue restructuring its agricultural sector as the economy moves towards globalization. China has a comparative advantage in horticulture, pork, poultry, fish and processed foods, and the export of these commodities will increase in the next two decades. To reap the opportunities resulting from trade liberalization, China needs to continue creating a favourable development environment so that agriculture will undergo a successful restructuring. 4) While rapid economic growth under trade liberalization will facilitate China's agriculture to shift towards sectors in which it has greater comparative advantage, the impacts may differ among farmers. Not every farmer in every region can respond appropriately to trade liberalization. The degree and speed of adjustment will vary among regions as well as farmers within the region. Farmers in many less-developed provinces in the west and north may not gain from trade liberalization. Last but not least, China's rapid economic growth under globalization will have more substantial implications on its non-agricultural sectors. China has a stronger comparative advantage in many non-agricultural sectors, in particular textiles, apparel and labour-intensive manufacturing.

E. International implications of China's rapid economic growth

China's rapid economic growth will provide both opportunities and challenges for the rest of the world. Overall, the opportunities are projected to far surpass the challenges. 1) China will significantly increase its imports of many land-intensive agricultural commodities (e.g. oilseed, feed, sugar and cotton) and also some labour-intensive products (e.g. tropical and subtropical fruits, processed foods, some pig and poultry parts). Increasing imports of these agricultural and food products will provide opportunities for many developing countries in South and Central America and some developed countries (e.g. the United States, Canada and Australia) to expand their production. 2) China's rapid economic growth will not be associated with a rise in the imports of rice and wheat, as the only major cereal that will experience a growth in import is maize used as feed. These results imply that China's rapid growth is unlikely to threaten the overall world staple food supply and rising staple food prices in the world market. 3) China's exports of many horticultural products and processed foods will rise over time. The rising exports of these commodities in which China has a comparative advantage will challenge those countries that are exporting the same commodities to world markets. 4) China will become more competitive in the textile and apparel sectors. This will have significant implications for many developing countries (e.g. India and other South Asian countries) that are currently exporting these products. Last but not least, China will significantly increase its imports of natural resource products. However, our simulation also shows that the rise in productivity and efficiency in the use of natural resources will considerably reduce imports of natural resource products.

F. Concluding remarks

Developing economies have to recognize the importance of both domestic and external policies in achieving sustainable growth. China's rapid growth would not have been possible without its domestic economic reforms, macroeconomic stability and its "open-door" policy. China's experience also shows that institutional innovation, technological changes, market reform and infrastructure development are critical to agricultural growth and the improvement of the nation's food security. While overall economic growth is a primary and essential condition for mass poverty reduction, the nature of growth, particularly agricultural growth in the initial stage of economic take off and non-farm employment during industrialization are other important factors shaping the trends in China's poverty reduction. Successful growth in the agriculture sector facilitates the economic transition from agriculture to industry/service, and from rural to urban economy.

While there are a number of challenges related to economic growth and income inequity, we are still optimistic regarding China's development in the future. China has been making significant efforts to balance its economic growth and income inequality. With increasing dependence on the external sector, China has been developing and may need more effort to enhance its long-term partnership with all trade partners.

Although China will not threaten world food security and domestic production will continue to grow and meet the increasing demand for most food and agricultural products, China may require more efforts to enhance its agriculture and rural sectors as well as non-farm employment of rural labour so that the rural/urban income disparity will not increase further. The efforts include but are not limited to: (i) investment in agricultural and rural infrastructure; (ii) investment in rural education; (iii) creating better R&D and a technology innovation system; (iv) supporting institutions related to farmers' associations and marketing; (v) sustainable use of limited water resources; (vi) avoiding environmental degradation related to the agricultural land base; (vii) improving the quality of all agricultural products and the ability to effectively implement and regulate quality standards to meet increasing demand from own domestic consumers and better compliance with international standards.

Our analyses also show that China's rapid economic growth will provide more opportunities than challenges to the rest of the world, and overall the rest of the world will gain from China's economic expansion; however this general conclusion may not hold for some countries. The rapid growth of China's economy will help those countries with a comparative advantage in many land-intensive products to expand their production and increase their exports to China. Developing countries can export agricultural products to China, particularly soybeans, other oilseed, maize, cotton, sugar, tropical and subtropical fruits, as well as some livestock products (e.g. milk, beef, mutton), although they have to compete with other exporters from developed countries such as the United States, Canada and Australia. While many other changes associated with China's economic growth are not analysed in this study, we believe that there are also more opportunities than challenges as the Chinese economy develops. The examples include but are not limited to education, international tourism, China's agricultural technology and China's capital investment in other countries.

1. Introduction

China's economy has experienced remarkable growth since economic reforms were initiated in 1979. Although there is a cyclical growth pattern, China's economy has outperformed almost all other countries in Asia and has been one of the fastest growing countries in the world since 1980 (World Bank 2002). The annual average growth rate of the GDP reached nearly 10 percent in the past two decades (NSBC 2004). The real GDP in 2004 was 10.3 times that in 1978. This growth is for an economy with 1.3 billion people (or more than 20 percent of world population) in 2004.

China's rapid economic growth has been associated with unprecedented progress in poverty alleviation and material well-being. In the past two-and-half decades, based on China's official poverty line, more than 230 million Chinese rural residents have escaped poverty, and the absolute level of poverty fell from 260 million in 1978 to less than 30 million in 2003 (NSBC 2004). The incidence of rural poverty has fallen equally fast, plunging from 32.9 percent in 1978 to less than 3 percent in 2003 (Figure 1).

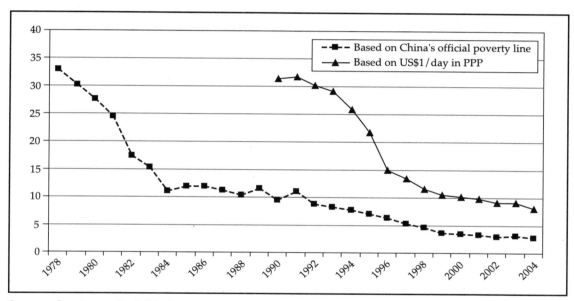

Source: See Appendix Table 1.

Figure 1. Poverty incidence (%) in rural China, 1978–2004

Food security, one of the central issues of concern to policy-makers in China, has also improved significantly since the late 1970s. At the national level, in contrast to many earlier analysts who expected that China would put pressure on world food security in the course of the rapid industrialization and liberalization of its economy, net food import growth has not occurred. In fact, even after more than 25 years of reform and rapid growth, China has continued to be a net exporter of food. In the meantime availability of food has increased significantly over time (NSBC 1995–2005). At the microlevel, China also has made remarkable progress in improving household food security and reducing the incidence of malnutrition during the past two decades. According to a publication by FAO (2002), the number of people who suffered from any sort of malnutrition in China declined from 193 million in 1990/1992 to 116 million in 1997/1999, or from 16 percent to 9 percent in total population.

The rapid growth has also been accompanied by significant structural changes in the economy. Rising income together with urbanization and other dynamics of the economy have resulted in major changes in demand and consumption patterns (Huang and Bouis 1996; Fan *et al.* 1995; Huang and Rozelle 1998), which have formed part of the driving force that stimulated the structural changes in the economy. Agricultural share in total economic output had declined from about 40 percent in 1970 and 30 percent in 1980 to 15 percent in 2004 (NSBC 2005), while the share of services has risen over time. Within the agriculture sector, considerable structural adjustments have also been observed as a result of changes in the pattern of food consumption.

While past accomplishments are impressive, there are still major challenges ahead. Income disparity, for example, rose with the economic growth. There are significant income disparities among regions, between urban and rural, and among households within the same location (Cai *et al.* 2002; World Bank 2002). Although the average annual growth rate of China's agriculture sector was much higher than population growth in the reform period, high input levels in many areas of China and diminishing marginal returns mean that increasing inputs will not provide large increases in output. In the future, many have predicted that almost all gains will have to come from new technologies that could significantly improve agricultural productivity (Fan and Pardey 1997; Huang *et al.* 2003a; Huang *et al.* 2002).

Trade liberalization might further challenge China's agricultural and rural economy. Debates on the impact of the World Trade Organization (WTO) on China's agriculture continue. Some argue that the impact of trade liberalization on China's agriculture will be substantial, adversely affecting hundreds of millions of farmers (Carter and Estrin 2001; Li *et al.* 1999). Others believe that, although some impacts will be negative and even severe in specific areas, the overall effect of accession to agriculture will be modest (Anderson *et al.* 2004; van Tongeren and Huang 2004; Martin 2002).

There is also concern regarding the implication of China's rapid economic growth on the rest of the world. Many perceive that China's economic growth and its transformation will have profound effects, not just for its own people but also for many others further afield. Such effects could be a combination of new market opportunities arising from enhanced purchasing power, and the greater competitiveness of China's economy as a producer of selected products. However, few studies have been found in the literature.

In exploring what the growth of China's economy might mean for China and the rest of the world, it is worth observing that China has a large agriculture sector. The performance in this sector is of great significance for future policies and strategies to achieve the Millennium Development Goals (MDGs), sustainable food security, agricultural and overall socio-economic development. First of all, China offers hope for a significant reduction in the overall numbers of the poor in the world despite the fact that even in the country poverty is entrenched in certain areas owing to various factors. Reduction in poverty in China would dramatically change the global numbers of the poor.

It is clear that rising income in China will in the first place create pressure for structural reform of its domestic agriculture/rural development and food sectors to cope with changing demand size and evolving consumer tastes. It is necessary to have a full understanding of the internal sectoral adjustments: Only with this knowledge is it sensible to assess the extent to which China will need external supplies to meet needs (due to domestic incapacity to cope or to compete) or will generate new surpluses directed at other countries. These sectoral adjustments are expected to also be significant in terms of the impact they are likely to have on other countries in Asia and around the world through trade and commerce both in terms of opportunities as markets and as exporters.

It is also expected that the continued growth of China will significantly affect the balance and direction of trade, trading opportunities and the degree to which the playing field is leveled for smaller countries abroad. It will call for timely diagnosis of the growth pattern in China so as to put policies in place to optimize gains and minimize losses and marginalization.

In sum, the rapid development of China has implications for its own policy-makers, as well as for policy-makers from other countries. In terms of domestic policy debates in China, the issues of importance remain rural poverty and farmer income, food security and safety, natural resource management, the environment and sustainability of the resource base. The overall goals of this study are to:

- Outline the main changes in agriculture, food security and rural development, including non-farm rural income opportunities that have been associated with overall economic growth and document the main policies and strategies that led to them;

- Extrapolate these trends in the future and assess the implications for internal food security;

- Assess the implications of the overall rapid economic growth of China for sustainable food security, agriculture and rural development in other countries, particularly in Asia but with significant attention also to the greater Pacific Rim.

Section 2 provides an overview of China's economic performance and agricultural and rural development in the context of economic growth, particularly with regard to major internal adjustments, past and ongoing, to cope with changes. Key development policies, strategies and institutional changes that have been associated with economic development are also discussed. Section 3 discusses the prospects for China's economic growth in the future. The major issues covered in this section include the national development plan, key driving forces and constraints to economic growth and the economic growth prospectus. Section 4 assesses the implications of rising income and technological changes on domestic demand, supply and trade of major agricultural products in the future. Section 5 assesses rapid economic growth and its impacts on future demand, supply and trade of major agricultural products in the rest of the world, with analysis of opportunities and challenges it poses to other countries, particularly in the Pacific Rim. The final section concludes the study with policy implications on sustainable food security, agriculture, rural development and natural resource management for both China and other developing countries, particularly for those countries in the Asia–Pacific Rim. Methodology applied in the impact analysis, data improvement and alternative economic growth scenarios that are used in this study are provided in Appendix 1.

2. Retrospective of China's economy and agricultural and rural development

2.1 Overall economic growth

China's leaders have implemented various reform measures that have gradually liberalized the institutional and market structure of the economy. Although there is a cyclical pattern in China's growth rates (Figure 2), China's economy has outperformed almost all other countries in Asia and has had one of the fastest growth rates in the world since 1980 (World Bank 2002).

In the early reform period, annual growth rates of the GDP increased considerably from 4.9 percent from 1970 to 1978 to 8.8 percent from 1979 to 1984 (Table 1). High growth was recorded in all sectors. Institutional reform that transferred collective agricultural production to individual household production was the main source of agricultural growth in the early reform period (Lin 1992; Huang and Rozelle 1996). The growth of agriculture provided the foundation for the successful transformation of China's reform economy (Perkins 1994). In the meantime, rising income in the initial years of reform stimulated domestic demand, and the high savings rate also was appropriately transferred into physical capital investments in non-agricultural sectors in both rural and urban areas, which led to annual growth rates of 8.2 percent in industrial GDP and 11.6 percent in services (Table 1). During this same period, as family planning effectively lowered the nation's population growth rate, the high economic growth also implied high per capita GDP growth. The annual growth rate of

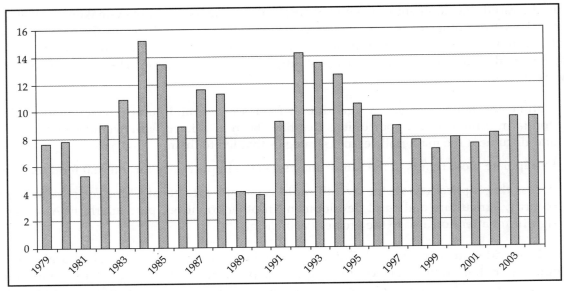

Source: NSBC (1990–2005).

Figure 2. Annual growth rate (%) of GDP, 1979–2004

Table 1. The annual growth rates (%) of China's economy, 1970–2004

	Pre-reform 1970–1978	Reform period			
		1979–1984	1985–1995	1996–2000	2001–2004
GDP	4.9	8.8	9.7	8.2	8.7
Agriculture	2.7	7.1	4.0	3.4	3.4
Industry	6.8	8.2	12.8	9.6	10.6
Services	Na	11.6	9.7	8.3	8.3
Foreign trade	20.5	14.3	15.2	9.8	25.8
Import	–	12.7	13.4	9.5	26.7
Export	–	15.9	17.2	10.1	25.0
Population	1.80	1.40	1.37	0.91	0.63
Per capita GDP	3.1	7.4	8.3	7.2	8.1

Note: Figure for the GDP (in real terms) from 1970 to 1978 is the growth rate of national income in real terms. Growth rates are computed using the regression method.

Source: NSBC, *Statistical yearbook of China.*

per capita GDP more than doubled between the pre-reform period, 1970–1978 (3.1 percent) and 1979–1984 (7.4 percent).

After reaching its peak growth in 1984 (15 percent), the pattern of rapid economic growth continued into the late 1980s (Figure 2) as economic reform had been gradually expanded from agricultural to non-agricultural sectors (Figure 2). In this period, instead of merely depending on urban sector expansion and reforming China's existing state-owned enterprises (SOEs), local leaders mobilized various resources (e.g. capital and labour) to develop rural township and village enterprises (TVEs). TVEs took off after the mid-1980s. In the meantime, management and incentive reforms and gradual structural changes in the urban economy, in response to demand changes under a more liberalized economy, also contributed to China's economic expansion. Capital formulation as a percentage of the GDP increased from about 32 percent from 1981 to 1982 to more than 38 percent from 1985 to 1986 (NSBC 2004). In fact, growth might have been too fast in the first few years after the mid-1980s.

In the late 1980s, in response to an overheated economy and unprecedented inflation rates, China's leaders were forced to adopt a set of stringent contractional macroeconomic policies (Naughton 1995). As a consequence, after China experienced two years of high inflation, economic growth slowed sharply from 1989 to 1990. The annual growth rate of GDP from 1989 to 1990 was about 4 percent only, the lowest rate over the entire reform period. After the brief slowdown period, the government responded promptly and implemented a series of policy measures to increase both domestic private and public investments as well as FDI. Policies to restimulate the economy included providing a better market environment for private sector development, fiscal and financial expansion, the devaluation of the exchange rate, trade liberalization and the expansion of special economic zones and higher agricultural prices (World Bank 1997). The economy quickly rebounded and the annual growth rate of the GDP accelerated to 14 percent in 1992 and maintained rates of 10 to 13 percent in the mid-1990s (1993–1996 — Figure 2). When the economy was growing at its top speed during the mid-1990s, inflation rates rose again.

Because the economy was growing rapidly, inflation was high in the mid-1990s. In order to avoid a repeat of the economic slowdown that occurred in the late 1980s, China's leaders implemented a range of measures aimed at achieving a soft landing (Zhu and Brandt 2001). As before, financial and credit policies were tightened. Administrative controls over new investments also were implemented. To keep the economy from stagnating too much, leaders increased urban wages, invested heavily in rural and urban infrastructure in an attempt to counterbalance the contractional measures. The growth decelerated gradually, but unlike the late 1980s, it only slowed marginally. During the late 1990s, economic growth remained high, more than 8 percent annually (Table 1 and Figure 2).

It is worth noting that despite the Asian financial crisis, an average annual growth rate of 8.2 percent from 1996 to 2000, was still remarkable (Table 1). China was able to keep the crisis from spreading into it borders, in part as a consequence of the more insulated nature of its financial sector. In addition, since the size of its domestic capital market was so large, China was better able to weather the international financial crisis. During this time also, its growth rates were among the highest in the world (NSBC 2002).

Moreover, in contrast to the stagnation of growth in the rest of the world, China's economic growth has been accelerated since the beginning of the twenty-first century. Annual GDP growth rose from 7.3 percent in 2001 to 9.5 percent in both 2003 and 2004 (Figure 2), with average growth rate of 8.7 percent from 2001 to 2005 (Table 1). It is projected that the growth rate will reach more than 9 percent in 2005, which implies that the size of China's economy will be 11 times as large as that in 1978 when China started to reform its economy.

2.2 Structural changes in China's economy

2.2.1 Overall change in economic structure

Rapid economic growth has been accompanied by significant structural changes in China's economy. Whereas agriculture accounted for more than 40 percent of the GDP in 1970, it fell to 30 percent in 1980, 20 percent in 1995 and only 15 percent in 2004 (Table 2). After a period of peaks and troughs of industrial share in the national GDP from 1970 to 1985, the share gradually started to increase after the late 1980s, rising from 42 percent in 1990 to 53 percent in 2004. In contrast to agriculture, the service sector has expanded rapidly. The share of the service sector in the national GDP increased from 13 percent in 1970 to 21 percent in 1980 and 32 percent in 2004 (Table 1). This trend is expected to persist in the coming years as China will continue to promote its structural adjustment policies and economic reforms in response to domestic demand and external trade pattern changes in the coming years.

Table 2. Changes in structure (%) of China's economy, 1970–2004

	1970	1980	1985	1990	1995	2000	2004
Share in GDP							
Agriculture	40	30	28	27	20	16	15
Industry	46	49	43	42	49	50	53
Services	13	21	29	31	31	33	32
Share in employment							
Agriculture	81	69	62	60	52	50	47
Industry	10	18	21	21	23	22	22
Services	9	13	17	19	25	28	31
Trade to GDP ratio	Na	12	23	30	40	44	70
Export/GDP	Na	6	9	16	21	23	36
Import/GDP	Na	6	14	14	19	21	34
Share in export							
Primary products	Na	50	51	26	14	10	7
Foods	Na	17	14	11	7	5	3
Share in import							
Primary products	Na	35	13	19	18	21	21
Foods	Na	15	4	6	5	2	2
Share of rural population	83	81	76	74	71	64	58

Source: National Statistical Bureau, *China statistical yearbook*, various issues; and *China rural statistical yearbook*, various issues.

Structural changes in economy have also been substantial in employment patterns. The share of employment accounted for by the industrial sector doubled from 1970 to 1985 and has remained at about 20 to 23 percent thereafter (row 5, Table 2). Employment share in the service sector had risen even more rapidly from 9 percent in 1970 to 19 percent in 1990 and 31 percent in 2004. Agriculture employed more than 80 percent of the nation's total labour force in 1970, which declined significantly to 60 percent in 1990 and less than 50 percent (including part-time agricultural labour) after 2000 (row 4, Table 2).

In rural areas, more than 40 percent of the labour force was employed in the non-agricultural sector in the late 1990s (deBrauw *et al.* 2002). Expanding non-agricultural employment has contributed substantially to the growth of farm household income since the late 1980s (Rozelle 1996). Non-agricultural farm household income exceeded agricultural income in 2000 for the first time and the share rose to 52.4 percent in 2004 (NSBC 2005).

There are many factors that have simultaneously contributed to China's structural changes in terms of economic compositions and employment. Rapid economic growth, urbanization (Huang and Bouis 1996), market liberalization (Lardy 1995; Huang and Rozelle 1998) and China's open-door policies (Branstetter and Lardy 2005), among many others, have significant impacts on consumption and demand (both internal and external) patterns. These, together with the rapid development of factor and output markets, largely explain the changes in China's economic structure in the past two to three decades (Brandt *et al.* 2005; Sonntag *et al.* 2005).

2.2.2 Demographic changes

During the three decades after 1950, China experienced an extraordinary population growth. Daunting prospects of feeding an ever-increasing population triggered the Chinese Government to enforce drastic population planning measures. At present, China's economic growth goes hand in hand with a rapid demographic transition process: Total fertility rates declined from 4.2 in the 1970s to below replacement level.

The factors fostering the fertility transition in China are largely attributable to the government's strict population policies and family planning programmes, as well as to profound socio-economic changes and massive urbanization trends. For the national total, the population increased from 552 million in 1950 to 830 million in 1970, which triggered China to start its family planning programmes. Since then the average annual growth rate of population has been falling from more than 2 percent from 1950 to 1970 to 1.8 percent from 1970 to 1978, and less than 1 percent after the late 1990s. By 2001 to 2004, the annual growth rate further fell to 0.63 percent only (Table 1).

After a long period of slow expansion of the urban economy, China's urbanization has started to take off. In contrast to rapid industrialization, due to urban–rural segmenting of institutional regulations, China's urbanization had proceeded rather slowly before 1980s. The rural population remained at about 81 to 83 percent in the 1970s (last row, Table 2). However, the process of urbanization has taken off and has been considered to have mighty potential for economic development since the mid-1990s. By 2004, the urban population accounted for 43 percent of the total population. It is anticipated that urbanization will accelerate in the next few decades thus making significant contributions to economic growth and further stimulating structural changes in China's economy.

2.2.3 More open economy

Rapid economic growth has also been associated with remarkable changes in China's international trade. Throughout the reform era, foreign trade has been expanding even more rapidly than the GDP. Annual growth rates of foreign trade reached nearly 15 percent in both the 1980s and the early 1990s (Table 1). China's foreign trade growth rate still grew at nearly 10 percent annually between 1996 and 2000 when the Asian and world economies were hit by the Asian economic crisis. After China's WTO accession, the growth of both imports and exports has been tremendous. The average annual growth rate of trade reached about 26 percent from 2001 to 2004 (Table 1).

With the rapid growth of China's external sector, foreign trade has been playing an increasing role in the national economy since the beginning of the reforms. China's export to GDP ratio increased from less than 6 percent in 1980 to 21 percent in 2001 and further to 36 percent in 2004 (row 8, Table 1). Over the same period, the import to GDP ratio also increased from 6 percent to 21 percent and 34 percent. These ratios indicate that China is ranked as one of the most open economies in the world.

China became the world's largest recipient of FDI in 2004. FDI inflows into China increased rapidly after 1979, and particularly since the early 1990s (Figure 3). It is worth noting that China has also begun to invest its capital overseas. China's FDI in other countries has increased significantly since the late 1990s though starting from a very low level. In 2003, China recorded US$2.85 billion investment in the rest of the world, which nearly doubled to US$5.5 billion in 2004.

The rapid expansion of China's external economy is largely explained by China's long-term development strategy to open its economy. Prior to economic reform, China adopted a highly centralized and planned foreign trade regime (Lardy 2001). Foreign trade rights were granted by the Ministry of Foreign Trade to only 12 SOEs or corporations with strictly state foreign trade plans. This system, however, has been substantially decentralized by granting more corporations or firms direct foreign trading rights. The number of trade firms rose to more than 2 200 in the initial period of reform (1980–1987, Huang and Chen 1999). By 2001 the government had granted trade rights to 35 000 firms, most being private trade corporations or production firms (Branstetter and Lardy 2005).

Significant reductions of export subsidy and import tariff have also occurred since the late 1980s. Because of the distorted domestic pricing system, the export subsidies were a common phenomenon

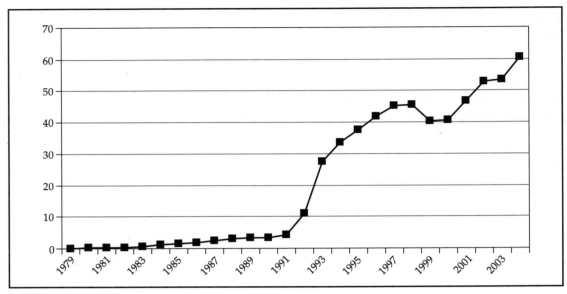

Source: NSBC (1990–2005).

Figure 3. Inward FDI in China (US$ billion), 1979–2004

under the planned foreign trade regime. The first effort to curb the rising trend of the subsidy was initiated in 1987 when China fixed its export subsidy for 1988 to 1990 to a level equal to about 4 percent of the total export value. By 1991, all export subsidies were phased out though China occasionally applied them for specific products (e.g. maize and cotton) to avoid a large fall of domestic prices before China's WTO accession (Huang *et al.* 2004). Reduction of import tariff has also been remarkable. China's average tariff was as high as 56 percent in the early 1980s, which was gradually reduced to 47 percent in 1991, 23 percent in 1996 and about 15 percent on the eve of WTO accession in 2001. Within the agriculture sector, significant reduction of import protection has also occurred. The simple average agricultural import tariff fell from 42.2 percent in 1992 to 23.6 percent in 1998 to 21 percent in 2001 (MOFTEC 2002).

China's openness to imports has progressed even faster than the decline in formal trade barriers might indicate. This is due to many special privileges that the government has extended to firms involved in export processing and strategic important commodity imports to balance domestic shortage. Thus, actual tariff revenues have been far below the average formal tariff rates. For example, the tariff revenues as a percentage of total import values was about 17 percent in the mid-1980s and only slightly more than 2 percent in 2004 (Lardy 2001; Branstetter and Lardy 2005).

Exchange rate policy has also changed significantly toward a market-oriented environment. Historically, the overvaluation of domestic currency for trade protection purposes reduced exportable incentives. Real exchange rates remained constant and even appreciated during the 30 years prior to reforms, but depreciated rapidly after reforms. From 1978 to 1994, the real exchange rate depreciated more than 400 percent. China also unified its two-tier foreign exchange rate systems (official exchange rate and swap rate) and the RMB has become convertible on the current account since 1996. Falling exchange rates increased export competitiveness and so have contributed to China's phenomenal export growth record. Following a modest appreciation, the exchange rate was effectively fixed at RMB8.3 to the United States donor in 1995. In 2005, China appreciated the RMB by about 2.5 percent (RMB to donor changed from 8.3 to 8.1); in the meantime China has also initiated a more market-oriented reform on its exchange rate policy.

China's policies on FDI have also changed noticeably since the beginning of its economic reform. For historical and ideological reasons, FDI in China was highly restricted prior to 1978. Since the passing of the Equity Joint Venture Law in late 1979, China has gradually liberalized its FDI regime, and the institutional framework has been developed to regulate and facilitate such investments. The liberalization of the FDI regime and the improved investment environment greatly increased the confidence of foreign investors in China. The changes in FDI policies and the increasing size of China's market have contributed to the rapid expansion of China's FDI inflows.

2.3 Agricultural and rural development

2.3.1 Agricultural production growth

The growth of agricultural production in China since the 1950s has been one of the main accomplishments of the country's development and national food security policies. Except during the famine years of the late 1950s and early 1960s, the country has enjoyed rates of production growth that have outpaced the rise in population.

After 1978, decollectivization, price increases and the relaxation of trade restrictions on most agricultural products accompanied the take off of China's food economy. Between 1978 and 1984, grain production increased by 4.7 percent per year; the output of fruit rose by 7.2 percent (Table 3). The highest annual growth rates came in the oilseed, livestock and aquatic product sectors, sectors that expanded in real value terms by 14.9, 9.1 and 7.9 percent, respectively.

Agricultural growth remained remarkable for most agricultural products from 1985 to 2000. Fishery production experienced the fastest growth from 1985 to 1995 (13.7 percent annual growth, Table 3). Although its annual growth rate fell in the following period, it still recorded 10.2 percent between 1996 and 2000. Over the same period, meat production and vegetable-sown areas expanded from 7 to 9 percent annually. Other cash crops such as oil crops, soybean and fruits also grew at rates much higher than population growth.

Overall growth of the agriculture sector remained at the annual rate of 3.4 percent from 2001 to 2004 and 1996 to 2000. Comparing the growth rates of individual commodities between these two periods, it appears that production (measured in quantity) growth of many individual agricultural

Table 3. The annual growth rates (%) of the agricultural economy, 1970–2004

	Pre-reform 1970–1978	Reform period			
		1979–1984	1985–1995	1996–2000	2001–2004
Agricultural GDP	2.7	7.1	4.0	3.4	3.4
Production:					
Grain	2.8	4.7	1.7	0.03	-0.2
Cotton	-0.4	19.3	-0.3	-1.9	6.5
Soybean	-2.3	5.2	2.8	2.6	2.4
Oil crops	2.1	14.9	4.4	5.6	0.6
Fruit	6.6	7.2	12.7	8.6	29.5
Meat	4.4	9.1	8.8	6.5	4.6
Fishery	5.0	7.9	13.7	10.2	3.5
Planted area:					
Vegetables	2.4	5.4	6.8	6.8	3.8
Orchards (fruit)	8.1	4.5	10.4	1.5	2.2

Note: Growth rates are computed using the regression method. Growth rates of individual and groups of commodities are based on production data.

Sources: NSBC (1985–2005) and MOA (1985–2005).

commodities fell, which may indicate that China's agricultural production has been shifting from aggregate production to value-added and quality food production.

2.3.2 Structural changes in agricultural production

China's agriculture has undergone significant changes since the early 1980s. Rapid economic growth, urbanization and market development are key factors underlining the changes. Rising income and urban expansion have boosted the demand for meat, fruit and other non-staple foods. These changes have stimulated sharp shifts in the structure of agriculture (Huang and Bouis 1996; Huang and Rozelle 1998). For example, the share of livestock output value rose 2.5 times from 14 percent to 35 percent between 1970 and 2004 (Table 4). Aquatic products increased at an even more rapid rate. One of the most significant signs of structural changes in the agriculture sector is that the share of crops in total agricultural output fell from 82 percent in 1970 to 51 percent in 2004.

Table 4. Changes in structure (%) of China's agricultural economy, 1970–2004

	1970	1980	1985	1990	1995	2000	2004
Share in agricultural output							
Crops	82	76	69	65	58	56	51
Livestock	14	18	22	26	30	30	35
Fishery	2	2	3	5	8	11	10
Forestry	2	4	5	4	3	4	4

Source: NSBC, *China's statistical yearbook*, various issues and *China rural statistical yearbook*, various issues.

Within the crop sector, the importance of the three major crops, rice, wheat and maize, has waxed and waned. The share of the major cereal grains increased from 50 percent in 1970 to a peak level of 57 percent in 1990 and then gradually declined to less that 50 percent in 2004 (Table 5). Most of the fall has been due to diminishing rice- and wheat-sown areas. In contrast, the shares of maize areas grew by more than 50 percent between 1970 and 2000 (Table 5). The rise in maize area, China's main feed grain, is correlated in no small way with the rapid expansion of the nation's livestock production during the same period.

Table 5. Shares of crop-sown areas, 1970–2004

	1970	1980	1985	1990	1995	2000	2004
Rice	22.1	23.1	21.9	22.3	20.5	19.2	18.5
Wheat	17.4	19.7	20.0	20.7	19.3	17.1	14.1
Maize	10.8	13.7	12.1	14.4	15.2	14.8	16.6
Soybean	5.5	4.9	5.3	5.1	5.4	6.0	6.2
Sweet potato	5.9	5.1	4.2	4.2	4.1	3.7	3.2
Cotton	3.4	3.4	3.5	3.8	3.6	2.6	3.7
Rapeseed	1.0	1.9	3.1	3.7	4.6	4.8	4.7
Peanut	1.2	1.6	2.3	2.0	2.5	3.1	3.1
Sugar crops	0.4	0.6	1.0	1.2	1.3	1.0	1.0
Tobacco	0.2	0.3	0.9	0.9	0.9	0.8	0.8
Vegetables	2.0	2.2	3.2	4.3	6.3	9.7	11.4
Others	30.1	23.5	22.5	17.4	16.3	17.2	16.7
Total	100.0	100.0	100.0	100.0	100.0	100.0	100.0

Source: NSBC, *China's statistical yearbook*, various issues; *China rural statistical yearbook*, various issues.

In addition to maize, other cash crops such as vegetables, edible oil crops, sugar crops and tobacco have expanded in area. In the 1970s, vegetables accounted for only about 2 percent of total crop area; by 2004, the share had increased by nearly six times (Table 5). The area devoted to edible oil also grew by two to three times. Field interviews reveal that the livelihood of the poor relies more on crops than livestock and fishery (when compared to richer farmers). Within the crop sector, poorer farmers produce more grains (particularly maize) than cash crops. These figures might imply that the poor have gained somewhat less than better off farmers from the diversification of agricultural production during the reform period.

2.3.3 Sources of production growth

Past studies have already demonstrated that there are a number of factors that have simultaneously contributed to agricultural production growth during the reform period. The earliest empirical efforts focused on measuring the contribution of the implementation of the household responsibility system (McMillan *et al.* 1989; Fan 1991; Lin 1992). These studies concluded that most of the rise in productivity in the early reform years was a result of institutional innovations, particularly the HRS (see Box 1), a policy that gave individual farmers control and income rights in agriculture.

Box 1. Land law in China

China initiated the Household Responsibility System (HRS) in 1979, which radically altered the organization of production in agriculture and the incentives facing rural households. By 1984, about 99 percent of agricultural land was contracted to all individual households, mostly on the basis of family size and the number of people in the household's labour force. At its conclusion, average farm size was about 0.6 ha. The size of farms varies among regions, ranging from more than 1 ha in Northeast and nearly 1 ha in North China to about 0.5 ha in Southwest and 0.2 to 0.3 ha in South China. Because the multiple cropping index (the number of crop seasons planted per year on a single plot of land) increases from one in the Northeast to two to three crops in South China, variations in sown area among China's regions are less than those of farm size. With the extension of land-use rights and residual income rights to households, agricultural production shifted from a collective-based to a family-based farming system. Land was not privatized, however. The ownership of land remained collective.

China's land rights are complicated and have been changing since its reform. The first term of the land-use right contract was stipulated for 15 years. The effects of such a land policy on the equitable distribution of land to farmers and its effect on food security and poverty alleviation have been obvious and well-documented. The land policy also has contributed greatly to efficiency. Specifically, the income and control rights contributed significantly to agricultural production and productivity growth in the early 1980s (Lin 1992; Huang and Rozelle 1996).

Although local leaders were supposed to have given farmers land for 15 years in the early 1980s and 30 years, starting in the late 1990s, collective ownership of land has resulted in frequent reallocation of village land. Many people have been concerned that such moves by local leaders could result in insecure tenure and negative effects on investment (Brandt *et al.* 2002). Many authors have shown, however, that in fact there has been little effect on either short- or long-term land productivity. There is still concern among officials that collective ownership and weak alienation and transfer rights could have other effects, such as impacts on migration and rural credit (Johnson 1995). As a result, China has recently passed a new land law, the Rural Land Contract Law (effective after March 1, 2003), which seeks to greatly increase tenure security.

Above all, the government has been searching for a mechanism that permits those that stay in farming to be able to gain access to additional cultivated land and increase their incomes and competitiveness. Even without much legal protection, researchers are finding increasingly more land is rented in and out (Deininger *et al.* 2005). In order to accelerate this process, the new Land Contract Law further clarifies the rights for transfer and exchange of contracted land. The new legislation also allows family members to inherit the land during the contracted period. The goal of this new set of policies is to encourage farmers to use their land more efficiently and increase their farm size.

More recent studies show that since the HRS was completed in 1984, technological change has been the primary engine of agricultural growth (Huang and Rozelle 1996; Fan 1997; Fan and Pardey 1997; Huang *et al.* 1999; Jin *et al.* 2002; also, see Box 2). Improvements in technology have by far contributed the largest share of crop production growth even during the early reform period. The results of these studies show that further reforms outside of decollectivization also have high potential for affecting agricultural growth. Price policy has been shown to have had a sharp influence on the growth (and deceleration) of both grain and cash crops during the postreform period. Favourable output to input price ratios contributed to the rapid growth in the early 1980s. However, this new market force is a two-edged sword. A deteriorating price ratio caused by slowly increasing output prices in the face of sharply rising input prices was an important factor behind the slowdown in agricultural production in the late 1980s and early 1990s. The higher opportunity cost of land has also held back the growth of grain output throughout the period, and that of cash crops since 1985.

Irrigation has played a critical role in establishing the highly productive agronomic systems in China (Wang 2000). The proportion of cultivated area under irrigation increased from 18 percent in 1952 to a level at which about half of all cultivated land had been irrigated after the early 1990s (NSBC 2001). However, rising demand for domestic and industrial water uses poses a serious constraint to irrigated agriculture and increasing water scarcity is being viewed as a major challenge to future food security and the well-being of people especially in the northern region. Wang *et al.*

Box 2. Agricultural productivity and technology in China

After the 1960s, China's research institutions grew rapidly, from almost none in the 1950s, to a system that now produces a steady flow of new varieties and other technologies. China's farmers used semi-dwarf varieties several years before the release of Green Revolution technology elsewhere. China was the first country to develop and extend the production of hybrid rice. Chinese-bred conventional rice varieties, wheat and sweet potatoes were comparable to the best in the world in the prereform era. China's TFP rose at a healthy rate of about 2 percent per year during the reform era (Jin *et al.* 2002). According to the work of Jin *et al.* (2002), technology is the most important source of TFP growth. Despite the breakdown of the extension system during the reform era, farmers continued to adopt new varieties produced by researchers. During the 1980s and 1990s China's producers were replacing varieties from about 20 to 25 percent of their sown areas during each cropping season. In other words, about every four to five years, China's farmers are completely turning over their technology portfolios.

In addition to the development of conventional agricultural technology, scientists and researchers have a strong commitment to plant biotechnology. A new source of plant biotechnology discoveries is emerging in China (Huang *et al.* 2002b; 2005a). Public investment in agricultural biotechnology has increased significantly since the mid-1980s. In 2003, the agricultural biotechnology research budget reached RMB1.6 billion (about US$200 million at the official exchange rate or more than US$800 million in PPP terms). Expenditures of this level demonstrate the seriousness of China's commitment to modern technology.

However, China's agricultural R&D system is also facing great challenges. Agricultural research in China is organized by the government. A nationwide reform in research was launched in the mid-1980s and accelerated after the late 1990s. The reforms attempted to increase research productivity by shifting funding from institutional support to competitive grants, supporting research useful for economic development and encouraging applied research institutes to support themselves by selling the technology they produce. Today, the record on the reform of the agricultural technology system is mixed. Empirical evidence demonstrates the declining effectiveness of China's agricultural research capabilities (Jin *et al.* 2002). Recognizing these challenges, China is now revisiting its reforms and formulating a new strategy aimed at re-establishing a more innovative agricultural technology system (for both research and extension) for sustainable agricultural growth.

(2005) showed that the water management reform has been helping to increase the efficiency of water use in North China, although the scope for such reform in the long term is somewhat limited.

2.3.4 Agricultural trade performance

While agricultural production was growing quickly, agricultural trade was growing even more so. Agricultural trade (both imports and exports) nearly tripled from 1980 to 1995 (Table 6). During this time, exports rose faster than imports. Since the early 1980s, China has been a net food exporter.

In the same way that trade liberalization has affected growth in the domestic economy (Lardy 2001), changes in the external economy have affected the nature of China's trade patterns (Huang and Chen 1999). As trade expanded, despite the overall positive growth of agricultural trade, the share of agriculture in total trade fell sharply because the growth of non-agricultural trade was much higher than that of agricultural trade. For example, the share of food exports (imports) in trade declined from 17 percent (15 percent) in 1980 to 3 percent (2 percent) only in 2004 (Table 2).

Disaggregated, product-specific trade trends show equally sharp shifts. This suggest that exports and imports are moving increasingly in a direction that is consistent with China's comparative advantages (Figure 4). In general, the net exports of land-intensive bulk commodities, such as grains, oilseed and sugar crops, have fallen reflecting the increase in imports. At the same time, exports of higher-valued, more labour-intensive products, such as horticultural and animal (including aquaculture) products have risen. Grain exports, accounted for nearly one-third of food exports in the mid-1980s. After the late 1990s, horticultural, animal and aquatic products accounted for about 70 to 80 percent of food exports (Huang and Chen 1999; Table 6).

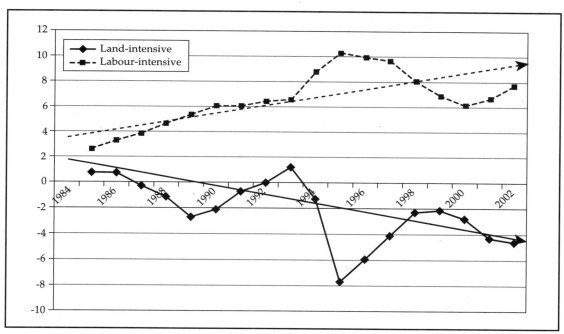

Source: Huang, *et al.* (2005).

Figure 4. Agricultural trade balance (net export) by land-intensive and labour-intensive products, US$ million

Table 6. Structure of China's food and feed trade (US$ million), 1980–2002

	1980	1985	1990	1995	2000	2001	2002
Exports:							
Live animals and meat	745	752	1 221	1 822	1 628	1 976	1 008
Dairy products	71	57	55	61	188	192	194
Fish	380	283	1 370	2 875	3 705	4 231	4 690
Grains, oils and oilseed	481	1 306	1 237	1 608	2 667	1 835	2 422
Horticulture	1 074	1 260	2 293	3 922	4 367	4 931	6 402
Sugar	221	79	317	321	173	156	227
Sum of above foods	2 972	3 737	6 493	10 609	12 728	13 340	14 943
Imports:							
Live animals and meat	6	24	68	115	696	659	706
Dairy products	5	31	81	60	218	219	274
Fish	13	44	102	609	1 212	1 319	1 558
Grains, oils and oilseed	2 472	1 065	2 535	6 760	4 163	5 343	5 825
Horticulture	104	92	113	259	677	866	838
Sugar	316	274	390	935	177	376	238
Sum of above foods	2 916	1 530	3 289	8 736	7 143	8 782	9 439
Net exports:							
Live animals and meat	739	728	1 153	1 707	932	1 317	302
Dairy products	66	26	-26	1	-30	-27	-80
Fish	367	239	1 268	2 266	2 493	2 912	3 132
Grains, oils and oilseed	-1 991	241	-1 298	-5 152	-1 496	-3 490	-3 403
Horticulture	970	1 168	2 180	3 663	3 690	4 065	5 564
Sugar	-95	-195	-73	-614	-4	-220	-11
Sum of above foods	56	2 207	3 204	1 873	5 585	4 558	5 504

Sources: Data for 1980–1995 are from Mathews (2002), based on UN COMTRADE statistics; data after 1995 are from various publications of China's National Statistical Bureau and China's Custom Authority.

2.3.5 Food security

Food security at the macronational level implies that adequate supplies of food are available through domestic production and/or through imports to meet the consumption needs of the country's population. China has experienced substantial increased per capita food consumption over the last three decades. Per capita food availability rose from 1 717 kcal per day in the early 1960s to 2 328 kcal between 1979 and 1981 (Table 7). By the late 1990s, per capita food availability had reached more than 3 000 kcal per day, a level that approaches that achieved in most developed countries. Hence it is clear that by the early reform period, China's food availability far exceeded the United States' minimum daily requirement of 2 100 kcal (WHO standard). Given China's status as a net food exporter, when examining the rise in domestic food availability, it is clear that the increase was almost exclusively achieved through increases in domestic production.

During the same period (between the 1960s and late 1990s), other indicators of nutrition also improved. For example, protein intake and fat consumption measures on a per capita per day basis increased significantly. Protein intake rose from 45 to 84 grams. Fat consumption increased from 17 to 82 grams. Table 7 also shows evidence that most of the improvement in the quality of China's diet was achieved after 1980. In the early 1960s, nearly 96 percent of calories came from grains and other non-livestock products. By the 1990s, the reliance on non-meat food products was reduced to about 81 percent. During the same period, the share of calories contributed by animal products rose from 4 to 19 percent (Table 7). Similar trends during the past four decades can be traced out for the changing sources of protein and fats.

Table 7. Per capita supply and sources of calories, protein and fat per day in China, 1961–2000

	1961–1963	1969–1971	1979–1981	1989–1991	1998–2000
Supply					
Calories	1 716.7	1 993.3	2 328.0	2 683.3	3 033.0
Protein (grams)	44.8	47.5	54.5	65.0	84.3
Fat (grams)	16.8	23.5	32.5	53.0	81.9
Sources (%)					
Calories					
– Vegetable products	95.9	94.1	92.6	88.4	81.3
– Animal products	4.1	5.9	7.4	11.6	18.7
Protein					
– Vegetable products	90.5	87.9	86.4	77.7	65.6
– Animal products	9.5	12.1	13.6	22.3	34.4
Fat					
– Vegetable products	66.1	56.8	53.4	49.0	41.4
– Animal products	33.9	43.2	46.6	51.0	58.6

Source: FAO database.

At the microlevel, household or individual food security depends on a number of factors. These are related, for the most part, to various forms of entitlements to income and food-producing assets. Also important are the links between domestic and external markets and the access of small, low-income and resource-poor producers and consumers to external markets.

Access to food in rural China has changed over time. In the early years of the reform, decollectivization policies gave all farm households in China a parcel of land. During this time, however, markets did not function well (deBrauw *et al.* 2004). As a result, most farmers produced mostly for their own subsistence. Access to food was primarily through the land that was allocated to farmers by the state.

As China has changed, so has the food economy and nowhere has the change been more noticeable than in access to food. From an economy that was mostly subsistence, in recent years China has one of the most commercialized rural economies when compared to other developing economies. On the average, the shares of marketed products in total production ranged from 54 percent for grain to more than 90 percent for fish (Huang *et al.* 2003b). Even the poorest of the poor also marketed nearly all products they produced, though the rate of commercialization is less than that of the richer Chinese farmers who have also increasingly purchased their food from the rural market.

Although China's rural consumers still face a number of uncertainties in access to food, these differ from other countries. In other countries, production risk is often thought to be one of the most important sources of risk that will affect rural residents. In China this is less likely. While China's farmers also face production risks, these may be less important relative to other nations. A much higher share of China's land (nearly 50 percent) is irrigated (NSBC 2001). A higher share of households (around 80 percent) is diversified by having at least one family member in the off-farm market (deBrauw *et al.* 2004). Giles (2000) shows that risks in China come from a number of non-traditional sources, such as wage and policy risks. With an increasing number of households relying on markets to procure their food, households also face rising market price risks.

Stability of food supplies and access to food by the poor are the other dimensions of food security. In this regard, the government has developed its own disaster relief programme. It also runs a national food-for-work scheme, although this is less for disaster relief and more for long-term investments. The nation's capacity to deal with emergencies has been demonstrated repeatedly during the reform period. For example, the government responded massively and in a timely fashion during the floods in 1990s. Through these reactions, China's government has proved that its capacity to deal with the consequences of natural disasters is adequate. During the 1980s and early 1990s, one of the major constraints that affected the stabilization of food supply in China was the poor marketing and transportation infrastructure (Nyberg and Rozelle 1999).

2.3.6 Off-farm employment

China's rural enterprises provide employment for millions of rural labourers who have been transferred out of the agriculture sector as agricultural productivity increases. Without the rapid growth of this sector in China, a huge employment problem would have been created in the past. Among different periods of rural enterprise development, township and TVE development before the late 1990s was unique and played a vital role in facilitating China's economic growth and increasing farmers' income (Box 3).

Off-farm work has emerged as the main source of income growth for rural households since the mid-1980s. By 2003 about half of China's rural labour force earned at least part of its income from off-farm jobs; more than 85 percent of households had at least one person working off-farm (Figure 5). Internal migration has become the most common way for rural labourers to get a off-farm job. More than 100 million migrants now reside and work away from their home villages. More than 75 percent of 16 to 20 year olds work off-farm in cities far removed from their homes. A veritable flood of young and relatively well-educated workers has been flowing towards China's cities and into industrial and service sector jobs in recent years. Self-employment opportunities in the rural economy also have risen rapidly during the past two decades, and the quality of these microenterprises has steadily improved. The firms, although household-based and extremely labour-intensive, provide employment for more than 80 million rural residents in more than 50 million households (Zhang et al. 2005).

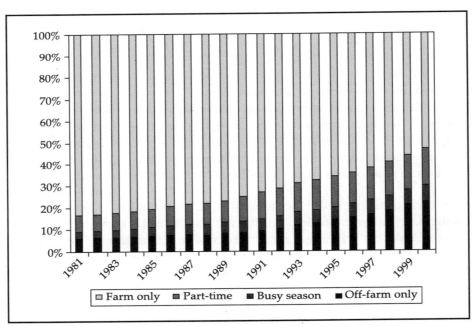

Source: Zhang, *et al.* (2005).

Figure 5. Level of participation in farming and non-farming activities, 1980–2000

Box 3. Rural enterprise development in China

China's experience with rural enterprises (REs) shows the importance of expanding non-agricultural sectors in the path of overall economic development. REs' share in the GDP increased from about 3 percent in 1970s to nearly 30 percent by the late 1990s. REs have also dominated the export sector since the mid-1990s and employed about one-third of rural labour.

Several factors assisted the growth of REs before the early 1980s. Putterman (1997) provided five major explanations for rural industrial growth in China's prereform economy: Abundant rural unskilled labour, the availability of rural skilled labour from returned urban-retired workers, initial capital accumulation by local brigades and communes for RE investment, rising demand for industrial products that were neglected by the state because of its imbalanced emphasis on heavy industry and entrepreneurial talents of the local brigade and commune leaders.

With the rise of non-township- and non-village-owned enterprises (e.g. private and cooperative enterprises) since the mid-1980s, the term township and village enterprise (TVE) was expanded to cover private, cooperative and other forms of enterprises in rural areas (but excluding SOEs located in rural areas). The annual growth rate of TVE output value in real terms was recorded at more than 24 percent from 1984 to 1995 (NSBC 1997). Total employment in the TVE sector rose from 52.1 million in 1984 to 128.6 million in 1995, with an annual increase of about 7 million. By 1995, the gross output value of REs accounted for 75 percent of the rural output and 50 percent of national industrial output (NSBC 1997).

Several policies have contributed to the rapid growth of TVEs since the mid-1980s. Otsuka *et al.* (1998) showed that a large difference in efficiency between REs and public ownership (SOE) contributed to the significant growth of TVEs in the 1980s and early 1990s. Within the TVE sector, the recognition of private (individual and cooperative) enterprises by the central government beginning in 1984 had also become a new engine of TVE growth in the late 1980s and 1990s. Before the 1980s, almost all rural enterprises or TVEs were operated under the leadership of local townships and village. The number of privately owned and cooperative enterprises reached 20.4 million in 1995, which accounted for 53 percent of total RE employment (NSBC 1997). Increasing rural saving was the other important source of RE development. Rural industrialization also benefited from trade liberalization, currency devaluation (a devaluation of over 300 percent in real terms from 1984 to 1994) and favourable FDI policies. REs became more export-oriented. Their export share in total exports increased from less than 5 percent in the early 1980s to 43 percent by 1995.

However, RE expansion reached a turning point in 1997 when overall employment recorded a decline for the first time. A World Bank study (1999) shows that it will be difficult for REs to maintain past growth momentum because the environment has fundamentally changed. The initial conditions that favoured the rapid development of rural industries no longer prevail. In the early years of RE growth, China was supply-constrained. Most consumer and industrial goods were in short supply. With the emergence of REs, product competition grew and the larger profits of previous years disappeared. As the size of rural industry expanded, the extent of government support in terms of state financial aid, credits and tax reduction was limited. Financial markets could not meet their current needs. REs also faced considerable challenges in updating technology, expanding scale and environmental pollution. Despite significant changes in institutional and management forms in the RE sector, the property rights and operational and management systems were still far from efficient. Recognizing some of the above problems, China has implemented ambitious TVE property rights reforms since the mid-1990s. Nearly all collectively owned REs have been privatized since then. With improving credit access and increasing FDI, the growth of REs resumed recently.

The shift of the rural population off the farm into wage-earning jobs and self-employment has generated large increases in productivity and has contributed to most of the increase in rural incomes since the mid-1980s. Large increases in productivity come from shifting low productivity workers from farms into higher productivity manufacturing and service sectors. Between the mid-1980s and in recent years, average per capita rural household income rose by 4 to 5 percent per year, almost all of it from the off-farm sector. However, Zhang *et al.* (2005) show that the poorest farmers gain least from off-farm employment and are still highly dependent on agricultural income.

2.3.7 The impacts of economic and agricultural growth on poverty

China's success in poverty reduction is well-recognized internationally. The poverty rate has fallen from more than 30 percent to less than 3 percent of the total rural population (Figure 1 and Appendix Table 1). Understanding the determinants of success in poverty alleviation in poor rural areas is important beyond its academic interest for several reasons. First, there are still nearly 30 million rural people living below the nation's poverty line and a much large number when the international standard of poverty line is adopted (Figure 1). Second, the pace of rural poverty reduction has slowed down significantly since the late 1990s as poverty levels decline. Last but not least, there could be important policy implications not only for China but also for other developing countries in their efforts to reduce poverty.

Previous studies in China have mainly focused on the impacts of the nation's poverty alleviation programmes and poverty investment policies. The effectiveness of targeting poverty and the impacts of the poverty alleviation programmes on the income of the poor are key issues that have been widely addressed in the literature (World Bank 1992; Park *et al.* 1996; Rozelle *et al.* 1998). However, the impacts of overall economic and agricultural growth and trade liberalizations on poverty have been largely overlooked. One exception is a recent study on the determinants of poverty reduction in rural China (Huang *et al.* 2005b).

Huang *et al.* (2005b) provide several interesting results on key factors that have determined the changes of rural poverty in China. First, their results show that the overall economic growth (measured by per capita GDP) has been a primary source of rural poverty reduction in China. The average elasticity of poverty incidence with respect to per capita GDP was estimated to be -0.7 from 1985 to 2002, which implies that a 1 percent increase of per capita GDP has led to a 0.7 percent decline in rural poverty incidence.

Second, economic growth is an essential and necessary condition for nationwide poverty reduction, but not a sufficient condition. The estimated elasticities of poverty incidence with respect to economic growth decline significantly with economic growth. Their decomposition analysis shows that economic growth played a dominant role in reducing poverty in the 1980s. However, as income grew, the impact and effectiveness of general economic growth on poverty reduction has weakened considerably since the mid-1990s.

Third, agricultural growth, not just overall economic growth, matters for poverty reduction. For example, higher agricultural growth is statistically significantly associated with a lower poverty incidence rate over time and across provinces. Given the same growth of GDP, a 1 percent increase of agricultural share in the GDP will lead to a nearly 1 percent drop in the poverty incidence rate (Huang *et al.* 2005b). This should not be a surprising result as agriculture is the main source of income of the poor. The result also suggests the importance of government investment in agriculture and rural infrastructure on poverty reduction.

Fourth, the division of rural and urban development has significant adverse effects on rural poverty reduction. A widened urban–rural income gap has affected poverty reduction not only directly but also indirectly through its impact on overall economic growth. This result confirms our expectation that a larger urban–rural income gap is associated with higher poverty incidence. In this regard, the growth has to be made more broadly based than in the past.

Fifth, the growth of the non-state industrial sector and the development of TVEs have also contributed to China's rural poverty reduction indirectly through their effects on overall economic growth.

Last but not least, while trade liberalization benefits the Chinese economy as a whole (including the agriculture sector), policy-makers should be concerned about poverty and equity effects. Trade liberalization may enlarge both inter- and intra-regional income disparities, though the impacts are small than other factors examined by Huang *et al.* (2005b). Pro-poor policies must be adopted to target those who are vulnerable during the course of trade liberalization.

2.3.8 The main challenges for China's agricultural and rural development

While the progress in agricultural and rural development has been notable, there are also many lessons and major challenges ahead. With the transition from a planned to a market-oriented rural economy mostly complete, China's main challenge has shifted to broader development issues. In the coming years, the development process will have to be fundamentally different from the efforts in previous times when meeting the nation's food needs, poverty reduction and economic growth were the main goals.

China's rapid economic growth and the rise in the nation's overall wealth have been accompanied by widening income inequality. Regional income disparity has been expanding since the 1980s (Cai *et al.* 2002; World Bank 2002). Eastern China has grown faster than Central and Western China. The rural reforms increased rural incomes at a faster pace than urban incomes during the early 1980s. This led to a decline of the urban to rural income ratio from 2.57 in 1978 to 1.86 in 1985. However, after the one-time impact of the rural institutional reforms was exhausted, urban income growth has been consistently higher than that of the rural sector. By 2004, per capita income in the urban areas was 3.21 times that in the rural areas (NSBC 2005). Rising income disparity within the rural areas has also emerged. For example, the Gini coefficients in rural areas increased from 0.24 in 1980 to 0.31 in 1990 and to 0.37 in 2003 (NSBC–Rural Survey Department 2004).

While successful technology innovations will help China to increase its agricultural productivity, China may face a great challenge in coming to grips with water scarcity. Water shortages and increasing competition from industry and domestic use do not provide much hope for large gains in the areas under irrigation and the total output from irrigation expansion (Lohmar *et al.* 2003). This is particularly important in the North China Plain where most of China's wheat and to some extent maize, are produced.

While the land policy helped China to increase agricultural productivity in the early reform period and contributed significantly to reduction of China's rural poverty, landholdings are so small that farming activities alone cannot continue to raise the incomes of most rural households. The challenge is how China can effectively establish linkages between rural and urban areas and encourage the large labour shift out of agriculture.

Trends in environmental degradation suggest that there may be considerable stress on the agricultural land base. While judicious use of modern technologies is essential for efficient food production globally, inappropriate uses, such as excessive application rates or imbalances in input combinations, result in serious environmental problems and food safety concerns. China is now the world's leader in both chemical fertilizer and pesticide consumption. In the past 30 years, while world total nitrogen fertilizer application increased by seven times, China's nitrogen use in crop production increased by 45 times (Sonntag *et al.* 2005). On average, nitrogen use per hectare is about three times higher than the world average. Pesticides have been used on a large scale since the 1960s to protect crops from damage inflicted by insects and diseases (Huang *et al.* 2000). Recently, China surpassed Japan as the world's leading pesticide consumer. Intensive fertilizer and pesticide use can have several adverse effects and concerns about contamination of farm produce and endangering of the agro-ecosystem as well as human health are rising. Environmental stresses have also been occurring such as soil erosion, salinization, the loss of cultivated land and decline in land quality (Huang and Rozelle 1995). Deng *et al.* (2005) show that although China did not record a decline in total cultivated land from the late 1980s to the late 1990s, average potential productivity of cultivated land, or *bioproductivity*, declined by 2.2 percent over the same period. In the meantime, a large decline in cultivated land was recorded after the late 1990s due to industrial development and urban expansion.

The leaders of China have recognized the constraints and challenges of sustainable agricultural and rural development. Recently, China has initiated the Five Balanced Development Strategies, which aim for balanced developments between rural and urban areas, between economic growth and social progress, among regions, between human intervention and environmental conservation and between internal and external economies. The Five Balanced Development Strategies are ambitious, and a number of the proposed strategies and reforms are bold. However, national leaders also realize that there are many barriers preventing them from achieving these lofty goals.

3. Prospects for China's economic growth in the future

Projection of economic growth in the long term is intricate as there is no useful model to conduct this kind of analysis. There is little information on future structural changes that may respond to economic growth and development policies. In this study, instead of using model-based scenarios for China's GDP growth, we adopt a more qualitative approach that takes into consideration the likely trends of the major driving forces of economic growth.

3.1 National development plan

In the Eleventh Five-Year Plan, 2006–2010 and the strategies for long-term economic development, China has set ambitious goals to metamorphose the nation into a "well-off society" (*Xaiokun Shehui*) in the next 20 years: double GDP in ten years; smooth transformation of the economy from transition to development and from agriculture to industry and services; sustainable management of the environment; and other social and political targets.

In order to achieve these goals, China's leaders have been pursuing a more sustainable development plan, the so-called Five Balanced (or integrated) Developments (FBD); i.e. developments between rural and urban areas, across regions; between economic and social aspects; between human activities, natural resources and environmental conservation; and between internal (domestic) and external economies. This FBD plan is backed by policies to stimulate the development of new technologies, education and urbanization, to make optimum progress in controlling deterioration of ecosystems and to move the nation to a more market-oriented and open economy.

3.2 Driving force prospective for economic growth

There is considerable potential for China's economic growth despite some development risks. Rapid growth is likely to continue in the coming decade though growth rates might decline gradually over time. New national leaders, who are strong reformists, took their positions in the government in early 2003. Several initiatives have been undertaken to boost China's economy. These include policies related to the strong implementation of macroeconomic stabilization, deepening market reforms, further liberalizing of the economy and emphasizing sustainable growth through increasing investment in R&D, education, health and infrastructure and resource and environmental protection. The following factors are generally considered to be the key driving forces underpinning China's economic growth in the future:

a) **Macroeconomic stabilization.** Macroeconomic stabilization is likely to be further strengthened. The national leaders consider that macroeconomic stability is one of the pre-conditions to generate long-term economic growth as it will provide a favourable environment for both domestic and foreign investment. A stabilized macroeconomic environment will also help the government to better foster development of the infrastructure and institutions necessary for sustainable growth. The stability system was well tested when China was seriously affected by the SARS epidemic and yet the economy recorded 9.5 percent growth in 2003.

b) **Physical capital.** A high domestic savings rate is likely to remain in the coming decade. Capital formulation was about 35 percent of the GDP in the 1980s and has increased enormously over time, from nearly 40 percent in the 1990s to 44.2 percent in 2003 and 2004 (NSBC 2005). The Development Research Center of State Council (DRC) projects that the current rate of investment in the coming ten years will be maintained (DRC 2002). These high investment rates indeed have also been experienced for a sustained time period in several Eastern Asian countries or regions such as Japan, Republic of Korea and Taiwan Province of China. High domestic savings rates, stable macroeconomic environment, increasing inflows of FDI and large markets are fundamental bases for high level investment in China's current as well as future economy.

c) **Labour force.** Cheaper rural surplus labour has facilitated China's economic growth and structural changes. There is still an abundant and enormous pool of rural labourers who are seeking non-farm employment. This continued shift of labour from the agricultural to non-agricultural sectors will further accelerate the growth of labour-intensive industries and service sectors in the coming decade, and will continue to provide cheap industrial products to consumers in both China and the rest of the world. Export of labour-intensive products will expand under more liberalized world trade (Ianchovichina *et al.* 2004).

d) **R&D spending.** According to the recent Eleventh Five-Year Plan, 2006–2010 and the Long Term Development Plan (2006–2020), the Boosting China's Development through Science and Education programme (*Ke Jiao Xing Guo*) will be further strengthened. The government investment in R&D is planned to grow more than the average growth of government fiscal revenue (State Council 2002). The growth in public investment in professional education (i.e. colleges and universities) has also increased substantially since the late 1990s (NSBC various issues). We expect that the total factor productivity increase contributed by technology changes in the future will exceed that in the past.

e) **Human capital.** In additional to the *Ke Jiao Xing Guo* development programme, the national leaders decreed a new development plan, *Yi Ren Wei Ben* (or people-oriented development) in 2003. The new plan emphasizes overall human development (not only professional education), in particular rural primary education. In order to implement this new development plan, an ambitious programme has been proposed to reduce or eventually eliminate primary school education fees throughout China, including Western China and other less-developed regions. Other programmes aimed to improve primary, secondary and professional education are under consideration.

f) **Market development and role of the government.** Emerging markets and evolving institutions in China's economy also show that China is preparing for sustainable growth in the first half of the twenty-first century. As China enters the twenty-first century, the rural economy is evolving to the point that it is ready to help China make the next step in modernization. Markets for labour, agricultural commodities, many inputs for farmers and rural industrial managers have flourished in recent years and are increasingly competitive and rational (Rozelle *et al.* 1999 and 2000). The direct provision of goods and services will be handled increasingly by the private sector. Meanwhile, the government is planning to thoroughly reform its administrative system and shift its role to providing public goods, overcoming market failures, and providing services that the private sector will not provide, but which will serve to further the transformation of China in the coming years (State Council 2003).

g) **Urbanization.** Urbanization and newly initiated rural small-town development programmes will facilitate China's economic structural changes, create employment for rural and urban labourers, increase farmers' income and promote rural and urban demand for industrial commodities and services. The International Institute of Applied Systems Analysis (IIASA) projects that the level of urbanization will fall within a range of 50 to 55 percent in 2020 compared to 36 percent in 2000 (Toth *et al.* 2003).

h) **Trade liberalization.** China's gains from economic globalization and trade liberalization will further boost its economic growth. Expanding labour-intensive industries, fostered also by new export opportunities, can contribute to China's development strategy that includes labour absorption into industries outside primary agriculture. Merchandise trade in the future will grow much faster than in the past (Ianchovichina *et al.* 2004). Moreover, the static impacts (i.e. merchandise trade) are probably only a small part of China's gains from trade liberalization; the dynamic effects such as capital accumulation and technology spillovers will be more substantial (van Tongeren *et al.* 2003).

i) **Foreign direct investment.** Although the growth rates of FDI inflow may or may not be as high as those recorded in the past two decades, China will remain one of the most attractive countries for FDI in the post-WTO era and at least in the coming decade. China has attracted substantial FDI in past decades. After 2002 China has become the most important recipient of FDI in the world. In the past two decades, FDI has been pouring into the coastal regions. Recently, China's regional development plan and its increasing investment in infrastructure in less-developed regions have begun to impact the direction of FDI in China. Zhang and Post (2003) show that there is increasing FDI towards the western part of China to exploit its rich resources and stimulate domestic demand. Given the size of the market and the expectation of strong economic growth in the future, China is very likely to remain one of the most favoured investment destinations in the world.

j) **Regional development programmes.** Under the FBD strategy growth in less-developed regions is expected to accelerate in the coming decades. In order to pursue overall development of the country, the central government has initiated several regional development programmes, particularly the Great Western Development Plan, Central China Development Program, Northeast China Development Program and new National Poverty Alleviation Program, to redirect resources towards less-developed regions. According to the nation's development plan, in the first ten years of this century, the major investments under regional development programmes include infrastructure, ecosystem and environmental conservation, and human resource development (Du 2003). We expect that implementation of the regional balanced development strategy will help the less-developed regions to catch up with the national growth path. This will create local employment and demand for commodities from the coastal region, and help China reduce income disparity among regions.

While we expect that high growth will remain in China for the next 20 years, there are other factors and uncertainties that may limit China's economic growth over time. These include:

a) There could be potential risks associated with internal macroeconomic stability if China's income disparity continues to widen;

b) The growth in labour supply will slow down in association with China's falling population growth rate and the changing age structure of the population (Toth, *et al.* 2003), which will lead to an increase in wages after certain years;

c) The aged population will grow faster, which will lead to a rise in the dependence ratio in coming decades;

d) As the dependence ratio rises, national savings propensity is likely to decline, which may impact the growth of domestic investment;

e)   After ten to 15 years, China will have basically finished the major tasks of its economic reforms that were initiated in the late 1970s. The gains from further economic reforms will be weak;

f)   With rapid economic growth, there will be considerable stress on environmental degradation if appropriate environmental protection policies are not emphasized; and

g)   There may be political risk and tension in the external environment, which could affect China's economic and political stability in the future (although this is highly unlikely). In recent years, after China emerged as one of leading importers of natural resources such as timber, fish meal, energy and minerals, some claim that there will be concerns about global food security (if China imports enormous amounts of food from the international market) and the natural resource base, for China's long-term rapid economic growth.

3.3 Economic growth prospects

Based on the above discussions, this subsection provides our prospects for China's economic growth in the first two decades of the twenty-first century. While our prospects are focused on the most likely growth scenario (baseline), we also formulate an alternative higher growth scenario (or high growth scenario) because one of the objectives of this study is to examine the local and global implications of China's rapid economic growth. The details of both the baseline growth scenario and high growth scenario for China from 2006 to 2020 are summarized in Table 8. For comparison, we also present the corresponding figures in the past 20 years (1985–2005).

Table 8. Projection of China's economy, 2001–2020

	Annual growth rate (%)					
	1985–1995	1996–2000	2001–2005	2006–2010	2011–2015	2016–2020
Baseline						
GDP	9.7	8.2	8.9	8.0	7.2	6.3
Per capita GDP	8.3	7.2	8.2	7.4	6.7	5.9
High growth						
GDP	9.7	8.2	8.9	7.6	6.6	6.7
Per capita GDP	8.3	7.2	8.2	8.2	7.4	7.5
Population	1.37	0.91	0.72	0.61	0.54	0.41
	Per capita GDP in					
	2000	2005	2010	2015	2020	
Baseline:						
RMB	7 086	10 528	14 974	20 612	27 454	
US$	856	1 300	1 849	2 545	3 389	
High growth						
RMB	7 086	10 528	15 613	22 331	30 638	
US$	856	1 300	1 927	2 757	3 782	
Population (billion)	1.267	1.308	1.348	1.382	1.409	

Note: Values are in 2000 constant prices.

Baseline scenario

The baseline scenario assumes that the average annual GDP growth rates from 2001 to 2005 would reach 8.9 percent in 2001 to 2005 and then slightly fall over the entire projection period. The higher growth of GDP in 2001 to 2005 than that in 1996 to 2000 is because the average annual growth rate already reached 8.7 percent in 2001 to 2004 and China's economy is likely to grow at more than 9 percent in 2005. After 2005, the annual growth rate is assumed to decline from 8.9 percent in 2001 to 2005 to 8 percent in 2006 to 2010, 7.2 percent in 2010 to 2015 and 6.3 percent in 2016 to 2020 (Table 8). By 2020, China's economy will be more than four times as large as that in 2000, which also implies that China will meet its development goal of doubling its economy every ten years in 2001 to 2020. By 2020, the national GDP will be nearly RMB39 trillion (in 2000 prices, or about US$4.8 trillion converted at the current exchange rate).

In this study, we adopt a recent population projection conducted by IIASA (Toth *et al.* 2003). Toth *et al.* forecast several population growth scenarios for China from 2001 to 2030. One of their scenarios, the Central Line Scenario, has been adopted in our study. For per capita GDP growth, which is derived by deducting population growth from total GDP growth, the likely growth scenario presents an annual growth rate of 8.2 percent in 2001 to 2005. Average annual per capita GDP growth rates will remain at about 7 to 8 percent in 2010 and 6 to 7 percent in 2020 (Table 8).

The growths of total GDP and population assumed under this scenario imply that China's per capita GDP in 2000 prices will rise from RMB7 084 in 2000 to RMB14 974 in 2010 and RMB27 454 in 2020, an increase of 387 percent in 2020 over 2000 (Table 8). If we apply the official exchange rates in 2000 for the base year and the current rate for 2020, per capita GDP will increase from US$856 in 2000 to US$1 849 in 2010 and US$3 389 in 2020. If we further consider the purchasing power, the above projection would mean that China's per capita income will be in between the current incomes of the middle- and high-income countries in 2020 (World Bank 2002).

Higher growth scenario

For the aims of this study, we are interested in the implications of China's more rapid economic growth. Therefore, instead of formulating a low growth scenario, we assume that China would be able to better implement its future economic reform and create even more favourable internal and external development environments than those assumed under the baseline scenario. Under the high growth scenario, we assume that the annual GDP growth rate will be increased by 10 percent compared to that under the baseline scenario in 2006 to 2020. That is, the GDP growth rate under the baseline will be 8.0 percent in 2006 to 2010, the corresponding rate under the high growth scenario will be 8.8 percent (8.0 x 1.1) in the same period (row 4, Table 8).

Under the high growth scenario, GDP will more than double in the first ten years. By 2020, total GDP will be about 4.8 times more than the GDP in 2000. If growth continues at the rates estimated under the high growth scenario in 2020 (row 4, Table 8), per capita GDP will reach RMB30 638 (or US$3 782 at the current exchange rate) in 2020.

Comparisons with other projections

Table 9 compares our GDP growth projections with previous studies. The annual growth rates of our baseline projection are relatively close to the forecasts by Li (2001) and OECF (1995) but higher than the rest of other projections. A higher GDP growth rate in our baseline than that of many other projections is explained by the fact that we incorporated the most updated and actual GDP growth rates in the recent four years (8.7 percent in 2001 to 2004, Table 1) and predicted a growth rate of 9.5 percent in 2005. While none of the other studies predicted a growth rate of more than 8.5 percent in 2001 to 2005.

Table 9. Previous projections of China's GDP growth in China in the early 21st century

Study	Projection period	Methodology	Assumption of annual GDP growth (%)
OECF (1995)	1995–2010	Expert justification	8.0
World Bank (1997)	1995–2020	General equilibrium model	6.0
IFPRI (2001)	1997–2020	Expert justification	6.0
LEI–CCAP (2003)	2001–2020	Expert justification	5.7
DRC (2002)	2001–2010	Model (not discussed) with expert justification	7.5
	2011–2020		6.1
Li (2001)	2001–2010	Model (not discussed) with expert justification	8.1
	2011–2020		6.4
This study (baseline)	2001–2010	No model but based on prospective of driving forces	8.4
	2011–2020		6.7

Earlier studies with 1995 as the base year and projected to 2020 seem to largely underestimate China's GDP growth. For example, World Bank (1997) forecast an average of 6 percent GDP annual growth in 1996 to 2020. Because China had already achieved 8.2 percent annual GDP growth in 1996 to 2000 and most likely reached 8.9 percent in 2001 to 2005, if 6 percent of the annual GDP growth is assumed for the average growth of the entire period of 1996 to 2020, this implies that China's annual GDP growth will be less than 4.4 percent in 2006 to 2020. Given the strong growth in 2001 to 2005 and the prospect of future growth driving forces discussed in the previous section, most observers are not expecting that China's economy will grow at a rate lower than 6 to 7 percent over the next five to ten years.

The recent performance of China's economy shows that China is on track towards its long-term goal. For example, the GDP grew 7.5 percent in 2001, and accelerated to 8.3 percent in 2002 and 9.5 percent in 2003 and 2004 (NSBC 2005). Recent various forecasts show that China's strong GDP growth will continue and there is no sign of deceleration of economic growth in the coming years (Ma 2004; Brandt *et al.* 2005). In sum, we believe that China can achieve its development goals for the next 20 years. Economic growth will remain high but will decline slightly after 2005.

4. China's agriculture, food economy and sustainable economic growth

The results of analyses presented in this section are based on the Global Trade Analysis Project (GTAP). A brief introduction to the model, improvements on data and parameters of the current GTAP model, and assumptions on macroeconomic development (e.g. GDP and population growth by country or region, total factor productivity [TFP] changes and factor endowments) are provided in Appendix 1.

The implications of China's rapid economic growth on domestic agriculture and food economy as well as sustainable economic growth are examined through several key indicators we simulated for 2001 to 2020. These include self-sufficiency levels, import, export, net export and relative trade shares in China and the world economy. We use 2001 as the base year instead of a more recent year because the data for the most updated version of GTAP are in 2001.

29

4.1 Major results from the baseline scenario

The results of baseline scenario analysis show that China will play a greater role in the world economy. Because of higher economic growth in China than in the rest of the world, China's GDP shares in the world will rise gradually, increasing from 3.8 percent in 2001 to 5.5 percent in 2010 and further to 6.8 percent in 2020 (Figure 6). By 2020, China will become the third largest economy in the world, just behind the United States and Japan. Both import and export will continue to expand. There will be a few agricultural and food commodities that could experience significant decline in self-sufficiency, but they will not affect China's food security (Table 10). By 2020, China's total exports will account for 8.5 percent of the global trade (column 1 and last row, Table 11), which was 5.5 percent in 2001. Accompanying China's rapid economic growth and its rising importance in the global economy, China's agricultural and food as well as overall economy will also experience significant structural changes.

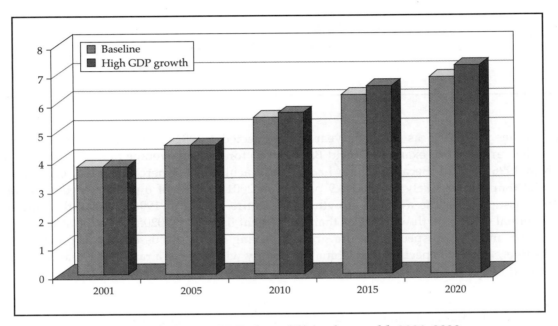

Figure 6. China's GDP share (%) in the world, 2001–2020

Table 10. Self-sufficiency level (%) in different scenarios in 2020

	Baseline	High GDP	High TFP
Rice	103	102	107
Wheat	95	92	97
Coarse grains	86	84	88
Oilseed	53	52	59
Sugar	72	71	75
Fibre	93	92	93
Horticulture	100	100	101
Beef and mutton	94	93	95
Pork and poultry	100	99	107
Milk	81	80	90
Fish	102	101	103
Processed food	101	100	103

Table 11. China's trade shares (%) in the world in 2020

	Export share			Import share			Net export share		
	Baseline	High GDP	High TFP	Baseline	High GDP	High TFP	Baseline	High GDP	High TFP
Food + feed crops	3.9	3.7	4.8	9.8	10.3	8.4	-5.9	-6.6	-3.6
Processed food	4.9	5.0	6.7	2.7	2.7	2.3	2.2	2.3	4.4
Animal products	6.1	5.5	12.3	6.7	7.5	4.4	-0.6	-1.9	7.9
Fibre	0.1	0.1	0.1	9.2	11.4	8.1	-9.1	-11.3	-7.9
Energy	0.2	0.2	0.5	7.1	9.0	4.6	-6.9	-8.8	-4.1
Minerals	2.0	1.6	2.4	23.4	29.4	18.7	-21.4	-27.8	-16.3
Textile/apparel	34.3	37.0	32.5	7.5	7.4	7.9	26.8	29.6	24.6
Manufacture	8.9	9.5	8.7	6.9	7.4	6.8	2.1	2.1	2.0
Services	2.0	2.2	1.8	6.2	6.2	7.0	-4.2	-4.0	-5.2
Total	8.5	9.0	8.4	6.9	7.4	6.8	1.5	1.6	1.5

Agricultural and food economy

Baseline projections show that self-sufficiency of all land-intensive crops except for rice will fall, but the fall will be very moderate for most commodities in the projection period (2001–2020) (Figure 7). This is what we should expect as many land-intensive crops in China have a less comparative advantage in the world markets.

Under the baseline scenario, the most significant increase in imports will be oilseed. The imports are projected to increase from US$6.4 billion in 2001 to US$10.8 billion in 2020 (Panel A, Figure 8). Because their exports will be minimal (Panel B), by 2020 oilseed self-sufficiency will further fall from 70 percent in 2001 to about 50 percent. Increasing import of oilseed is mainly because of the rising domestic demand for both edible oils and feed. This should not be surprising given China's experience in soybean import in the past five years. After China liberalized soybean trade by eliminating nearly all its trade distortions (both tariff and non-tariff measures), annual import of soybean surged from virtually zero in the late 1990s to more than 2 500 million tonnes in 2005.

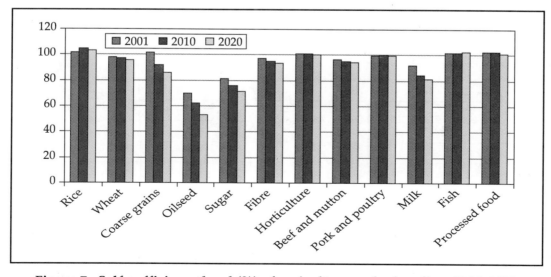

Figure 7. Self-sufficiency level (%) of agriculture under baseline, 2001–2020

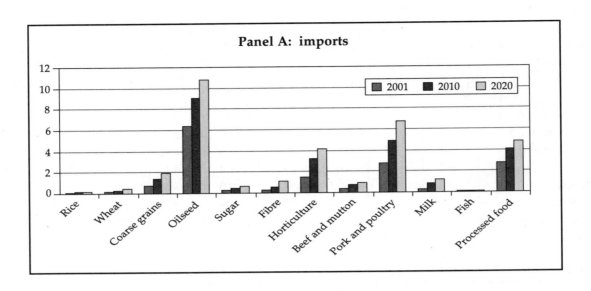

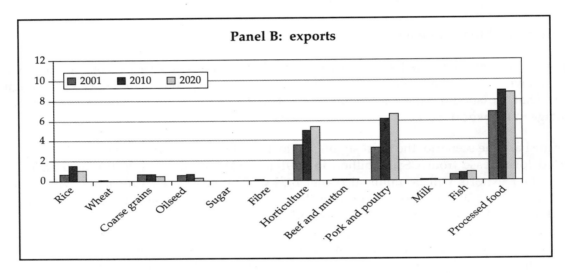

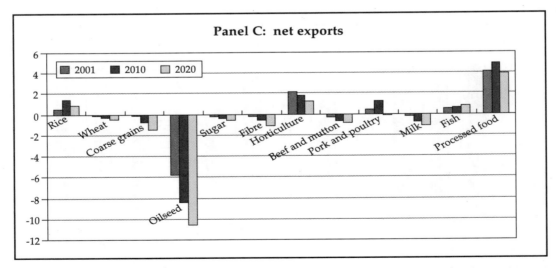

Figure 8. Agriculture and food trade (US$ billion) under baseline, 2001–2020

With rapid economic growth and trade liberalization, China's domestic sugar production will also fall far behind its domestic demand. Sugar imports will rise over time. Its self-sufficiency level will be the second lowest just after oilseed among all crops (Figure 7). Although the total import value of sugar will be much less than many other agricultural and food products (Panel A, Figure 8), sugar imports will account for about 30 percent of domestic consumption (Table 8).

The production of cotton and other plant-based fibre is projected to expand over time, mainly through their productivity growth, but it will also fall behind domestic demand. Similar to many other crops, fibre imports will rise with gradually falling self-sufficiency levels (Figure 7). More imported fibres are required to meet demand from China's rapidly expanding textile and apparel sector, which has created and will continue to generate employment for millions of rural people.

Among cereals, most of the imports are for feed grain (Panel A, Figure 8). By 2020, China will import nearly 20 percent coarse grains, mainly maize, to meet increasing demand from the expansion of the domestic livestock sector. Although China will continue to import wheat, its import will be minimal because per capita demand for wheat is projected not to increase in 2010 to 2015 and will fall thereafter (Appendix Table 4). Rice is the only cereal that will expand its export and maintain a net export commodity from 2001 to 2020. But rice export is projected to be only moderate. The average annual net export of rice will remain at about US$1 billion in 2010. For food grains (rice and wheat), our results show that China's rapid economic growth will not have any significant impacts on their trade.

On the other hand, China will export relatively labour-intensive products such as vegetables, fruits, fish and processed foods. The largest export will be recorded in processed foods (Panel B, Figure 8). While China may import many horticultural products, the exports will exceed the imports. Very low levels of net exports for horticulture and livestock products in the coming decades projected under our baseline differ from many other projections based on partial equilibrium models (Huang *et al.* 2003b; Rosegrant *et al.* 2001), but are consistent with several studies that applied CGE models (Li. *et al.* 1999; Ianchovichina and Martin 2004; Anderson *et al.* 2004). Although the basic conclusions are similar, the variations of magnitude need further investigation.

In terms of the importance of China's agricultural and food trade in global markets, it differs notably among commodities and between imports and exports (Figure 8). China will play a greater role in world markets for both importable commodities (e.g. oilseed, livestock products, processed foods, coarse grain, fibre, sugar) and exportable commodities (e.g. processed foods, pork and poultry, horticulture, fish). Some products figure significantly in both imports and exports due to the aggregation of commodity groups. For example, China imports large volumes of chicken feet and pig innards (or offal) but also export meats due to the price premium of animal feet/innards over meats in the domestic markets. Increasing imports of tropical and subtropical fruits will be associated with more export of Chinese vegetables and fruits to world markets (Figure 8). But in terms of net export or import of the aggregate commodity group, only edible oils (net import), processed foods (net export) and horticulture (net export) are significant. Net imports of oilseed reached 17 percent of world trade in 2001, which will be further raised to more than 25 percent in 2020 (Appendix Figure 1). Its net imports as a percentage of world production will also increase from less than 3 percent to nearly 5 percent over the same period (Appendix Figure 2).

In sum, China's economic growth and trade liberalization will facilitate domestic structural changes in agriculture. China's agriculture will gradually shift from land-intensive sectors with less comparative advantage to labour-intensive sectors with more comparative advantage. While self-sufficiency levels of many commodities will fall with economic growth under a more liberalized trade environment, food grain (excluding feed grain) and overall food self-sufficiency will remain high.

Other sectors

China has a comparative advantage in many non-agricultural sectors. This is particularly true in the textile, apparel and manufacturing sectors. Under the baseline scenario, we project that China will continue to dominate and play a greater role in the world textile and apparel sectors in the coming decades. Currently in this sector, China produces 30 percent more than its domestic demand and exports it to world markets (Figure 9). After 2010, the export as percentage of domestic consumption will further increase to about 40 percent (Figure 9). Its net export will reach US$20 billion in 2010 and about US$40 billion in 2020 (Figure 10). The export share of manufacturing goods will also increase rapidly from 5.5 percent in 2001 to 8.9 percent in 2020 (Table 11).

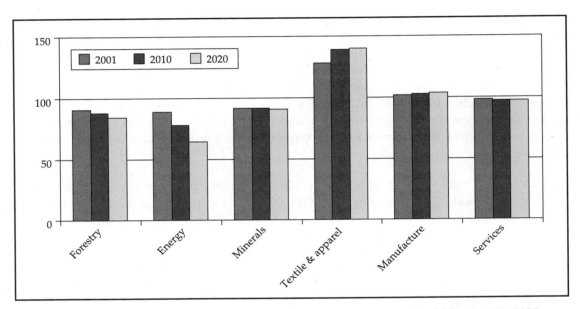

Figure 9. Self-sufficiency rates of non-agricultural sectors in China, 2001–2020

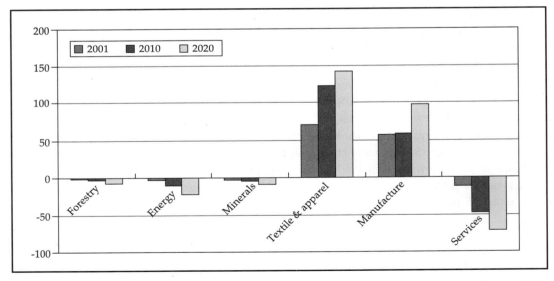

Figure 10. Net exports (US$ billion) of non-agricultural sectors in China, 2001–2020

As we would expect, the imports of forestry products, energy and minerals will rise (Figure 10) and their self-sufficiencies will fall (Figure 9) with economic growth. However, the projected increases in imports of these commodities are not dramatic but moderate and reasonable given the size of China's economy and its lack of these resources. It is worth noting that interpretations of self-sufficiency ratios for forestry should be viewed with caution. China imports large volumes of woods/timber but also exports substantial furniture and other processed wood-based products. However, these export products are not included in the "forestry" sector but in the "manufacturing" sector in the GTAP database and modeling. Despite this data grouping problem, our baseline projection shows that the self-sufficiency of the "forestry" sector will remain as high as 83 percent in 2020 (compared with 91 percent in 2001 (Figure 9). If we would include furniture and other wood-based processed products in the forestry sector, the net imports of forestry products would be minimal. Among all resource-based industries, a significant rise in energy imports projected in the coming decades is worthy of concern. Under the baseline, that is, if the government policy would not respond to the rapid increase of energy imports, the self-sufficiency of energy would fall from 92 percent in 2001 to less than 67 percent in 2020 (Figure 9). We will return to the energy import issue later in this section when we discuss the high TFP growth scenario.

4.2 Major results from China's high GDP growth scenario

Several interesting results are generated from the comparison of the results of the high growth scenario with those of the baseline scenario. First, the simulations show that the higher growth of China's economy will not have significant impacts on overall food and agricultural economy in China. Although a higher growth of China's economy is associated with a lower rate of self-sufficiency in nearly all agricultural and food commodities, the changes will be minimal (Table 10). Rising domestic demand resulting from additional income growth in the future will be less than that of the past. Food income elasticities have been falling and will continue to fall with the rapid growth of China's economy. After 2010, all cereal grains will have negative income elasticities (Appendix Table 4). Increases in income will lead to decline in cereal consumption. Table 10 shows that, in comparing columns 1 and 2, the rates of self-sufficiency decline only 1 percent for all agricultural and food commodities except for coarse grain (2 percent) and wheat (3 percent). The small impact of the higher economic growth on agriculture and food security is also reflected in the small changes in China's net exports of food and feed (Figure 11), and very small changes in China's import or export shares of agricultural and food commodities in the world markets (Table 11).

Second, with higher GDP growth, China will further restructure its agricultural and food economy in favour of the commodities with a greater comparative advantage. For example, the export shares of the land-intensive food and feed crop sectors in world trade will decline and their import shares will rise (Table 11). The high GDP growth scenario reduces the export share of animal products (6.1 percent in the high GDP growth scenario, compared to 5.5 percent in the baseline) because of their positive income elasticities. As a whole, the net export (or net import) of food and feed will decline (increase) by about US$4 billion compared to the baseline in 2020 (Figure 11 and Table 13).

Third, China would further exploit its comparative advantage in textile and apparel and manufacturing sectors under the higher economic growth assumption. Table 11 shows that export shares of textile and apparel would increase from 34 percent in the baseline to 37 percent under the high growth scenario. As the import shares are similar to those of the baseline, the net export shares rise from 27 to 30 percent, and the net export value increases by about US$15 billion (Figure 11). Although the change is not as great as textile and apparel, the exports of the manufacturing sector change in the same direction (Figure 11).

Last but not the least, China's imports of energy and mineral products would further rise with higher economic growth. For example, the shares of China's net imports in world trade in 2020 for energy and minerals will rise from 6.9 and 21.4 percent in the baseline to 8.8 and 27.8 percent in the high GDP growth scenario, respectively (columns 7 and 8, Table 11). Whether or not such a high

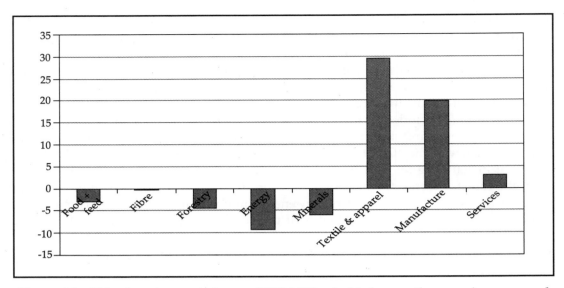

Figure 11. China's net export change (US$ billion): high growth scenario compared to the baseline in 2020

level of dependence on imports for energy and minerals would undermine the sustainability of the Chinese economy is an issue that has attracted much attention within and outside China.

4.3 The impact of China's higher TFP growth

The above two subsections have examined two of the major concerns for food security and the sustainability of natural resources under China's rapid economic growth. For the first concern, we seem to have reached a conclusion that China will be able to produce a sufficient amount of food to meet its increasing demand under an economy with rapid growth. Moreover, even if one would consider the levels of food imports for some commodities under both baseline and high growth scenarios to be too high for security, there are still alternatives such as productivity enhanced investment that will help China to further improve its production. The analyses presented above also show that rising dependence on natural resource imports could become a bottleneck for China's rapid and sustainable economic growth if there are no policy responses. However, the Chinese Government has recognized such problems and has taken various measures to improve the efficiency of resource use particularly through restructuring economic and technological changes in those sectors that intensively use the natural resources.

In this subsection, we explore the likely impact of technological changes on China's food security and its dependence on imports of natural resources with specific focus on energy and minerals. In this context, the high TFP growth scenario, is used. This scenario assumes that all assumptions for the baseline scenario in China and the rest of the world are maintained except for the TFP assumptions for China. In China, we assume that average productivity will be increased by about 5 percent in ten years. This is equivalent to additional productivity growth of 0.47 percent annually. Similar to other scenarios, productivity growth will also start in 2006 and continue to 2020. It is worth noting that this is a very moderate change in productivity growth. Under this assumption, by 2020 TFP will be only about 7.3 percent higher than that under the baseline scenario. More detailed discussions of the high TFP growth scenario are provided in Appendix 1.

The results from the high TFP growth scenario are compared with those simulated under the baseline scenario and are presented in Tables 12 and 13 and Figure 11. Our analyses show that China could substantially increase its food supply and reduce (increase) its food imports (exports) through a very moderate change in agricultural productivity (the last column, Table 10). Under the high TFP

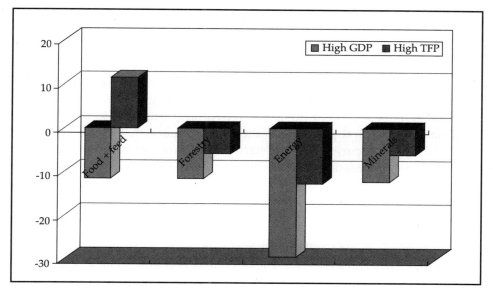

Figure 12. Net export of food and natural resource products (US$ billion) under high growth and high TFP scenarios in China in 2020

growth scenario, China could become a net food and feed exporter and the export value would reach US$11 billion in 2020 (Figure 12). It is worth noting that the additional assumption under the high TFP growth scenario (compared to the baseline) for agricultural and food production is that China's agricultural productivity would rise by 5 percent in ten years. This should not be considered as a strong assumption given the recent rapid growth of government investment in agriculture in general and R&D in particular (Rozelle *et al.* 2005).

China could also significantly reduce its dependence on imports of natural resources through innovations in input-saving technology. By 2020, energy imports will be reduced from US$29 billion (the baseline) to US$13 billion (the high TFP growth scenario, Figure 12). Similarly, the high TFP growth scenario will also substantially reduce the imports of minerals (Figure 12). Reducing energy and mineral imports under the high TFP growth scenario implies there will be a significant reduction in import dependence for natural resources. Table 11 further shows that the net import shares of China in world trade will decline to 4.1 percent only (from 6.9 percent in the baseline) for energy and 16.3 percent for minerals (from 21.4 percent in the baseline, Table 11).

5. Implications of China's rapid economic growth for the rest of the world

The Chinese economy has been increasingly integrated into the world economy since its economic reform. The integration has occurred in both commodity trade and FDI between China and the rest of the world. In 2003, China ranked first in the world in terms of inward flows of FDI, second in terms of absolute purchasing power and sixth in terms of real GDP (United Nations 2005). The increasing inflows of FDI have stimulated China's economic growth and promoted China's international trade. In this section, we examine the impact and implications of China's economic growth on the rest of the world in the future. We will first discuss the implications of China's rapid growth upon the rest of the world from our baseline analysis. Then further implications from higher GDP and productivity growth scenarios will follow.

5.1 Major results from the baseline analysis

The main conclusions on the implications of China's rapid economic growth from our baseline analysis are that China's growth will provide more opportunities than challenges to the rest of the world, and overall the world will gain from China's economic expansion. As regards food and agriculture, China's economic growth under a more liberalized global economy will help countries with a comparative advantage in land-intensive agricultural products to expand their production and export additional agricultural products to the Chinese markets. China's economic growth will not affect the world's food security. For the natural resource sector, resource-rich countries can take advantage of China's increasing imports of energy and minerals to support their economic growth.

Agricultural and food security

Under the baseline scenario, China will significantly increase its imports of many land-intensive agricultural commodities (e.g. oilseed, feed, sugar, cotton) and also some labour-intensive products (e.g tropical and subtropical fruits, processed foods, some parts of pig and poultry) (Panel A, Figure 8). Increasing imports of these agricultural and food products will provide opportunities for many developing countries in South and Central America and some developed countries (e.g. United States, Canada and Australia) to expand their production and exports. For example, the exports of agricultural and food products from South and Central America to China will be more than doubled, from US$3.9 billion in 2001 to US$8.5 billion in 2020 (the row of SAM, Table 12). The North American Free Trade Area (NAFTA) can also gain substantially from rising Chinese imports of oilseed and feed. China's imports from NAFTA will rise from US$4.7 billion in 2001 to US$9.6 billion in 2020.

China's rapid economic growth will not be associated with a significant rise in imports of many staple foods. As China's economy grows, demand for rice, wheat and other cereal foods will not increase or even fall after 2010. The only major cereal that will experience a growth in import is maize used as feed. These results imply that China's rapid growth will not affect world food security.

Table 12. Agriculture and food trade in other countries/regions with China, 2001–2020 (US$ billion)

Regional aggregations*	Import from China			Export to China			Net export to China	
	2001	2020	Change in 2020 over 2001 (%)	2001	2020	Change in 2020 over 2001 (%)	2001	2020
China: HK + TW	1.7	2.1	23	0.1	0.2	177.3	-1.6	-1.9
India	0.2	2.4	1 179	0.1	0.3	79.1	0.0	-2.1
Japan + Republic of Korea	6.7	6.6	-1	0.5	1.5	217.3	-6.2	-5.1
SE Asia	1.4	4.0	176	2.1	2.9	39.6	0.6	-1.1
Other Asia	0.5	1.3	141	0.2	0.3	41.5	-0.4	-1.1
AusNzl	0.2	0.2	39	2.0	4.4	112.8	1.9	4.1
NAFTA	1.7	2.1	19	4.7	9.6	102.5	3.0	7.5
SAM	0.2	0.3	38	3.9	8.5	119.6	3.6	8.2
EU15	2.2	2.3	5	1.0	2.3	130.5	-1.2	0.0
CEEC	0.2	0.2	-14	0.1	0.2	171.2	-0.1	0.0
Russian Federation	0.3	0.5	61	0.2	0.7	185.4	0.0	0.2
ROW	1.1	2.1	97	0.5	1.1	131.6	-0.6	-1.0
Total	16.4	24.0	47	15.4	31.9	107.1	-1.0	7.8

* Details in Appendix Table 2.

Horticultural products are the most heterogeneous commodities that China will both export and import in large volume. The countries that are projected to have a significant increase in vegetables and fruits exported from China are mostly the developed countries and regions such as Japan, Republic of Korea, European Union and North America, and some relatively developed countries in Southeast Asia. On the other hand, China will also import substantial horticultural products, particularly tropical and subtropical fruits, from Southeast Asia, South and Central America, NAFTA, Australia and New Zealand. Their production and export to China will expand with China's economic growth.

China's economic development and trade liberalization also provide great opportunities for multilateral trade with China in the livestock sector (Figure 8). While China may increase exports of pork and poultry to East Asia (e.g. Japan and Republic of Korea), European Union and NAFTA, imports from Australia, New Zealand, NAFTA and Southeast Asia are expected to rise substantially.

China has been a net food exporter since the late 1980s (Table 7) and contributed significantly not only to its own domestic food security but also to that of the rest of the world, particularly the developing countries. In future, although we project that for food and feed as a whole China will shift from its current status as a net exporter to a net importer, net imports will be only about US$7.8 billion in 2020 (the last column, Table 12). South and Central America (SAM) is the region that will have the largest net export value to China. The net export from SAM to China will reach US$8.2 billion in 2020 (Table 12). Besides the SAM region, the net export from NAFTA (US$7.5 billion) and Australia/New Zealand (US$4.1 billion) to China will also be substantial. China will also export food and feed to many other Asian countries valued at about US$10 billion in 2020 thus contributing to food security in the region.

In sum, the shifting of China's agricultural structure in the coming decade under rapid economic growth will generate more trade in the agricultural and food sectors. This will provide opportunities for many countries to adjust their production structures in order to reap the benefits of expanded markets in China. Due to trade liberalization (not China's economic growth), rising exports of several agricultural commodities in which China has a comparative advantage will challenge countries that are exporting the same commodities to the world markets. The impact of China's rapid economic growth on world agricultural and food markets is smaller that what many may have expected. Finally, China's rapid growth will not result in any significant increase in imports of rice, wheat and food maize, which are the most important crops for food security in developing countries.

Non-agricultural sectors

As projected under our baseline scenario, China will become more competitive in the manufacturing and textile and apparel sectors. The trade surplus of these two sectors will increase over time (Figure 10 and Table 13). However, the trade flows differ between these two sectors. As Table 13 has shown, China is a net exporter of textile and apparel products with all trade partners. NAFTA, European Union, Japan and Republic of Korea, as well as Hong Kong Special Administrative Region and Taiwan Province of China are six main economic regions that will import large amounts of textile and apparel products from China (Table 13). Total imports of these five regions will account for nearly 80 percent of China's exports. This could challenge the local textile and apparel sectors in these regions if they do not adjust their economic structures to better cope with China's rapid economic growth and trade expansion. With respect to manufactured goods, China has a trade surplus and will continue to increase the surplus with its major trade partners except for three regions (Japan and Republic of Korea, Russian Federation and Southeast Asia) (Table 13). By 2020, China will have a trade deficit (net import) of US$70 billion in manufactured goods from the above three regions. By contrast, NAFTA, European Union, Hong Kong Special Administrative Region and Taiwan Province of China are the three largest importers of Chinese manufacturing products (more than 80 percent in 2020), which could also have important policy implications for structural changes in these regions.

In the next two decades China will significantly increase the import of natural resource products (Table 13). Oil imported from the Middle East (including in the rest of the world, ROW, in Table 13) and the Russian Federation and minerals imported from Australia, NAFTA and South America will rise substantially (Table 13). Increases in energy and mineral imports would further trigger the pressure for their rising world prices, which would impact not only the world's economic structure, but also world agriculture through its effects on key agricultural inputs (e.g. fertilizer, agricultural machinery). But as we will show in the next subsection, these impacts should not be exaggerated because China's total imports of energy and minerals account for only a small share of the global production.

Table 13. Net export of energy, minerals, textile and apparel, manufactory and services to China (US$ billion)

Regional aggregations	Energy		Minerals		Textile & apparel		Manufactory*		Services	
	2001	2020	2001	2020	2001	2020	2001	2020	2001	2020
China: HK + TW	-0.6	-0.1	-0.1	-0.1	-9.2	-14.6	-7.6	-11.7	13.4	43.2
India	-0.2	-0.2	0.3	0.8	0.1	-0.3	-0.8	0.9	0.1	0.4
Japan + Republic of Korea	-2.1	-0.3	0.1	0.8	-11.2	-15.7	26.7	43.9	-0.8	-0.9
SE Asia	0.6	1.2	-0.2	0.1	-1.3	-1.8	7.0	18.4	0.3	2.8
Other Asia	0.0	0.2	0.2	0.4	-1.2	-1.3	-2.1	-2.7	0.0	0.1
AusNzl	0.1	0.4	1.2	2.7	-2.2	-3.3	-1.5	-3.2	0.0	0.3
NAFTA	-0.2	0.1	1.1	2.8	-22.7	-45.9	-64.6	-111.4	-0.2	7.2
SAM	0.0	0.2	1.1	2.9	-2.2	-3.6	-2.5	-5.9	-0.2	0.2
EU15	-0.2	0.3	1.0	2.6	-12.1	-33.1	-11.4	-16.9	-0.9	12.2
CEEC	0.0	0.0	-0.1	0.2	-1.4	-2.4	-2.2	-3.4	0.2	0.9
Russian Federation	0.3	2.0	0.0	0.1	-1.7	-4.0	5.9	7.6	-0.3	-0.7
ROW	5.8	18.4	0.9	2.0	-5.9	-15.5	-3.6	-11.8	0.2	5.3
Total	3.4	22.1	3.9	10.4	-70.8	-141.6	-56.7	-96.2	11.9	70.9

* Details in Appendix Table 3.

5.2 The implications of China's high economic growth

Under the high GDP growth scenario, China will generate more trade and nearly all countries or regions will gain from the faster growth of China's economy. The signs and sizes of gains for each region from additional growth in China depend on the nature of its economic structure. Those countries that are largely complementary to China's economy will gain more from China's growth. Otherwise, when a country has a similar economic structure as that of China, adverse consequence could occur. Detailed comparisons of impacts on output, trade and corresponding welfare due to China's higher economic growth (compared to the baseline) are presented in Table 14, Figure 11 and Table 15, respectively.

Table 14 shows that all regions will gain in terms of food and feed production from China's faster growth (the first three rows, Table 14). With further restructuring of China's economy and rising food demand resulting from higher economic growth (compared to the baseline), the imports of food and feed in China will rise. A 10 percent increase in the annual growth rate of the GDP (e.g. from 8 percent to 8.8 percent) and holding all other factors constant, China's food and feed net imports (exports) will increase (decline) by about US$3 billion in 2020. The rising imports in China will push the world price upwards and increase production of food and feed in all countries, particularly exporting countries (Table 14).

Table 14. Percentage output changes in different regions in 2020 due to China's higher economic growth (compared to baseline)

	HK + TW	India	SE Asia	Japan + Republic of Korea	Other Asia	AusNzl	NAFTA	SAM	Enlarged EU	Russian Federation	ROW
Food + feed crops	0.4	0.1	0.4	0.3	0.1	0.5	0.4	0.5	0.3	0.5	0.3
Processed food	0.1	0.1	0.1	0.2	0.1	0.2	0.1	0.2	0.1	0.3	0.2
Animal products	0.4	0.0	0.6	0.4	0.2	0.6	0.4	0.3	0.3	0.6	0.4
Fibre	-2.0	-0.9	-0.8	0.4	-1.1	-0.5	0.0	-0.5	4.4	-0.7	0.0
Forestry	1.1	0.5	4.0	0.9	1.4	6.6	1.6	1.3	4.8	17.1	5.0
Energy	3.1	2.7	3.3	4.0	3.9	2.9	2.7	2.7	3.0	3.0	3.1
Minerals	1.3	9.1	2.2	1.4	6.7	8.8	1.2	6.8	1.5	1.0	2.8
Textile & apparel	-3.6	-1.0	-3.3	-2.5	-2.0	-3.5	-1.6	-1.6	-2.6	-2.6	-2.6
Manufactory	0.6	0.1	0.2	0.3	0.2	-0.6	0.0	-0.1	0.2	-1.1	-0.4
Services	0.1	-0.2	0.1	0.2	-0.2	0.5	0.0	0.1	0.1	0.8	0.2
Total	0.12	-0.09	0.09	0.17	-0.16	0.49	0.05	0.13	0.10	0.77	0.20

Table 15. Welfare change in different regions in 2020 due to China's higher economic growth (compared to baseline)

	Aggregate welfare effect (EV) US$ billion	Change in welfare (%)
China	226.2	10.6
The rest of world	14.8	0.09
China: HK + TW	1.3	0.22
India	-1.4	-0.15
Japan + Republic of Korea	1.4	0.07
SE Asia	0.4	0.07
Other Asia	-0.2	-0.06
AusNzl	1.3	0.51
NAFTA	1.4	0.03
SAM	1.1	0.10
EU15	0.8	0.03
CEEC	-0.2	-0.05
Russian Federation	2.7	0.82
ROW	6.2	0.44
Total	241.0	1.31

While higher economic growth in China will generate more domestic demand for final consumer goods, it will also result in both higher exports and imports of manufactured and textile and apparel products. The world prices of these commodities are projected to fall accordingly. The consumers in large importing countries or regions (i.e. NAFTA, European Union, Japan and Republic of Korea, Hong Kong Special Administrative Region and Taiwan Province of China) will gain from the lower world prices. For those countries or regions that export manufacturing products to China (e.g. Japan and Republic of Korea, Southeast Asia), their production will rise (Table 14). However, countries with the same export structures to China may be hurt by lower prices. This may explain why India and some other Asian countries will incur slightly negative effects (ranging from 0.01 percent to 0.02 percent in 2020) from China's higher economic growth (10 percent increase in the annual growth rate, see Section 4.3).

Our simulations also show that the production structure in other countries will adjust accordingly as China's economic growth accelerates. This is reflected in the differences of production changes across sectors in each region (Table 14). Whether a country or region can reap gains from China's economic expansion as those presented in this section will depend on how flexible and efficient their economies are in responding to world market changes triggered by China's economic growth.

One concern that might arise from China's more rapid economic growth is the corresponding increase in the imports of products in the forestry, energy and mineral sectors (Figure 11). While rising resource imports may further provide economic growth opportunities for countries exporting these products, it could also challenge the conservation efforts in these countries. In addition, there may be potentially negative effects on other resource-importing countries as world prices will rise with China's imports.

To have a better understanding of the overall impact of China's rapid economic growth on the rest of the world, welfare analysis is applied. Table 15 shows that global welfare will increase by about US$241 billion in 2020 under China's high growth scenario (compared to the baseline), of which about US$226 billion (93.7 percent) occurred in China and nearly US$15 billion in the rest of the world (6.3 percent). In terms of the GDP, the rest of the world (the whole world excluding China) will have additional annual growth of 0.12 percent in 2020 (compared with the baseline). Therefore, rapid economic growth in China is an important engine of world economic development.

Table 15 also shows that nearly all regions could gain from China's economic expansion. India and other South Asian nations are exceptions. The changes of welfare indicate that regions that are complementary with China will gain more from China's higher economic growth (Table 15). For example, the Russian Federation, Australia, South America and the Middle East (including the ROW group) will gain more than many other countries because China will significantly increase its imports of energy and minerals as well as many agricultural products from these regions compared to other regions. The exporting countries gain from increases in both price and volume associated with China's commodities. This will further expand welfare gains by raising the return of endowments, enhancing efficiency of allocation etc.

On the other hand, countries seeking to expand exports of products similar to those of China would be adversely affected. India and other South Asian countries such as Bangladesh and Sri Lanka belong to this group. Like China, these countries are also major exporters of textiles and apparel. Textile and apparel exports accounted for 24 percent (India) and 54 percent (other South Asian countries) of their total exports (Appendix Table 8). Moreover, manufacturing products exported from India and some other Asian countries have a high degree of substitutability with those from China. Therefore these countries would encounter increasing competition from China in the world markets in the coming decades.

5.3 Implications of China's higher TFP growth

The key issue analysed in the higher TFP growth scenario is the extent to which China could lower its imports of food and feed as well as products related to natural resources through technological changes. The analysis hereunder reveals that China could significantly ease concerns with respect to both food security and resource dependence.

Under China's high TFP growth scenario, our analysis shows that the rise in China's agricultural productivity and nature resource-use efficiency will considerably reduce imports of these products (Figure 10). With a very moderate change in agricultural technology, increases in domestic production could shift China from a food and feed net importer to exporter. While China will continue to import forest products under the high TFP growth scenario, their import will be reduced by more than half (Figure 12). For the energy and mineral sector, the high TFP growth scenario will enable China to save these inputs substantially. Net imports of energy will be reduced by nearly 60 percent and account for about 4 percent of total world production in 2020. This level of import should not seriously affect China's economic growth and the world's energy security. Similarly, for minerals, imports will be reduced by nearly half (Figure 12) and their share of net imports will fall to 3.2 percent of the total world production in 2020 (Figure 13).

Reducing imports of food, energy and minerals in China under the high TFP scenario will lower world prices of these commodities and therefore adversely affect production and export among exporting countries. By 2020, the world prices of food and forestry will have dropped by about 2 to 3 percent and energy and mineral products by 3 to 7 percent (Table 16).

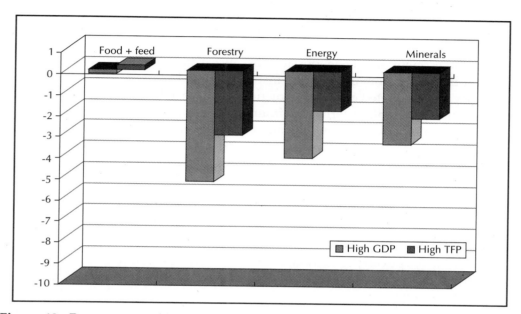

Figure 13. Percentages of China's net export in world total production under high GDP growth and high technology scenarios in 2020

Table 16. The world price change in 2020 (compared to baseline) (%)

	High GDP growth	High TFP growth
Food + feed crops	0.54	-1.66
Processed food	0.05	-2.11
Animal products	0.46	-2.58
Fibre	1.96	-1.54
Forestry	4.57	-3.19
Energy	2.39	-3.13
Minerals	12.03	-7.17
Textile & apparel	-0.72	0.18
Manufacture	-0.02	-0.36
Services	-0.07	-0.14
Total	0.04	-0.43

6. Concluding remarks

Two and half decades of economic reform in China have achieved remarkable economic growth. During the 1980s and 1990s, China has become one of the fastest growing economies in the world. The GDP grew at about 10 percent annually in the past 20 years. Over the course of the reform period, both rural and urban incomes have increased noticeably. Rising income has also been associated with a substantial reduction of poverty and significant improvement in food security.

China's experience shows the importance of both domestic and external policies in achieving sustainable growth. China's rapid growth would not have been possible without its domestic economic reforms, macroeconomic stability and its "open-door" policy. The rapid economic growth has been realized through high capital investments, gradually releasing constraints for abundant rural labour for non-farm employment, technological changes and external economic expansion. High growth of investment has been possible because China has high domestic saving rates and also enjoys a massive inflow of FDI. The institutional and market-oriented reforms improved economic efficiency and facilitated economic structural changes in line with shifts in market demand. A stable internal and favourable external environment also provided better prospects for China's economic growth and market expansion. The successful growth in the agriculture sector facilitates the economic transition from agriculture to industry/services and from the rural to the urban economy. The growth in agricultural productivity enabled China to release its large pool of abundant rural labour, providing cheap labour for the nation to industrialize its economy.

China's experience also shows that institutional innovation (particularly land tenure), technological changes and market reform and infrastructure development are critical to the improvement of the nation's food security. China's experience further shows that overall economic growth is a primary and essential condition for poverty reduction, but not a sufficient condition for continuous reduction of poverty. Important factors shaping trends in China's poverty reduction are agricultural growth in the initial stage of economic development and the subsequent growth in non-farm employment with the expansion of industry.

While there are a number of challenges related to economic growth, we are still very optimistic about China's future growth. With rapid growth of its economy which is increasingly dependent on the external sector, China needs to continue to enhance its long-term partnership with trade partners. A stable and favourable external economy and political environment will be critical for the sustainable development of China's economy. On the other hand, any country that is seeking to embrace globalization cannot afford to ignore this "rising dragon" economy in Asia.

The high level of China's food security, even under a rapid economic growth scenario, suggests that China's massive import of food is not likely to occur. China can still significantly increase its food production through new technological innovations. However, more effort will be needed to cope with the increasing scarcity of water in many parts of Northern China.

In restructuring its agricultural economy China will need: (i) to create better R&D and technology innovation systems, (ii) better management of water resources, (iii) to avoid environmental degradation and (iv) support institutions, such as farmers' associations. China should also increase its efforts to improve the quality of all agricultural products and capacity to effectively implement and regulate quality standards to meet increasing demand from own domestic consumers and better compliance with international standards. Meanwhile, policy-makers should be concerned about the poverty and equity effects of trade liberalization and the need to encourage farmers in poorer agricultural and inland areas to shift their production (where appropriate) to more competitive agricultural products and/or to take other off-farm jobs to improve their livelihoods.

It is also worth noting that gains in non-agricultural sectors from trade liberalization far surpass those for agriculture. On the other hand, China's rising dependence on forestry products, energy and minerals presents one of the biggest challenges that China will face in the coming decades. The challenge exists even if the imports of these commodities are not projected to be too spectacular. Meeting this challenge will require substantial and long-term efforts in technological innovation, economic restructuring, investments, seeking new resources and establishing strategic partnerships with major trade partners.

The results from this study also provide significant policy implications for many countries that are currently China's major trade partners or those seeking greater economic and trade relations with China. The main conclusions on the implications of China's rapid economic growth are that China's growth will provide more opportunities than challenges to the rest of the world. Overall the rest of the world will gain from China's economic expansion though this general conclusion may not hold for some countries. China is set to play an increasing role in international trade, which should benefit both developed and developing countries.

For those countries whose economic structures are complementary to China, there will be emerging opportunities offered by China's increasing imports due to its rapid growth and integration into the world economy. While countries that have similar export structures to that of China and are competing for the same export markets will have to make extra efforts to restructure their economies and invest more in domestic infrastructure to lower production and marketing costs.

The rapid growth of China's economy will help those countries with a comparative advantage in many land-intensive products to expand their production and increase their exports to China. Developing countries can export agricultural products to China, particularly soybeans, other oilseed, maize, cotton, sugar, tropical and subtropical fruits, as well as some livestock products (e.g. milk, beef, mutton), although they have to compete with other exporters from developed countries such as the United States, Canada and Australia.

While we recognize a number of limitations in using GTAP to simulate the impacts of China's rising economy, we believe the major trends and results that are generated from this study. We also recognize that there are many challenges such as tourism, educational services, agricultural technology transfer and policy responses that cannot be analysed under the current framework.

Methodology, data and assumptions

The main analytical tool used in this study is a model for global trade, which is based on the GTAP. In this Appendix, after a brief introduction of the model, the efforts to improve GTAP's database and parameters for China are discussed. Finally, assumptions on macroeconomic development such as GDP and population growths by country or region, TFP changes and factor endowments are discussed.

A1. The Global Trade Analysis Project (GTAP)

We used the well-known GTAP as our analytical framework to assess the implications of China's rapid economic growth for agriculture and food security in both China and the rest of the world. The GTAP is a multi-region, multi-sector computable general equilibrium model, with perfect competition and constant returns to scale. The model is fully described by Hertel (1997). It has been used to generate projections of policy impacts in the future (Arndt *et al.* 1997; Hertel *et al.* 1999; van Tongeren and Huang 2004).

In the GTAP model, each country or region is depicted within the same structural model. The consumer side is represented by the country or regional household to which the income of factors, tariff revenues and taxes are assigned. The country or regional household allocates its income to three expenditure categories: private household expenditures, government expenditures and savings. For the consumption of the private household, the non-homothetic Constant Difference of Elasticities (CDE) function is applied. Firms combine intermediate inputs and primary factors, land, labour (skilled and unskilled) and capital. Intermediate inputs are composites of domestic and foreign components, and the foreign component is differentiated by region of origin (the Armington assumption). On factor markets, the model assumes full employment, with labour and capital being fully mobile within regions, but immobile internationally. Labour and capital remuneration rates are endogenously determined at equilibrium. In the case of crop production, farmers make decisions on land allocation. Land is assumed to be imperfectly mobile between alternative crops, and hence allowed for endogenous land rent differentials. Each country or region is equipped with one country regional household that distributes income across savings and consumption expenditures to maximize its utility.

The GTAP model includes two global institutions. All transport between regions is carried out by the international transport sector. The trading costs reflect the transaction costs involved in international trade, as well as the physical activity of transportation itself. Using transport inputs from all regions, the international transport sector minimizes its costs under the Cobb–Douglas Production Function. The second global institution is the global bank, which takes the savings from all regions and purchases investment goods in all regions depending on the expected rates of return. The global bank guarantees that global savings are equal to global investments.

The GTAP model does not have an exchange rate variable. However, by choosing as a numeraire index of global factor prices, each region's change of factor prices relative to the numeraire directly reflects a change in the purchasing power of the region's factor incomes on the world market. This can be directly interpreted as a change in the real exchange rate. The welfare changes are measured by the equivalent variation, which can be computed from each region's household expenditure function.

Taxes and other policy measures are represented as *ad valorem* tax equivalents. These create wedges between the undistorted prices and the policy-inclusive prices. Production taxes are placed on intermediate or primary inputs, or on output. Trade policy instruments include applied most-favoured nation tariffs, antidumping duties, countervailing duties, export quotas and other trade restrictions. Additional internal taxes can be placed on domestic or imported intermediate inputs and may be applied at differential rates that discriminate against imports. Taxes could be also placed on exports and on primary factor income. Finally, relevant taxes are placed on final consumption, and can be applied differentially to consumption of domestic and imported goods.

The GDP can be treated either endogenously or exogenously in simulations. Normally, the GDP is treated as an endogenous variable when analysing the impacts of trade liberalization or other policy shocks (e.g. technology changes, resource endowment changes and fiscal or financial policy changes). However, the GDP also can be treated as an exogenous variable when one uses the GTAP to analyse the impacts of overall economic growth on the performance of individual sectors, trade and others. In this case, technology variables become endogenous if capital investment is exogenous, or capital investment become endogenous if technological change is exogenous.

A2. Data improvements

The GTAP database contains detailed bilateral trade, transport and protection data characterizing economic linkages among regions, linked with individual country input–output databases which account for intersectoral linkages among the 57 sectors in each of the 87 regions. The database provides quite detailed classification on agriculture, with 14 primary agricultural sectors and seven agricultural processing sectors. All monetary values of the data are in US$ million and the base year for the version (Version 6) used in this study is 2001. For the purposes of this study, the GTAP database has been aggregated into 14 regions and 18 sectors. The regional and sectoral aggregations are summarized in Appendix Tables 2 and 3.

Before we applied the GTAP Version 6, we carefully examined its database and parameters for China and made substantial improvement to several aspects related to agricultural input and output ratios, demand parameters, trade policies and production values. For a global model such as GTAP, some data defects for a country like China are not surprising. Major data improvements to GTAP Version 6 include:

1) Input–output tables in the agriculture sector. In this study, we overcome some of the shortcomings in the GTAP database by taking advantage of data that have been collected by the National Development and Reform Commission (NDRC) and government organizations. Using a sampling framework with more than 30 000 households, the NDRC collects data on the costs of production of all of China's major crops and livestock. The data set contains information on quantities and total expenditures on labour and material inputs as well as expenditure on a large number of miscellaneous costs such as tax, transportation and marketing costs. Each farmer also reports output and the total revenues earned from the crops or livestock. The data have previously been used in analyses on China's agricultural supply and input demand (Huang and Rozelle 1996; World Bank 1997). The comparison of the input shares of agricultural production in the original database and improved ones are summarized in Appendix Table 4. In doing so, we also ensure the balance and consistency of overall input–output relationships among sectors.

2) Demand elasticities in the base year. A major effort has been made to improve income and price demand parameters in the base year (2001). We incorporated the most updated and empirically estimated price and income elasticities of demand for various foods in China for the base year (2001) into GTAP Version 6. For comparison, Appendix Table 5 summarizes major adjustments that have been made in this study. In general, the original GTAP has much lower own-price elasticities of demand for various foods than those that we found in the empirical studies (Fan *et al.* 1995; Huang and Bouis 1996; Huang and Rozelle 1998). We also find that the income elasticities of demand for cereal, edible oils, livestock products and fish are relatively high in the GTAP's original database, while they are relatively low for other commodities such as sugar, horticultural products, processed foods and most non-agricultural products and services (Appendix Table 4).

3) Income elasticities in the projection period. We assume that income elasticities of demand for various foods and non-food commodities will change with income growth. This is a reasonable and essential assumption for a study that makes a long-term projection/simulation. In general, we assume that food income elasticities decline with income growth (Appendix Table 4), which is based on several empirical studies in China by researchers (Huang and Bouis 1996; Huang *et al.* 1991; Huang and David 1993; Huang and Rozelle 1998) and has also widely been applied in other simulation models (e.g. Huang and Chen 1999; Huang and Li 2003).

4) Trade distortions. A number of studies have estimated the magnitude of agricultural price distortions using the available series on domestic and international prices. Unfortunately, the results obtained have varied widely. Huang, *et al.* (2004) adopted a new approach based on policy impacts from detailed interviews with participants in China's agricultural markets and trades rather than on readily available price series. This approach provides a much clearer indication of the implication of agricultural trade policies than would otherwise be possible. Their results have been used in several recent studies on the impacts of the WTO on China's economy (Bhattasali *et al.* 2004; Anderson *et al.* 2004; Ianchovichina and Martin 2004). We adjusted both import and export tariff equivalents of agricultural commodities in the base year (2001) based on results from the Huang *et al.* (2004) study. Detailed adjustments are provided in Appendix 5.

A3. Assumptions under different scenarios

The central issue of this study is to assess the implications of China's rapid economic growth in China and the rest of the world, particular in the Asia and Pacific region. Towards this end three scenarios have been developed. They are baseline (A), China's high growth scenario (B) and China's high productivity growth scenario (C).

A3.1 The baseline scenario

Initial GDP growth. For initial assumptions on GDP growth over the next 20 years (2001–2020) for all countries except China and India, we adopted World Bank projections. World Bank projection on global and regional GDP growths has been widely used in many similar studies (e.g. Walmsley *et al.* 2000; van Tongeren and Huang 2004). In the meantime, we also incorporated economic growth prospects for Asia with information from *Economic outlook* (Asian Development Bank 2002). The assumptions on annual growth of the GDP for 2001 to 2020 are based on the prospects of China's economic growth presented in Section 3. Initial GDP growths for all countries are used to calibrate the implicit assumptions of technology changes (e.g. TFP) embodied in these initial GDP growths given the input–output tables for individual countries or regions. After the embodied TFP growths are estimated and used as exogenous assumptions in the model, the GDP is treated as endogenous in the final analysis.

Population and labour. Population data for 2001 to 2020 for all countries except for China are from the United Nations' population projection. China's population projection is from a recent study by IIASA (Toth *et al.* 2003). We apply IIASA's population projection for China as it provides more detailed structure of population by age for the period we studied. Assumptions on skilled and unskilled labour forces are presented in Appendix Table 6.

Natural resource endowments. No effort has been made to develop a comprehensive database on natural resource endowments for China and the rest of the world. In this study, we directly adopted those assumptions that were embodied in a recent LEI–CCAP's study (van Tongeren and Huang 2004). They assumed that the annual growth rate of natural resource endowment will be 0.3 percent for all countries, including China.

Physical capital. Assumptions of physical capital growth are from Wellesley *et al.* (2000) and van Tangerine and Huang (2004). There are several methods to keep the capital endogenously based on

48

the static model (Francois *et al.* 1996; Walmsley 1998). However, it usually assumes the initial and final results are stable states and the return rates of capital in the beginning and the final stage equally. Therefore it was not suitable to simulate short-term steps (five years) in our simulations. Moreover such a method also assumes that capital is freely mobile among countries and does not trace the ownership.

Recursive dynamic simulation. The baseline is constructed through the recursive dynamic approach. We implemented the simulation using four steps (2001–2005, 2006–2010, 2011–2015 and 2026–2020) to reflect the change of endowment in different countries and periods. This procedure has been used in several other studies (Hertel *et al.* 1999; van Tongeren and Huang 2004). Comparing these methods, we keep the long-term trade balance of different countries as fixed. The basis for this assumption is that investment must be financed solely from domestic savings and thus capital is not mobile across regions (Walmsley 1998). If we do not trace the ownership and pay the foreign capital inflow back, this will cause large foreign capital inflow via trade deficits. Although it is not as perfect as the recent dynamic GTAP model, which allows capital free mobility among countries and traces the foreign ownership, there is no public version available, and it requires the creation of a new accounting database to reflect the foreign capital inflow, which is beyond the scope of this study. On the other hand, under our approach, the equivalent variable (EV) can be directly interpreted as a change in welfare.

Trade and other policies. The baseline projection also includes a continuation of existing policies and the effectuation of important policy events related to international trade as they are known to date. The important policy changes are: implementation of the remaining commitments from the GATT Uruguay Round agreements; China's WTO accession between 2001 and 2005; global phasing out of the Multifiber Agreement under the WTO Agreement on Textiles and Clothing (ATC) by January 2005; European Union enlargement with Central and Eastern European Countries (CEECs); and possible trade agreement in Doha negotiations from 2005 to 2010. For the baseline projection, this results in a number of assumptions with regard to import tariffs, TRQs, production and export subsidies. Because there are still high uncertainties about the results of the current Doha Round negotiations, we assume the possible outcome by simply averaging the offers provided by the United States, European Union and CAIRNS proposals in 2004. Details of these assumptions are adopted from van Tongeren and Huang (2004); some of key parameters on China's trade liberalization are provided in Appendix Table 7.

A3.2 China's high GDP growth scenario

Under China's high GDP growth scenario, all assumptions under the baseline scenario are held except for China's GDP growth and physical capital investment in the whole projection/simulation period. For China's GDP growth, the baseline GDP growths are replaced by those associated with China's high growths (row 3, Table 8; Figure 14). We analysed China's high growth scenario (compared with the baseline scenario) in order to examine questions such as: What will be the likely impacts of more rapid growth in the Chinese economy on other countries? Which countries or regions could benefit or might lose from China's growth? What are the implications of more rapid economic growth in China on agriculture and food security in China and the rest of the world.

For physical capital, given exogenous assumptions of GDP and TFP growths, China's capital investment could be determined endogenously. For other countries, the GDP growths are endogenous and capital grows similarly to the baseline.

A3.3 China's higher TFP growth

Under China's high TFP growth scenario, all assumptions for the baseline scenario in China and the rest of the world remain except for the TFP assumptions for China. There are several logical processes underlining this scenario. China's strategies to simulate its economic growth and sustainable

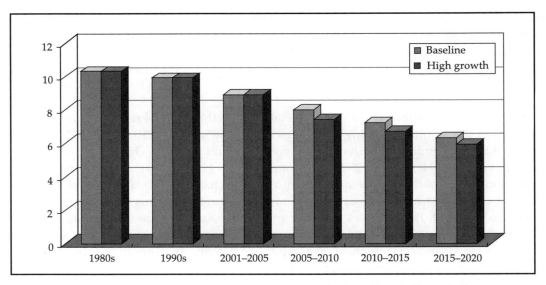

Figure 14. Annual growth rates (%) of GDP in China, 1981–2020

development may be further reinforced in the future (see Section 3.2). To minimize any potential or perceived risks associated with domestic food security and resource constraints for its rapid economic growth, China may make more effort to improve its production of food and other sectors that use large shares of natural resources such as land, water, forestry, energy and minerals. If China's rapid economic growth results in significant implications for the world's food security or surges in imports of natural resources from the rest of the world, it is unlikely to assume that there would be no policy response from China's leaders in the long term.

To understand the implications of technological changes on food security and other aspects of the economy, under the high TFP scenario we assume there will be a small increase in the productivity of several sectors. This is formulated as follows: On the top of the baseline scenario, we assume that: 1) agricultural and forestry sectors will experience neutral productivity-enhanced improvements; 2) the manufacturing sector will have biased energy-saving technology improvement; and 3) the service sector will follow a similar productivity improvement as that in the manufacturing sector. We further assume that average productivity will be increased by about 5 percent in ten years. This is equivalent to additional productivity growth of 0.47 percent annually. Similar to other scenarios, productivity growth will also start in 2006 and continue to 2020. It is worth noting that this is a very moderate change in productivity growth. Under this assumption, by 2020, TFP will be only about 7.3 percent higher than that under the baseline scenario. However, the implications for further TFP increase are straightforward.

Appendix figures

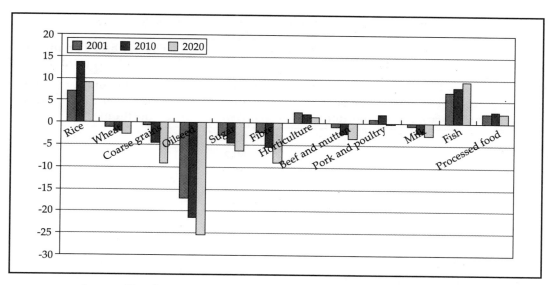

Appendix Figure 1. Net export of agriculture as percentage of
world trade under the baseline, 2001–2020

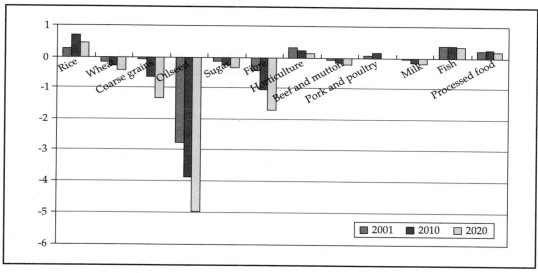

Appendix Figure 2. Net export of agriculture as percentage of
world output under the baseline, 2001–2020

Appendix tables

Appendix Table 1. Rural poverty in China, 1978–2004

Year	Poverty based on China's official poverty line			Poverty based on international standards ($1/day in PPP)	
	Poverty line (yuan/year)	Number of the poor (million)	Poverty incidence (%)	Number of the poor (million)	Poverty incidence (%)
1978		260	32.9		
1979		239	30.2		
1980		218	27.6		
1981		194	24.4		
1982		140	17.5		
1983		123	15.3		
1984	200	89	11.0		
1985	206	96	11.9		
1986	213	97	11.9		
1987	227	91	11.2		
1988	236	86	10.4		
1989	259	102	11.6		
1990	300	85	9.4	280	31.3
1991	304	94	11.0	287	31.7
1992	317	80	8.8	274	30.1
1993	350	75	8.3	266	29.1
1994	440	70	7.7	237	25.9
1995	530	65	7.1	200	21.8
1996	580	58	6.3	138	15.0
1997	640	50	5.4	124	13.5
1998	635	42	4.6	106	11.5
1999	625	34.1	3.7	96.7	10.5
2000	625	32.1	3.4	94.2	10.1
2001	630	29.3	3.2	90.3	9.8
2002	627	28.2	3.0	86.5	9.2
2003	637	29.0	3.1	85.2	9.1
2004	668	26.1	2.8	75.9	8.1

Sources: Poverty data for 1978–1988 are from World Bank (China: Strategies for Reducing Poverty in the 1990s, 1992); 1989–2004 data are from the Rural Social and Economic Survey Service of the NSBC, various issues.

Appendix Table 2. Regional aggregations

	Description	Original GTAP v6 regional aggregation
China	Mainland, China	Mainland, China
HK	Hong Kong SAR	Hong Kong, China
TW	Taiwan Province of China	Taiwan, China
JapKor	Japan and Republic of Korea	Japan, Republic of Korea
SEA	Southeast Asia	Indonesia, Viet Nam, Malaysia, Philippines, Thailand, Singapore
India	India	India
OthAsia	Other Asia	Bangladesh, Sri Lanka, rest of South Asia, rest of Southeast Asia
AusNzl	Australia and New Zealand	Australia, New Zealand
NAFTA	North American Free Trade Area	Canada, United States, Mexico
SAM	South and Central America	Central America, Caribbean, Colombia, Peru, Venezuela, rest of Andean Pact, Argentina, Brazil, Chile, Uruguay, rest of South America, rest of the Caribbean
EU15	European Union	Austria, Belgium, Denmark, Finland, France, Germany, United Kingdom, Greece, Ireland, Italy, Luxembourg, Netherlands, Portugal, Spain, Sweden
CEEC	Central European Associates	Hungary, Poland, Albania, Bulgaria, Croatia, Cyprus, Czech Republic, Malta, Romania, Slovakia, Slovenia, Estonia, rest of Europe
Russia	Russian Federation	Russian Federation
ROW	Rest of World	Switzerland, rest of Efta, Turkey, rest of Middle East, Morocco, rest of North Africa, Malawi, Mozambique, Tanzania, Zambia, Zimbabwe, other Southern Africa, Uganda, rest of Sub-Saharan Africa, former Soviet Union, Botswana, rest of Sacu, rest of world

Appendix Table 3. Sector aggregation

	Description	Original GTAP v6 sector aggregation
Rice	Rice, paddy and processed	Paddy rice, processed rice
Wheat	Wheat	Wheat
Cgrains	Coarse grains	Cereal grains (nec)
Oilseed	Oilseed and vegetable oils	Oilseed, vegetable oils and fats
Sugar	Sugar raw and processed	Sugar cane, sugar beet, sugar
Pfb	Plant-based fibre	Plant-based fibre
Othcrop	Horticulture and other crops	Vegetables, fruit, nuts, crops (nec)
Ctl	Cattle and red meat	Cattle, sheep, goats, horses and their meat
Oap	Pig & poultry-white meat, wool	Animal products (nec), wool, silk-worm cocoons, meat products
Milk	Raw milk and dairy products	Raw milk, dairy products
Fish	Fish	Fish
Ofood	Food products (nec)	Food products (nec), beverages & tobacco products
Forestry	Forestry	Forestry
Energy	Energy	Coal, oil, gas
Minerals	Minerals	Minerals
Texlea	Textiles and leather	Textiles, apparel, leather products
Manu	Manufactory	Wood and paper products, publishing, metal products, motor vehicles and parts, transport equipment (nec) petroleum, coal products, chemical rubber plastic prods, mineral products (nec), ferrous metals, metals (nec), electronic equipment, machinery and equipment (nec), manufacture (nec)
Serv	Services	Electricity, gas manufacture, distribution, water, construction, trade, transport (nec), sea transport, air transport, communications, financial services (nec), insurance, business services (nec), recreation and other, public admin/ defence/health/educat, dwellings

Appendix Table 4. The adjusted own-price and income elasticities for China

	Own-price elasticity		Income elasticity				
	GTAP 2001	Adjusted 2001	GTAP 2001	Adjusted 2001	2005	2010	2015
Rice	-0.08	-0.27	0.4	0.04	0.03	-0.05	-0.10
Wheat	-0.06	-0.29	0.4	0.06	0.05	0.00	-0.10
Coarse grains	-0.06	-0.26	0.4	-0.35	-0.35	-0.38	-0.41
Oilseed	-0.16	-0.57	0.8	0.42	0.41	0.34	0.28
Sugar	-0.07	-0.60	0.4	0.55	0.50	0.42	0.35
Fibre	-0.22	-0.50	1.1	1.06	1.06	1.06	1.06
Horticulture	-0.12	-0.65	0.4	0.53	0.53	0.45	0.40
Beef and mutton	-0.26	-0.78	1.2	0.66	0.65	0.50	0.42
Pork and poultry	-0.37	-0.65	1.2	0.56	0.55	0.47	0.40
Milk	-0.25	-0.89	1.2	1.05	1.04	0.88	0.76
Fish	-0.28	-0.67	1.2	0.80	0.79	0.69	0.58
Processed food	-0.28	-0.55	0.9	1.12	1.04	1.08	1.12
Forestry	-0.26	-0.26	1.3	1.20	1.20	1.20	1.20
Energy	-0.27	-0.27	1.3	1.29	1.29	1.29	1.29
Minerals	-0.26	-0.26	1.3	1.25	1.25	1.25	1.25
Textile and apparel	-0.29	-0.29	1.1	1.25	1.11	1.00	1.00
Manufacture	-0.41	-0.41	1.3	1.26	1.20	1.20	1.20
Services	-0.48	-0.48	1.2	1.30	1.30	1.30	1.30

Appendix Table 5. Comparison of I-O parameters (%) in the original GTAP and adjusted ones

	Rice	Wheat	Coarse grains	Pork & poultry
GTAP Version 6 database in 2001				
Rice	47	0	0	9
Wheat	0	21	0	12
Course grains	0	0	54	1
Oilseed	3	0	0	9
Sugar	0	0	0	0
Fibre	0	0	0	0
Other crops	1	0	0	3
Cattle and red meat	1	0	0	0
Pig, poultry, wool	2	2	1	27
Milk	0	0	0	0
Fish	8	0	0	0
Other foods	1	2	1	25
Forestry	0	1	1	0
Energy	0	0	0	0
Minerals	0	0	0	0
Textile and apparel	1	1	1	0
Manufacture	20	51	30	3
Services	15	22	12	10
Total	100	100	100	100
Adjusted database in 2001				
Rice	9	0	0	2
Wheat	0	17	0	2
Course grains	0	0	13	14
Oilseed	0	0	0	4
Sugar	0	0	0	0
Fibre	0	0	0	0
Other crops	2	0	0	2
Cattle and red meat	2	0	0	40
Pig, poultry, wool	4	2	1	0
Milk	1	0	0	0
Fish	0	0	0	0
Other foods	2	2	2	16
Forestry	1	1	1	0
Energy	0	0	0	0
Minerals	0	0	0	0
Textile and apparel	1	1	1	0
Manufacture	49	64	69	4
Services	29	12	12	14
Total	100	100	100	100

Appendix Table 6. The assumptions on annual growths (%) of China's factor endowment and capital stock under the baseline in 2002–2005

	2002–2005	2006–2010	2011–2015	2015–2020
Land	-0.30	-0.30	-0.30	-0.30
Labour	2.75	2.50	2.06	2.06
Unskilled labour	1.40	1.20	0.70	0.70
Skilled labour	3.90	4.90	5.50	5.50
Capital stock	9.21	8.73	8.47	8.34

Source: Walmsley *et al.* (2000); van Tongeren *et al.* 2004.

Appendix Table 7. Summary of import and export tariff equivalent in China, 2001–2020

	Import tariff equivalent %					Export tariff equivalent %				
	GTAP	2001	2005	2010	2020	GTAP	2001	2005	2010	2020
Rice	1	4	1	1	1	0	-9	-5	-3	0
Wheat	1	2	1	1	1	0	0	0	0	0
Coarse grains	88	9	1	1	1	0	31	0	0	0
Oilseed	85	4	3	1	1	0	0	0	0	0
Sugar	19	35	21	13	9	0	0	0	0	0
Fibre	3	5	1	1	1	0	14	0	0	0
Horticulture	20	35	12	8	5	0	-10	-6	-3	0
Beef and mutton	15	45	12	8	5	0	-5	-3	-2	0
Pork and poultry	8	20	12	8	5	0	-18	-10	-6	-2
Milk	20	50	11	7	5	0	0	0	0	0
Fish	12	14	12	8	5	0	-18	-9	-6	-3
Processed food	22	22	17	15	15	0	-9	-5	0	0
Forestry	0	0	0	0	0	0	0	0	0	0
Energy	0	0	0	0	0	0	0	0	0	0
Minerals	1	1	0	0	0	0	0	0	0	0
Textile & apparel	19	19	12	12	12	-5	-5	-2	0	0
Manufacture	12	12	6	6	6	0	0	0	0	0
Services	0	19	9	9	9	0	0	0	0	0

Source: CCAP. Similar assumptions were also used in van Tongeren and Huang (2004); Ianchovichina and Martin (2004).

Appendix Table 8. The national import and export share of different commodities in different regions in 2001

	China	Hong Kong SAR, China	Taiwan Province of China	JapKor	SEA	India	Other Asia	AusNzl	NAFTA	SAM	EU15	CEEC	Russian Federation	ROW
Export structure														
Food + feed crops	1.5	0.0	0.2	6.5	0.3	3.6	6.2	6.0	2.7	13.2	1.5	1.4	0.6	3.1
Processed food	1.8	0.3	1.0	3.9	0.6	3.2	2.5	4.8	2.1	8.1	3.2	2.5	2.6	2.5
Animal products	0.9	0.0	0.3	0.9	0.0	0.9	0.9	15.6	1.6	2.8	2.2	2.0	0.4	0.9
Fibre	0.0	0.0	0.0	0.1	0.0	0.0	0.5	1.2	0.2	0.2	0.0	0.0	0.1	0.5
Forestry	0.0	0.0	0.0	0.1	0.0	0.2	0.8	0.6	0.1	0.1	0.1	0.3	1.5	0.3
Energy	1.0	0.0	0.0	0.1	0.0	3.4	6.4	10.2	2.3	9.2	0.6	0.6	36.6	26.0
Minerals	0.3	0.0	0.0	2.0	0.0	0.7	0.6	6.0	0.3	4.1	0.2	0.2	0.6	1.2
Textile & apparel	24.3	11.0	10.6	23.9	4.6	7.6	53.5	1.7	2.7	7.2	4.7	9.9	1.1	5.7
Manufacture	64.4	10.0	78.9	42.3	85.2	66.2	11.5	34.8	67.8	40.2	67.2	63.7	48.2	41.5
Services	5.8	78.6	8.9	20.3	9.1	14.2	17.1	19.2	20.1	14.8	20.3	19.5	8.2	18.3
Total	100.0	100.0	100.0	100.0	100.0	100.0	100.0	100.0	100.0	100.0	100.0	100.0	100.0	100.0
Import structure														
Food + feed crops	2.3	1.5	1.8	4.5	2.6	2.2	9.2	1.1	1.4	3.3	2.3	2.1	5.4	4.1
Processed food	1.0	2.5	1.9	0.4	4.0	2.1	3.5	2.9	2.0	3.0	3.0	2.9	3.9	3.1
Animal products	1.3	2.2	1.0	1.0	2.4	1.2	1.6	0.6	0.9	1.2	2.1	1.2	4.4	1.8
Fibre	0.1	0.1	0.3	1.0	0.2	0.4	1.4	0.0	0.0	0.2	0.1	0.2	0.5	0.1
Forestry	0.6	0.0	0.2	0.9	0.4	0.1	0.1	0.0	0.0	0.0	0.1	0.1	0.0	0.1
Energy	2.7	0.3	6.4	16.4	10.5	4.0	2.9	2.4	4.6	3.6	3.7	5.3	1.7	3.4
Minerals	1.5	0.1	0.6	2.2	1.5	0.4	0.5	0.3	0.2	0.4	0.5	0.7	0.8	0.5
Textile & apparel	8.0	19.0	2.3	2.1	6.5	3.4	14.2	5.6	7.1	5.9	6.0	7.9	7.6	6.2
Manufacture	67.8	55.3	73.7	51.7	51.5	70.0	51.6	68.0	69.9	63.8	61.2	66.1	49.0	61.4
Services	14.5	19.0	11.8	19.8	20.4	16.5	15.1	19.0	13.7	18.4	21.0	13.5	26.6	19.4
Total	100.0	100.0	100.0	100.0	100.0	100.0	100.0	100.0	100.0	100.0	100.0	100.0	100.0	100.0

Bibliography

ADB (Asian Development Bank). 2002. *China's current economy and prospects: 2001.* Asian Development Bank, PRC, Beijing. In Chinese.

Anderson, K., Huang, J. & Ianchovichina, E. 2004. Will China's WTO accession worsen farm household income? *China Economic Review,* 15(2004): 443–456.

Arndt, C., Hertel, T., Dimaranam, B., Huff, K. & McDougall, R. 1997.China in 2005: implications for the rest of world. *Journal of Economic Integration,* 505–547, Dec. 1997.

Bhattasali, D., Li, S. & Martin, W. (eds.). 2004. *China and the WTO: accession, policy reform, and poverty reduction strategies.* Washington, DC, World Bank and Oxford University Press.

Brandt, L., Huang, J., Li, G. & Rozelle, S. 2002. Land rights in China: facts, fictions, and issues. *The China Journal,* 47: 67–97.

Brandt, L., Rawski, T.G. & Lin, G. (eds.). 2005. *China's economy: retrospect and prospect.* Asian Program Special Report No. 129. Washington, DC, Woodrow Wilson International Center for Scholars.

Branstetter, L. & Lardy, N. 2005. China's embrace of globalization. *In* L. Brandt, T.G. Rawski & G. Lin, eds. *China's economy: retrospect and prospect.* Asian Program Special Report No. 129, Washington, DC, Woodrow Wilson International Center for Scholars.

Cai, F., Wang, D. & Du, Y. 2002. Regional disparity and economic growth in China: the impact of labor market distortions. *China Economic Review,* 11 (2002).

Carter, C.A. & Estrin, A. 2001. *China's trade integration and impacts on factor markets.* University of California, Davis, January (mimeo).

deBrauw, A., Huang, J., Rozelle, S., Zhang, L. & Zhang, Y. 2002. China's rural labor markets. *The China Business Review,* March–April 2002: 2–8.

deBrauw, A., Huang, J. & Rozelle, S. 2004. The sequencing of reform policies in China's agricultural transition. *The Economics of Transition,* 12, 3 (2004): 427–465.

Deininger, K., Jin, S. & Rozelle, S. 2005. Rural land and labor markets in the process of economic development: evidence from China. *In* B.H. Sonntag, J. Huang, S. Rozelle & J.H. Skerritt, eds. *CCICED Task Force, China's agricultural and rural development in the early 21st century.* Australian Government, Australian Centre for International Agricultural Research, 2005.

Deng, X., Huang, J., Rozelle, S. & Uchida, E. 2005. Cultivated land conversion and potential agricultural productivity in China. Forthcoming in *Land use policy.*

DRC (Development Research Center of State Council). 2002. The coming 50 years of China's economy: discussion on trends of development and policy tropism. *New Economy Weekly,* May 2002: 1–5.

Du, P. 2003. *Four basic judgments on the development of China's regional economy in the next 20 years.* Working Paper, Institute of Regional Development and Economy, National Development & Reform Commission.

Fan, S. 1991. Effects of technological change and institutional reform on production growth in Chinese agriculture. *American Journal of Agricultural Economics,* 73: 266–275.

Fan, S. 1997. Production and productivity growth in Chinese agriculture: new measurement and evidence. *Food Policy* 22: 213–228.

Fan, S. & Pardey, P. 1997. Research productivity and output growth in Chinese agriculture. *Journal of Development Economics,* 53: 115–137.

Fan, S., Wales, E.J. & Crame, G.L. 1995. Household demand in rural China: a two-stage LES-AIDS model. *American Journal of Agricultural Economics,* 77: 54–62.

FAO (Food and Agriculture Organization of the United Nations). 2002. *The state of food insecurity in the world 2001.* Rome, FAO.

Francois, J.F., MacDonald, B.J. & Nordström, H. 1996. *Trade liberalisation and capital accumulation in the GTAP Model.* GTAP Technical Paper No. 7.

Giles, J. 2000. *Risk and rural responses in China.* Working Paper, East Lansing, MI, Michigan State University.

Hertel, T.W. & Martin, W. 1999. *Would developing countries gain from inclusion of manufactures in the WTO negotiations?* GTAP Working Paper, Purdue University.

Hertel, T.W. (ed). 1997. *Global trade analysis: modelling and applications.* Cambridge University Press.

Huang, J. & David, C.C. 1993. Demand for cereal grains in Asia: the effect of urbanization. *Agricultural Economics,* 8: 107–124.

Huang, J. & Rozelle, S. 1995. Environmental stress and grain yields in China. *American Journal of Agricultural Economics,* 77: 853–864.

Huang, J. & Bouis, H. 1996. *Structural changes in demand for food in Asia.* Food, Agriculture, and the Environment Discussion Paper, Washington, DC, International Food Policy Research Institute.

Huang, J. & Rozelle, S. 1996. Technological change: rediscovery of the engine of productivity growth in China's rural economy. *Journal of Development Economics,* 49(2): 337–369.

Huang, J. & Rozelle, S. 1998. Market development and food consumption in rural China. *China Economic Review,* 9: 25–45.

Huang, J. & Chen, C. 1999. *Effects of trade liberalization on agriculture in China: institutional and structural aspects.* Bogor, Indonesia, United Nations ESCAP CGPRT Centre.

Huang, J., Rozelle, S. & Rosegrant, M. 1999. China's food economy to the 21st century: supply, demand, and trade. *Economic Development and Cultural Change,* 47: 737–766.

Huang, J., Qiao, F., Zhang, L. & Rozelle, S. 2000. *Farm pesticide, rice production, and the environment.* EEPSEA Research Report 2001–RR3. Singapore, IDRC.

Huang, J., Rozelle, S. & Pray, C. 2002a. Enhancing the crops to feed the poor. *Nature,* 418: 678–684.

Huang, J., Rozelle, S., Pray, C. & Wang, Q. 2002b. Plant biotechnology in China. *Science,* 295: 674–677.

Huang, J. & Li, N. 2003. China's agricultural policy analysis and simulation model – CAPSiM. *Journal of Najing Agricultural University,* 3(2): 30–41.

Huang, J., Hu, R. & Rozelle, S. 2003a. *Agricultural research investment in China: challenges and prospects.* Beijing, China's Finance and Economy Press.

Huang, J., Li, N. & Rozelle, S. 2003b. Trade reform, household effects and poverty in rural China. *American Journal of Agricultural Economics,* 85(5): 1292–1298.

Huang, J., Rozelle, S. & Chang, M. 2004. Tracking distortions in agriculture: China and its accession to the World Trade Organization. *World Bank Economic Review,* 18(1): 59–84.

Huang, J., Hu, R., Rozelle, S. & Pray, C. 2005a. Insect-resistant GM rice in farmer fields: assessing productivity and health effects in China. *Science,* 308: 688–690.

Huang, J., Zhang, Q. & Rozelle, S. 2005b. *Macroeconomic policies, trade liberalization and poverty in China.* CCAP Working Paper. Beijing, Center for Chinese Agricultural Policy, Chinese Academy of Sciences.

Ianchovichina, E. & McDougall, R. 2000. *Theoretical structure of dynamic GTAP.* GTAP Technical Paper No. 17. Purdue University.

Ianchovichina, E., Martin, W. & Fukase, E. 2003. Assessing the implications of merchandise trade liberalization in China's accession to WTO. *World Bank Economic Review,* forthcoming.

Ianchovichina, E. & Martin, W. 2004. Economic impacts of China's accession to WTO. *In* D. Bhattasali, ed. *China and the WTO: accession, policy reform, and poverty reduction strategies.*

Jin, S., Huang, J., Hu, R. & Rozelle, S. 2002. The creation and spread of technology and total factor productivity in China's agriculture. *American Journal of Agricultural Economics,* 84(4): 916–939.

Johnson, D.G. 1995. *Is agriculture a threat to China's growth?* Working paper No. 95: 04. Office of Agricultural Economics Research, University of Chicago, April, 1995.

Lardy, N. 2001. *Integrating China in the global economy.* Washington, DC, Brookings Institution.

Lardy, N.R. 1995. The role of foreign trade and investment in China's economic transition. *China Quarterly,* 144: 1065–1082.

Li, J. 2001. *Development trends of China's economy in the 21st century. National economy management.* Working paper. Beijing, Development Research Center. In Chinese.

Li, S., Zhai, F. & Wang, Z. 1999. *The global and domestic impact of China joining the World Trade Organization.* Project Report. China, Development Research Center, the State Council.

Lin, J.Y. 1992. Rural reforms and agricultural growth in China. *American Economic Review,* 82: 34–51.

Lohmar, B., Wang, J., Rozelle, S., Huang, J. & Dawe, D. 2003. China's agricultural water policy reforms: increasing investment, resolving conflicts, and revising incentives. Economic Research Service, Agriculture Information Bulletin, No. 782.

Ma, J. 2004. Greater China economic outlook for 2004. *Asian Emerging Markets Monthly.*

Maijl, V.H., Tongeren, V.F., Huang, J., & Li, N. 2002. *A baseline projection for China's agriculture and global trade: 2001–2020.* LEI/CCAP working paper.

Martin, W. 2002. Implication of reform and WTO accession for China's agricultural policies. *Economies in Transition,* 9(3): 717–42.

Mathews, A. 2002. The possible impacts of China's WTO accession on the WTO agricultural negotiations. Trinity Economic Paper No. 15, Department of Economics, Trinity College Dublin.

McMillan, J., Walley, J. & Zhu, L. 1989. The impact of China's economic reforms on agricultural productivity growth. *Journal of Political Economy,* 97: 781–807.

MOA (Ministry of Agriculture). *China agricultural development report, 2000 and 2002.* Beijing, China's Agricultural Press.

MOFTEC (Ministry of Foreign Trade and Economic Cooperation). 2002. *Foreign trade and economic yearbook of China.* China Statistical Press.

Naughton, B. 1995. China's macroeconomy in transition. *The China Quarterly,* 144: 1083–1104.

NBSC (China National Statistical Bureau). *China statistical yearbook.* Various issues from 1995 to 2005. Beijing, China Statistical Press.

NSBC (Rural Survey Department, National Statistical Bureau of China). *China rural household survey yearbook.* Various issues from 1982 to 2004. Beijing, State Statistical Press.

Nyberg, A. & Rozelle, S. 1999. *Accelerating China's rural transformation.* Washington, DC, World Bank.

OECF (Overseas Economic Cooperation Fund) & Research Institute of Development Assistance. 1995. *Prospects for grain supply-demand balance and agricultural development policy in China.* Discussion paper No. 6. Tokyo, Japan.

Otsuka, K., Liu, D. & Murakami, N. 1998. Industrial reform in China: past performance and future prospects. Oxford, New York, Clarendon Press.

Park, A., Rozelle, S., Wong, C. & Changqing, R. 1996. Distributional consequences of fiscal reform on China's poor areas. *China Quarterly,* 147: 1001–32.

Perkins, D.H. 1994. Completing China's move to the market. *Journal of Economic Perspectives,* 8(2): 23–46.

Putterman, L. 1997. On the past and future of China's township and village-owned enterprises. *World Development,* 25 (4): 639–1654.

Rosegrant, M.W., Paisner, M.S., Meijer, S. & Witcover, J. 2001. *Global food projections to 2020.* Washington, DC, International Food Policy Research Institute. (IFPRI).

Rozelle, S. 1996. Stagnation without equity: changing patterns of income and inequality in China's post-reform rural economy. *The China Journal,* 35: 63–96.

Rozelle, S., Park, A., Benziger, V. & Ren, C. 1998. Targeting poverty investments and economic growth in China. *World Development,* 26(12): 2137–2151.

Rozelle, S., Li, G., Shen, M., Hughart, A. & Giles, J. 1999. Leaving China's farms: survey results of new paths and remaining hurdles to rural migration. *China Quarterly,* 158: 367–393.

Rozelle, S., Park, A., Huang, J. & Jin, H. 2000. Bureaucrat to entrepreneur: the changing role of the state in China's transitional commodity economy. *Economic Development and Cultural Change,* 48(2): 227–252.

Rozelle, S., Huang, J. & Otsuka, K. 2005. The engines of a viable agriculture: advances in biotechnology, market accessibility and land rentals in rural China. *The China Journal,* 53: 81–111.

Sonntag, B.H., Huang, J., Rozelle, S. & Skerritt, J.H. 2005. *China's agricultural and rural development in the early 21st century.* Australian Government, Australian Centre for International Agricultural Research, 2005.

State Council. 2002. *The report on the 16th China's communist party national representative conference.* Beijing.

State Council. 2003. *The report on economic conference of China's central communist party and the state council.* 27–29 November, 2003. Beijing.

Toth, F.L., Cao, G.Y. & Hizsnyik, E. 2003. *Regional population projections in China.* International Institute for Applied System Analysis, Interim Report, IR-03-042.

Van Tongeren, F. & Huang, J. 2004. *China's food economy in the early 21st century.* Report #6.04.04. The Hague, Agricultural Economics Research Institute (LEI).

Van Tongeren, F., van Meijl, H., Huang, J. & Li, N. 2003. *Evaluation of Doha Development Round proposals: important gains for China.* Working paper. The Hague, Agricultural Economics Research Institute.

Walmsley. T.L. 1998. *Long-run simulations with GTAP: Illustrative results from APEC trade liberalization.* GTAP technical paper No. 9.

Walmsley, T.L., Betina, V.D. & Robert, A.M. 2000. *A base case scenario for the dynamic GTAP model.* West Lafayette, Center for Global Trade Analysis, Purdue University.

Wang, J. 2000. *Property right innovation, technical efficiency and groundwater management: case study of groundwater irrigation system in Hebei, China, 2000.* Chinese Academy of Agricultural Sciences. (Ph.D. thesis)

Wang, J., Huang, J., Huang, Q. & Rozelle, S. 2005. Privatization of tubewells in north China: determinants and impacts on irrigated area, productivity and the water table. *Hydrogeology Journal,* 2005.

World Bank. 1992. *China: strategy for reducing poverty in the 1990s.* World Bank, Washington, DC, World Bank.

World Bank. 1997. *China 2020: development challenges in the new century.* Washington, DC, World Bank.

World Bank. 1999. *China rural development study. A World Bank country study.* Washington, DC, World Bank.

World Bank. 2002. World development indicators 2002. Washington, DC, World Bank.

Zhang, L., Zhang, J. & Rozelle, S. 2005 Self-employment, entrepreneurship and growth in Rural China. *In* B.H. Sonntag, J. Huang, S. Rozelle, & J.H. Skerritt, eds. *China's agricultural and rural development in the early 21st century.* Australian Government, Australian Centre for International Agricultural Research, 2005.

Zhang, X. & Post, J. 2003. *Trade and FDI in China: limited role of the Netherlands.* Working paper. The Hague, Agricultural Economics Research Institute.

Zhu, X. & Brandt, L. 2001. Soft budget constraints and inflation cycles: a positive model of the macro-dynamics in China during transition. *Journal of Development Economics,* 64(2): 437–457.

PART II

Indian agriculture and scenario for 2020

Bibek Debroy
PHD Chamber of Commerce and Industry

Laveesh Bhandari
Indicus Analytics

Contents

Contents *(continued)*

Tables

Contents *(continued)*

Abbreviations and acronyms

AEZ	Agricultural export zone
AMS	aggregate measurement of support
AOA	(Uruguay Round) Agreement on Agriculture
APMC	Agricultural Produce Marketing Committee
APTFYP	Approach Paper to the Tenth Five Year Plan
ASEAN	Association of South East Asian Nations
BBIN	Bangladesh, Bhutan, India and Nepal
BIMARU	Bihar, Madhya Pradesh, Rajasthan, Uttar Pradesh
BIMSTEC	Bay of Bengal Initiative for Multi Sectoral Technical and Economic Cooperation
BPL	below the poverty line
BRGF	Backward Regions Grant Fund
CACP	Commission on Agricultural Costs and Prices
CARG	compounded annual rate of growth
CEPA	Comprehensive Economic Partnership Agreements
CSO	Central Statistical Organization
CSS	centrally sponsored scheme
DDA	Doha Development Agenda
DRC	domestic resource cost
ECA	Essential Commodities Act
EPC	effective protection coefficient
ERC	Expenditure Reform Commission
ESC	effective subsidy coefficient
FCI	Food Corporation of India
FSSA	Food Safety and Standards Authority
FTA	Free Trade Agreement
GATT	General Agreement on Tariffs and Trade
GDP	gross domestic product
GMP	good manufacturing practices
GNP	gross national product
GTAP	Global Trade Analysis Project
GURT	Genetic Use Restriction Technology
HACCP	Hazard Analysis and Critical Control Point
HCR	head count ratio
HYV	high-yielding variety
IAAP	Intensive Agricultural Area Programme
IADP	Intensive Agricultural District Programme
IAY	Indira Awas Yojana
ICAR	Indian Council of Agricultural Research
ICOR	incremental capital/output ratio
ICRIER	Indian Council for Research on International Economic Relations
IFPRI	International Food Policy Research Institute
ITC	Indian Tobacco Company
KCC	Kisan Credit Cards
KVK	Krishi Vigyan Kendra
LDC	less-developed countries
MERCOSUR	*Mercado Común del Sur* or Southern Common Market

MFN	most-favoured nation
MSP	minimum support price
MTNs	multilateral trade negotiations
NAFTA	North America Free Trade Agreement
NCAER	National Council of Applied Economic Research
NCMP	National Common Minimum Programme
NDA	National Democratic Alliance
NDDB	National Dairy Development Board
NFWP	National Food for Work Programme
NHDP	National Highway Development Programme
NPC	nominal protection coefficient
NREGA	National Rural Employment Guarantee Act
NSAP	National Social Assistance Programme
NSS	National Sample Survey
NTB	non-tariff barrier
PDS	public distribution system
PFA	Prevention of Food Adulteration (Act)
PMGSY	Pradhan Mantri Gram Sadak Yojana
POL	petroleum, oil, lubricants
PPP	purchasing power parity
PRI	Panchayati Raj Institutions
PTA	Preferential Trade Agreement
PURA	Provision of Urban Amenities in Rural Areas
QR	quantitative restriction
RRB	regional rural bank
RSVY	Rashtriya Sama Vikas Yojana
RTA	Regional Trade Agreement
SAARC	South Asian Association for Regional Cooperation
SAFTA	South Asian Free Trade Area
SEB	State Electricity Board
SEZ	Special Economic Zone
SGAAS	Steering Group on Agriculture and Allied Sectors
SGRY	Sampoorna Gramin Rozgar Yojana
SGSY	Swarnajayanti Gram Swarozgar Yojana
SHG	self-help group
SPS	sanitary and phyto-sanitary
TPDS	targeted public distribution system
TRIPs	trade-related intellectual property rights
TRQ	tariff rate quota
TRQs	tariff rate quotas
UNCTAD	United Nations Conference on Trade and Development
UPA	United Progressive Alliance
VAT	value-added tax
WTO	World Trade Organization

Executive summary

The objectives of the study are mainly to understand the dynamics of the agriculture sector within India, how it is likely to emerge in coming years and how other countries in the region or otherwise can gain from greater interaction with India.

This study draws from the literature, government reports as well as policy documents to bring out specific issues related to agriculture apropos increasing its potential for contributing to development. The impact of India's agriculture sector on the rest of the world is an important aspect in this context. Forecasts for domestic production and consumption as well as the potential exports and imports of various agricultural commodities obtained using the Global Trade Analysis Project (GTAP) model are considered. The implications for other countries, both as potential trade partners and in general are also discussed.

The paper first discusses the evolution of the Indian economy with a special focus on the agriculture sector. Since independence there have been three major phases — before the Green Revolution, the Green Revolution years and deceleration after the Green Revolution. The success of the Green Revolution provides us with some important insights: The government, even for a country as diverse and heterogeneous as India, can play an important role in setting the agriculture sector on a course towards high growth. It has done so in the past, *inter alia* by promoting suitable technology nationwide, supplying ample credit and manifold extension services, declaring a minimum support price and a scheme for government purchasing, subsidizing fertilizer and pesticides, and increasing investment in small irrigation projects. Despite their relatively low capital base, Indian farmers, including small and marginal farmers, responded positively to the opportunities offered by technology and the incentives put in place by the government. Impressive strides were made in other subsectors such as fisheries and livestock, meeting the diverse food needs of the growing population. A critical success factor was the coordinated approach by the government in establishing numerous agricultural research institutions and a well-knit extension system.

However, all of these efforts could not disseminate the benefits of the new technologies to all parts of the country, given the diversity in crops and resource constraints, particularly water, in less well-endowed areas. In the 1990s, in the wake of the policy reforms in response to the macroeconomic crisis, there was a slackening of public investment in research and infrastructure. Risk mitigation measures — so necessary for continued and stronger diversification — were also not in place. The coordinated approach worked best during crises (for example lack of food or foreign exchange) that resulted in heavy dependence on external largesse. But once the crisis was over, the necessary follow-up measures were not forthcoming.

One of India's significant successes in the past few decades has been massive reduction in poverty levels at a time when the population was expanding rapidly at about 2 percent *per annum*. Was the Green Revolution responsible for this? Although this is not debated here, the Green Revolution as well as improvements in the dairy industry, fisheries and animal husbandry, were quite instrumental. The greatest increases in productivity occurred in the 1970s and 1980s. The greatest reduction in poverty occurred in the 1980s and 1990s, which were also a period of high economic growth and economic liberalization. The Green Revolution facilitated the availability of agricultural commodities; it also increased incomes for many cultivators who could access the available technologies. When the high-income growth phase occurred, poverty levels fell significantly, as high-yielding varieties benefited both producers directly and consumers indirectly. In other words, enhanced production by itself may not have generated the required impact on poverty, although it was a necessary factor, but when greater income growth came later, the impact on poverty was significant.

Section 3 discusses current population, economic growth and demand patterns and future prospects. It also discusses productivity issues to provide a backdrop to the assumptions used for the GTAP model that is used to forecast food production and consumption scenarios in India.

1

Between 10 and 13 percent of the Indian export basket of goods (excluding services) comes from agriculture and is worth around US$7 billion a year. Tea, coffee, rice, wheat, sugar and molasses, tobacco, spices, cashew nuts, oilmeal, fresh fruit and vegetables, meat and marine products are the major export items. India's export shares in global exports are high for items like tea, coffee, tobacco, spices, sugar, rice and fish. Contingent on domestic reforms, there is enormous potential for meat products, fruit and vegetables and processed foods. Imports of agricultural products account for between 4.5 and 5.5 percent of India's imports of goods (excluding services), worth US$2 to 3 billion, with pulses, cashew nuts, other fruit and nuts and edible oils being the major items. Rice is the largest agricultural commodity export and India is currently among the top three nations in quantity terms. India is a minor exporter of wheat and by-products and this share is expected to fall further.

Oil and oilseed imports are likely to increase in quantity and value. India is going to become an even more important exporter of cotton garments, and therefore importer of cotton, accounting for 18 percent of global plant-based fibre imports by 2020. Meat is not a significant export, and India will remain a net exporter, although marginal, of fish products.

Sections 4 and 5 discuss the agenda for reform related to land, water, credit, markets, diversification and taxation separately. For poor farmers, land and its ownership is the most significant asset and form of collateral. Since the 1990s, conversion of agricultural land to other uses has increased because of urbanization and population pressure. Land redistribution in many states has not really changed the status of small and marginal farmers. Apart from improper land utilization, there are salinization and waterlogging constraints. A considerable area of land is also subject to litigation and land ceiling laws have not been repealed. Land consolidation on the basis of efficiency has been hampered by poor documentation and confusion over land rights.

Barely one-third of agricultural land is irrigated, so Indian agriculture remains dependent on monsoons. Irrigation fuelled the success of the Green Revolution, but since the 1990s projects remain incomplete or on paper only owing to lack of funds. Credit has similarly remained out of reach for many farmers despite initiatives taken by the government, as well as non-government entities, especially for small farmers with poor access, knowledge and collateral. A concomitant issue is the continued absence of a comprehensive crop insurance scheme.

Intermediation is a serious problem that plagues Indian agriculture. The abundance of intermediaries not only wastes produce but also keeps farmers at the bottom of the food chain. The plethora of laws aggravates the situation. Nine different ministries are concerned with food processing and there are 22 related Acts and Orders. Encouraging diversification through producers' organizations and greater private sector participation would be of major assistance.

The National Common Minimum Programme, a politico–economic agenda that guides new government policy decisions, lists several important reforms. Some are underway. Now an integrated food-processing law is being prepared and the Essential Commodities Act (ECA) has been drastically amended. All Orders issued by state governments under the ECA have almost been repealed. Contract farming, because it is equated with corporate farming, is controversial, but many states have amended their Agricultural Produce Marketing Committee (APMC) laws, to allow direct marketing, contract farming and the establishment of private markets in the private or cooperative sectors.

But if reforms have not matched actual expectations, there is a reason. Constitutionally, most agriculture-related areas are state government subjects and it is difficult for the central government to provide incentives for such reforms. The major exceptions to this principle are foreign trade policy, agricultural credit and insurance, major irrigation projects, fertilizer policy and research and development.

Reform needs can be therefore be summarized as follows:

- Create infrastructure: For irrigation, for marketing and distribution, and for transportation and storage;
- Adequate public investment in research;
- Change laws that will enable the free flow of goods and services;
- Allow for greater flexibility in production and trade;
- Appropriate regulatory measures and enforcement of environmentally sustainable development of agriculture;
- Enforcement of food quality standards and food safety;
- Ensure availability of credit by not only targeting public sector banks, but moving from cost to accessibility;
- Stop unsustainable exploitation of water and use of land.

A greater decentralized and market-oriented approach is emerging, albeit slowly. In the past, whether for technology development, provision of extension services or seed generation, initiatives in the private corporate sector were scarce. Although it is too soon to tell, this appears to be changing. Owing to the open economy, liberalization, greater ease in setting up and operating domestic firms, rapidly growing demand, improvement in infrastructure and government subsidies, many different privately backed activities are occurring across India. Most are currently small in size and are widely scattered. However, they have the potential to generate dynamic changes, as many are bottom-up responses to requirements and appear to be scaleable. Moreover, the government still continues to and will continue to play an important role. In part as a beneficiary, where it continues to subsidize many if not most agricultural inputs, and regulates and controls many activities. Moreover, new technologies are being developed by government scientific research agencies. Although private research and development (R&D) in the agriculture sector is at a nascent stage, it appears to be growing. The diversity of India's agroclimatic zones and highly educated human resource pool provide many opportunities for developing an array of technologies specific to different conditions and soil types.

Although there is great potential for private R&D, it cannot completely replace public R&D. Moreover, issues such as conservation of local varieties and import of newer varieties need to be addressed. Although the legal structure exists through the Protection of Plant Varieties and Farmers' Rights Act, its enforcement needs to be strengthened.

Section 5 delves into issues related to multi- and bilateral trade. It discusses India's trade with the rest of the world commodity-wise and points to specific opportunities for other countries. India has many regional trade agreements (RTAs) and Comprehensive Economic Partnership Agreements (CEPAs). FTAs (free trade agreements) are covered by Article XXIV of the General Agreement on Tariffs and Trade (GATT), although India's RTAs are notified under a 1979 enabling clause that requires less trade to be liberalized than through Article XXIV. Multilateral liberalization is preferable to discretionary regional liberalization, even if negotiating the latter is easier although it will soon become irrelevant. The focus ought to shift to cross-border movements of labour and capital, non-trade barriers, double tax avoidance agreements, investment agreements and cross-border liberalization of services.

As things stand currently, India is unlikely to be in a position to tap global potential. However there is no particular reason for India to fear a deluge of agro-imports. Barring isolated sectors, India is cost competitive in agricultural products.

What can other countries learn from India's experience? The critical differentiating factor between India and many other countries, in the view of the authors, is not that India has greater population or land mass. But that agroclimatically, culturally and economically, India is a highly diverse and heterogeneous country. Moreover it has a decentralized system of governance. Hence coordinated efforts by the central government are difficult to manage and sustain in an environment where flexibility is important. The alternative option is a system where the government leaves the role of coordination to the market mechanism and limits itself to ensuring price stability, rural development, environmental and standards' regulations and property rights. India appears to be moving in this direction.

Doubtless there will be high levels of increase in demand for agricultural products on account of both increases in population and high economic growth. These will generate rapid increases in the demand for food products, although of course to varying degrees for different items. At the same time, India is a major producer of most of the commodities that it consumes. Agricultural productivity appears to be stagnating but there is much that could happen to put productivity back on a high growth path.

1. Background

Agriculture is important to the Indian economy. At a speech delivered on 27 October 2005 at a National KVK (*Krishi Vigyan Kendra*) Conference, the present Prime Minister quoted a former Prime Minister.[1] "Long ago, Jawaharlal Nehru once said "Everything else can wait but agriculture cannot wait....And I should begin by stating that our Government attaches the highest importance to achieve a 4 percent average growth rate in agricultural production." The share of agriculture in national income (gross domestic product) is a shade lower than 20 percent now and will only fall further.[2] The percentage of the working population that reports itself as earning a living primarily from agriculture is now around 57 percent. It should also be noted that agricultural performance during the first three years of the Tenth Five Year Plan (2002–2007) has been nowhere near that target trend of 4 percent, actual growth having been more like 1.6 percent.

Following the reforms of the 1990s, initially introduced in 1991, there have been outstanding successes in the Indian economy and these cannot be disputed. (1) The external sector is doing very well. (2) The rate of GDP growth has risen. (3) Despite some quibbling about data, the percentage of the population below the poverty line has declined and so has the occurrence of hunger. (4) There is no evidence that income distributions have deteriorated.[3] (5) Educational indicators have improved, not only literacy rates, but also gross enrolment ratios. (6) The rate of population growth has begun to slow down and is currently around 1.8 percent[4], implying a faster increase in per capita income. (7) The savings rate has increased to around 28 percent.[5] (8) With dependency ratios dropping, there is a demographic dividend to be reaped. Overall, the Indian economy appears to be in an enviable position.

But concerns remain. The benefits of economic growth have not been evenly distributed. Traditionally, India's less-advanced states have been known as the BIMARU (Bihar, Madhya Pradesh, Rajasthan, Uttar Pradesh). After the bifurcation of some states, the states in this category are now Bihar, Madhya Pradesh, Chhattisgarh, Jharkhand, Uttar Pradesh, Orissa and Rajasthan, with some evidence of deprivation also in the northeast. Despite the benefits of the liberalization of the 1990s, employment growth has tended to stagnate and this is fundamentally a rural sector problem. Commercialization and diversification of agriculture is tending to increase but at a slow pace. Agriculture's profitability has been squeezed, with increases in input prices eroding any increases in output prices. There has been exposure to risk and uncertainty, without the development of risk mitigation instruments. The rural sector's failure to create jobs has resulted in economic refugees' migration to urban areas. Public investments in agriculture have slowed down and this is also applicable to research and extension services. While required reforms are on the agenda, they continue to be on paper only, with minimal implementation. This is partly due to India being a constitutionally federal country, with most agricultural issues being state-government subjects. These endogenous and systemic problems explain much of the opposition in opening up agriculture, within or outside the World Trade Organization (WTO) negotiating system.

However, it is not that the Indian state does not have the capacity to push the agriculture sector along a higher growth path. The great successes of the past have shown that indeed when there is motivation and a concerted effort, resources can be found and programmes for overall agricultural and rural development have been instituted. But concentrated, synchronized and coordinated efforts are difficult to sustain over time.

Overview of Indian agriculture

On the eve of Independence, Indian agriculture had experienced many years of relatively low growth and by many accounts even deceleration in both productivity and output growth. From annual agricultural output growth of greater than 1 percent in the late 1800s, the first half of the

1900s saw annual growth plummet to about 0.3 percent *per annum*. Growth in grain yields has been estimated at between -0.4 to -0.6 percent annually from 1916 to 1946 (Blyn 1966).

It is generally agreed that a combination of (1) structure of land rights and (2) resource endowments generated a set of incentives that worked against increases in productivity. The argument is that those who had ownership rights and access to capital did not have the right set of incentives to invest in productivity enhancing measures. Why this occurred has been the topic of much debate and will not be revisited here (see Roy 2000). The more important question is why this continued in the period following Independence. The answer is that class structure and resource endowments take time to change.

Subsequently Indian agriculture has witnessed significant positive changes. Growth of net domestic products from agriculture averaged 1.87 percent from 1950 to 1967, increased to about 2.25 percent in 1966 to 1981 and further increased to about 3.3 percent in 1980 to 1999. However it now appears to be stagnating, as is discussed in later sections. The growth in production can be broadly ascribed to (1) growth in factor inputs and (2) growth in productivity. The first phase was more a result of an increase in factor inputs and the latter was driven by increases in productivity (see NCAER 2001). It is debatable whether the early twenty-first century will witness stagnation or a continued increase (Figure 1).

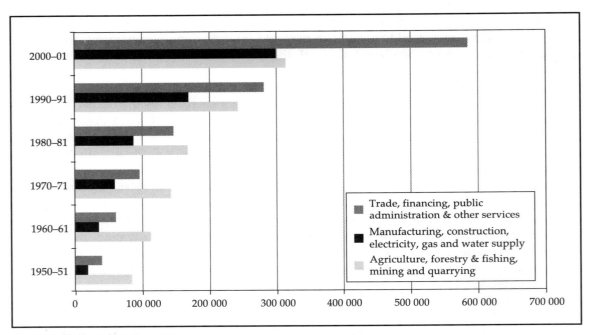

Source: NCAER (2001).

**Figure 1. Trends in sectoral output — net domestic product
(1993 constant, Rs10 million)**

At the same time the Indian economy overall is also growing faster. Moreover the dependence of the overall economy on agricultural growth is now much lower. According to estimates from Indian Council for Research on International Economic Relations (ICRIER) about 45 percent of the historical variation in growth can be accounted for by variations in agricultural output (Virmani undated). But growth evidence from the early 2000s suggests that high levels of dependence belong to the past.

However, high growth is essential, with increases in population, incomes and nutritional requirements being various aspects. The ability to advance progress and the lifestyles of a large mass of the population is an important component. The experience of China is relevant here. A recent International

Food Policy Research Institute (IFPRI) report summarizes the issue well (Gulati *et al.* 2005): "The comparative study shows that agriculture-led reform and development not only provide the necessary conditions for the manufacturing and service sectors to grow and reform, but also lead to larger reductions in poverty given the same rate of growth. The Chinese reform starting with agriculture ensured that the majority of the population benefited from the initial reforms, as the population was overwhelmingly dependent on the primary sector. The breathtaking reduction of poverty, from 33 percent of the population in 1978 to 3 percent in 2001, is primarily attributed to the acceleration of agricultural growth during the same time period."

India's experience however has been rather tame in comparison. The reasons are apparent. For one, the governance structure is quite different. There have been few effective policy measures in agriculture despite policy documents stating otherwise. This does not mean that policy-makers do not appreciate the importance of agriculture. But a combination of factors ranging from the fiscal situation, India's infamous infrastructure bottlenecks, manifold laws and coordination failures have contributed to the situation. The politico–economic argument of entrenched lobbies is one of the more frequently cited reasons. But not the only one. India had fewer price distortions, and fewer controls on deliveries at the very outset, and therefore agricultural reforms were not as critical as they may have been in China.

The objectives of this study are to:

- Outline the main changes in agriculture, food security and rural development, and document the main policies and strategies that led to them;

- Extrapolate these trends in the future and assess the implications for food security;

- Assess the implications of the overall rapid economic growth of India for neighbouring countries and generally.

This study draws from the literature, government reports, as well as policy documents to highlight the specific issues related to agriculture with a view towards increasing its potential to contribute to development. The impact of India's agriculture sector on the rest of the world is an important aspect in this context. Forecasts for domestic production and consumption as well as potential exports and imports of various agricultural commodities obtained using the Global Trade Analysis Project (GTAP) model are considered.[6] The implications for other countries, both as potential trade partners and generally are discussed.

Section 2 discusses the evolution of the Indian economy with a special focus on the agriculture sector. Following independence there have been three major phases — before the Green Revolution, the Green Revolution years and subsequent deceleration. How these phases occurred, and what implications they may have for developing countries in general and India in particular are discussed.

Section 3 discusses how population, economic growth and demand patterns exist in India and how they are expected to behave in the near future. It also discusses productivity issues; the objective being to provide a backdrop to the assumptions used for the GTAP model that is used to forecast the food production and consumption scenario in India.

Section 4 discusses the agenda for reform; for this purpose it discusses issues related to land, water, credit, markets, diversification and taxation separately. Section 5 discusses the current agenda, constraints and the emerging private sector. Section 6 delves into issues related to multi- and bilateral trade. It then provides a commodity-wise discussion of India's trade with the rest of the world and points to specific opportunities for other countries. Conclusions are drawn in Section 7.

2. Economy and agricultural economy: growth and deceleration

India has a land area of about 328 million ha and a coastline of about 7 000 km. Of the total land area about 165 million ha are arable and 54 million ha belong to the net irrigated area (GOI 2005a). Ranging from the Himalayas in the north to the Thar desert in the west and the tropical climate in the south, there is a wide range of climatic conditions within the country.

2.1 Growth

There are various ways to disaggregate the temporal trend of India's growth experience, for instance, the decadal system. Alternatively, one can use the five-year plan framework, as India has a system of five-year plans.[7] Real annual average GNP growth was 3.7 percent during the First Plan (1951–1956), 4.2 percent during the Second Plan (1956–1961), 2.8 percent during the Third Plan (1961–1966) and 3.4 percent during the Fourth Plan (1969–1974) (GOI 2004–2005). The period up till the mid-1970s is often described by the term "Hindu rate of growth", a term coined for an annual average real growth of 3.5 percent, a rate that India never seemed to cross till the mid-1970s. From the second half of the 1970s, growth rates inched up, especially in the 1980s, to an annual average real growth approaching 5.5 percent. For instance, the Fifth Plan (1974–1979) produced average growth of 5.0 percent, the Sixth Plan (1980–1985) 5.5 percent and the Seventh Plan (1985–1990) 5.8 percent. As a trend, the new Hindu rate of growth became 5.5 percent. Some reforms were introduced in the late 1970s and 1980s, particularly in the second half of the 1980s. Faced with a balance of payments crisis in 1990 to 1991, more substantive economic reforms were introduced in the 1990s, beginning with 1991. Following these reforms, the Eighth Plan (1992–1997) produced average growth of 6.8 percent and the Ninth Plan (1997–2002) 5.6 percent. The Tenth Plan (2002–2007) has a target growth rate of 8 percent and the NCMP (National Common Minimum Programme) of the United Progressive Alliance (UPA) Government mentions growth of between 7 and 8 percent. The 8 percent target during the Tenth Plan is now impossible to achieve. The first three years have produced 4.2 percent in 2002 to 2003, 8.5 percent in 2003 to 2004 and 6.8 percent in 2004 to 2005, with around 7.5 percent expected in 2005 to 2006. Growth in 2006 to 2007 will have to cross 10 percent for the 8 percent goal of the Tenth Plan to be reached — an unlikely situation.[8]

2.2 Poverty

How does growth affect poverty and unemployment in a relatively poor country like India beyond direct antipoverty programmes? Income poverty is certainly not the only indicator of poverty, but it is an important one. Table 1 shows the incidence of poverty in India (GOI 2003–2004a). The poverty ratio or head count ratio is based on the percentage of population below the national poverty line.[9] This national poverty line is not the same as the international PPP (purchasing power parity) standard of US$1.00/day, but is close to it. Data for computing poverty ratios are obtained through surveys and the National Sample Survey (NSS) organization conducts sizeable and reliable surveys approximately once every five years. The NSS collects data on consumer expenditure, not income. Similar to surveys elsewhere in the world, the aggregate of consumption expenditure obtained in household surveys falls short of the aggregate of consumption expenditure obtained through national accounts. Ideally, one ought to make adjustments for this gap, but ultimately all such adjustments tend to be subjective. Nationwide, there are significant inter-regional variations.

Income poverty has dropped significantly, especially since the early 1980s (Table 1). This is understandable, and has largely been a function of growth. Income and expenditure distributions have not deteriorated. Depending on the year, the Gini coefficient of rural consumption expenditure distributions has varied between 0.25 and 0.30, while the Gini coefficient for urban consumption expenditure distributions has varied between 0.32 and 0.34. Therefore, because distributions have not declined, growth has induced trickle-down poverty reduction effects. In addition, because income distributions are typically log normal, sharp drops are possible when the thick part of the distribution

Table 1. Incidence of poverty

Year	Rural poverty ratio (%)	Urban poverty ratio (%)	Combined poverty ratio (%)	Absolute number of rural poor (million)	Absolute number of urban poor (million)
1977–78	53.1	45.2	51.3	264.3	64.6
1983	45.7	40.8	44.5	252.0	70.9
1987–88	39.1	38.2	38.9	231.9	75.2
1993–94	37.3	32.4	36.0	244.0	76.3
1999–2000	27.1	23.6	26.1	193.2	67.1

Source: GOI (2003–2004a).

passes above the poverty line. Arguably, that is precisely what has been happening in the 1990s and this trend should continue for the next decade also.

The decline in the combined poverty ratio from 36.0 percent in 1993 to 1994 to 26.1 percent in 1999 to 2000 was one of the sharpest drops ever witnessed.[10] But despite the reduction, the absolute numbers of the poor were quite large, particularly in rural India, where, in 1999 to 2000, almost 200 million individuals were BPL (below the poverty line). In addition, the rural poverty ratio was higher than the urban poverty ratio.[11] There are significant regional variations within India, such as between states or between districts. Also there are states where the rural poverty ratio is lower than the urban ratio. This was evidenced in Andhra Pradesh, Gujarat, Haryana, Karnataka, Madhya Pradesh, Rajasthan and Tamil Nadu in 1999 to 2000. However there were other states where the rural poverty ratio in 1999 to 2000 exceeded 30 percent, for example Assam, Bihar, Madhya Pradesh, Orissa, Uttar Pradesh and West Bengal as well as some northeastern states.

All of this evidence indicates that high growth is a significant force behind high poverty reduction. Neither government poverty alleviation programmes nor other direct policy instruments appear to have made a significant dent in poverty levels on a large enough scale. At the same time, there are too many state-level and within state variations in both poverty levels and their trends, indicating that if poverty has to be impacted through other means, then location-specific models need to be built around the socio-economic and other peculiarities of specific villages and urban communities.

2.3 Unemployment

The last NSS survey was held in 1999 to 2000 and is somewhat dated now.[12] It revealed a labour force of 363.33 million and a workforce of 336.75 million, with an unemployment rate of 7.2 percent. With a significant share of the workforce employed in the rural sector, unemployment figures may not reveal a great deal. The problem is more of underemployment. Again, there are significant variations in unemployment rates across states. Unemployment rates exceeded 10 percent in states such as Kerala, Tamil Nadu and West Bengal. What is worrying is that the annual average growth in employment has slowed down. While the average annual growth rate in employment was 2.89 percent between 1983–1987–1988 and 2.50 percent between 1987–1988 and 1993–1994, it was 1.07 percent between 1993–1994 and 1999–2000.

This deceleration is largely because in the 1990s agriculture failed to create jobs. While this is recognized and increasing rural employment is important in the present UPA government's agenda, notwithstanding the emphasis on agricultural reforms, it is fair to say that the emphasis is not on creating employment through crop output. Instead, the emphasis is on creating employment through off-farm activities and within farm activities, through non-crop diversification.

2.4 Broad sectoral trends

Sectoral compositions of the GDP are not constant. They change over time. In 2003 to 2004, agriculture and allied activities (the primary sector), accounted for 21.71 percent of the GDP, compared to 59.20 percent in 1950 to 1951, 54.75 percent in 1960 to 1961, 48.12 percent in 1970 to 1971, 41.82 percent in 1980 to 1981 and 34.93 percent in 1990 to 1991.[13] This relative decline, particularly marked in the 1990s, has been due to the increased importance of the services sector, rather than increasing importance of the secondary sector. This classification of the primary sector also includes mining and quarrying. In 2003 to 2004, mining and quarrying accounted for 2.3 percent of the GDP.[14] That is, with mining and quarrying excluded, agriculture, forestry and logging and fishing accounted for 19.8 percent of the GDP. The forestry and logging share was 0.01 percent of the GDP and the fishery share was also 0.01 percent. Thus, agriculture contributed 19.6 percent of the GDP.[15]

2.5 Trends in the agriculture sector

There were three distinct periods in the evolution of Indian agriculture and agricultural policy after Independence. The first period was before the Green Revolution up to the mid-1960s (Phase 1). The second period was the Green Revolution from the mid-1960s till the late 1980s (Phase 2). The third phase continues from then to the present day (Phase 3).

2.5.1 Phase 1

The first period saw the government focusing policy on the following:

- irrigation,
- land reforms,
- community development, and
- restructuring of rural credit institutions.

Land reforms involved abolition of intermediaries, tenancy reforms, acquisition of surplus land through ceilings on holdings and redistribution and consolidation of holdings; success varied across states (Deshpande *et al.* 2004). Land reforms quite successfully altered agrarian structures in states like Kerala, West Bengal and Karnataka, but failed to do so in states such as Bihar, Orissa and Rajasthan. Changes in agrarian structures occurred in Punjab, Haryana, Western Uttar Pradesh, Tamil Nadu and Andhra Pradesh.[16]

A Community Development Programme was started in 1952, for integrated village development by coordinating the development of agriculture, animal husbandry, infrastructure and extension at the block level. Also in 1952 the National Extension Programme was spliced into the Community Development Programme, incorporating provision of technical inputs. The Intensive Agricultural District Programme (IADP), started in selected potential districts in 1960 and 1961, aimed to provide a package of high-yielding inputs (seed, fertilizers, plant protection measures, etc.) to farmers. The Intensive Agricultural Area Programme (IAAP), started in selected potential blocks in 1964 and 1965 aimed to provide technological inputs for identified crops.

Whether these changes were successful or not depends upon how one benchmarks success. Compared to the low or negative growth in the period immediately preceding Independence, they were successful. Both productivity and output increased during most of the period. However, progress in productivity improvements was not commensurate with the requirements even during good monsoon years. There were institutional constraints in providing inputs like high-yielding varieties, fertilizers and irrigation, coupled with a switch during the Second Plan (1956–1961), with reduced investments in agriculture as fallout. In other words, the government was unable to inject the required financial resources, or develop adequate institutional back-up to enable widespread and sustained implementation. Moreover, the government was also unable to effect improvements in technology and the usage of improved seeds, inputs and methods did not occur until much later.

On the positive side the first phase did succeed in other aspects that facilitated later changes. Land reforms (although limited to some states and discussed elsewhere), assigning ownership rights to tenants, consolidation of holdings, among others, were important measures that started during this period and have continued to a varying extent to the present day. The establishment of many agricultural technology institutions and the birth of a widespread extension services system also transpired during this time (although it is now ineffective in many states). Most importantly, administrative systems were developed during this period with the capacity to take on the challenge of the Green Revolution when the technologies finally became available.

The mid-1960s witnessed a succession of exogenous negative shocks that had a major impact on agricultural output: a war with China in 1962, a war with Pakistan in 1965 and successive monsoon failures in 1965 to 1966 and 1966 to 1967. India had to resort to large-scale imports of food.

2.5.2 Phase 2

The Green Revolution package was based on increased availability/access to:

- high-yielding varieties (HYV) of seeds,
- fertilizers,
- irrigation,
- biochemicals,
- extension services,
- availability of credit,
- establishment of marketing and price-support mechanisms for farmers.

This was spliced with a price-support policy. The government's role in ensuring the availability of complementary inputs for HYV seeds was quite significant. Ahluwalia summarizes it well, "[it] required a comprehensive strategy for agricultural change requiring active Government intervention in many dimensions..." (Ahluwalia undated).

A sustained effort was needed to expand irrigation with a shift from major to medium and minor irrigation projects. It was necessary to move the banking system into rural areas to provide credit for the purchase of biochemical inputs needed for HYVs. Nationalized banks were given the task of upgrading their rural operations and they succeeded to a large extent. Primary agriculture markets were regulated and some of the usurious practices of traders stopped. Extension services were set up and backed by numerous agricultural research establishments. Development of appropriate varieties was critical given the heterogeneity in agroclimatic conditions. The ability of the government to effect adequate coordinating mechanisms was also quite important. Provision of credit was facilitated through the nationalization of banks. Fertilizer availability and accessibility was expanded through subsidies and was juxtaposed by public and private sector expansion in manufacturing. Moreover price support was instituted at remunerative prices. This coordination role cannot be understated. While subsidized inputs were becoming available and productivity increases were rapid and concentrated, the price-support mechanism ensured that incomes for farmers increased. The three key characteristics of the mandate were: simultaneous handling of constraints in supply and marketing, a coordinated approach and recognition of heterogeneity in agroclimatic conditions. This approach can be assigned most of the credit for the success of the Green Revolution.

Table 2 shows growth rates in area, production and productivity of major crop groups. The asterisks in the table indicate the major contributing factors behind increase in production during that period. As Table 2 indirectly suggests, from 1949–1950 to 1964–1965, non-foodgrain was the major component of crop production and for both foodgrain and non-foodgrain, production growth primarily transpired through area expansion. This was reversed from 1967–1968 to 1980–1981. During this period, expansion of production for both foodgrain and non-foodgrain occurred through productivity

Table 2. Growth rates in area, production and productivity of crop groups
(annual percentage change)

Crop groups		1949–50 to 1964–65	1967–68 to 1980–81	1979–80 to 1989–90	1991–92 to 1999–2000
Foodgrain	Area	1.35[†]	0.38	-0.11	-0.17
	Production	2.82	2.15	3.54	1.94
	Productivity	1.36	1.33[†]	3.33[†]	1.52[†]
Non-foodgrain	Area	2.44[†]	0.94	1.21	1.37
	Production	3.74	2.26	4.02	2.78
	Productivity	0.89	1.19[†]	2.47[†]	1.04[†]
All crops	Area	1.58[†]	0.51	0.21	0.25
	Production	3.15	2.19	3.72	2.28
	Productivity	1.21	1.28[†]	2.99[†]	1.31[†]

[†] Major contributing factors behind increases in production.
Source: GOI figures, but reproduced from Despande *et al.* (2004).

increases, area expansion having slowed down. This trend continued from 1979–1980 to 1989–1990, with productivity increases becoming sharper and the area under foodgrain actually declining. However, in the last few years, productivity growth has slackened, and so has growth in production, particularly of foodgrain.

However the Green Revolution had several positive aspects: (1) As foodgrain production increased faster than the population growth rate, per capita availability of food increased. Per capita net availability of cereals and pulses was 394.9 grams in 1951, 468.7 grams in 1961, 468.8 grams in 1971, 454.8 grams in 1981, 510.1 grams in 1991 and 416.2 grams in 2001 (GOI 2004–2005). (2) Per capita income generation in agriculture increased. (3) Agriculture was better protected from the ravages of drought. (4) There was greater commercialization and diversification, with cropping patterns changing in favour of commercial crops and moving away from coarse cereals, even for small and marginal farmers. (5) Capital accumulation rose, including investments from the private sector. (6) While there may have been some reservations about the initial distributional impact of the Green Revolution package, the benefits became more broad-based in subsequent years.

Table 3 shows that many holdings are marginal (less than 1 ha) or small (between 1 and 2 ha). Barring pulses and coarse cereals, all other crops seem to have benefited from the new technologies. In addition, there was a paradigm shift from foodgrain towards commercial crops and even fruits and vegetables, this diversification being at the expense of pulses and coarse cereals. Although a large percentage of small and marginal farmers is still dependent on foodgrain, there was some diversification among small and marginal farmers. For instance, the share of cereals in area cultivated by small and marginal farmers declined from 71.44 percent in 1970 to 1971 to 70.57 percent in 1980 to 1981 and 66.22 percent in 1990 to 1991; the share of fruit and vegetables increased in area from 2.43 percent in 1970 to 1971 to 3.25 percent in 1980 to 1981 and 3.71 percent in 1990 to 1991 (Despande *et al.* 2004).[17] Thus it can be argued that there has been a degree of commercialization and diversification among small and marginal farmers but this could have been greater.

However there are some qualifiers. The first is that the coordinated approach did not lead to the spread of the benefits of the new technologies across India. Only a few areas benefited. It is difficult for a central government to introduce measures and mechanisms that are fine-tuned to the requirements of each state and district.[18], Success was based on the term "provision" — *inter alia* provision of credit, HYVs, subsidized fertilizers and extension services. These had a negative long-term impact on the development of market-backed services and commodities. Lastly, the new technologies were biased towards high usage of water for irrigation. As many parts of the country were not irrigated, power-operated motorized tubewells sprung up across the country. Crops such

Table 3. Distribution of landholdings (% of total holdings and total area)

Year	Marginal (< 1 ha)	Marginal (< 1 ha)	Small (1–2 ha)	Small (1–2 ha)	Semi-medium (2–4 ha)	Semi-medium (2–4 ha)	Medium (4–10 ha)	Medium (4–10 ha)	Large (> 10 ha)	Large (> 10 ha)
	% holdings	% area	% holdings	% area	% holdings	% area	% holdings	% area	% holdings	% area
1960–61	60.06	7.59	15.16	12.40	12.86	20.54	9.07	31.23	2.85	28.24
1970–71	62.62	9.76	15.49	14.68	11.40	21.92	7.83	30.75	2.12	22.91
1980–81	66.64	12.22	14.70	16.49	10.78	23.38	6.45	29.83	1.42	18.07
1990–91	69.38	16.93	21.75	33.97	5.06	17.63	2.84	17.64	0.95	13.83

Source: Despande *et al.* (2004).

as rice in Punjab and sugar cane in Maharashtra have become quite important even though surface water is limited in some of these areas. The result has been a rapid fall in water levels.

2.5.3 Phase 3 and the agricultural anomaly

In the 1980s, when the balance between demand and supply of cereals (foodgrain) was in sight, the overall goal of agricultural strategy/policy shifted from "maximization of production of foodgrain" to "evolution of a production pattern in line with the demand pattern". The implication of this shift is that the emphasis of the policy shifted from foodgrain to other agricultural commodities like oilseed, fruit and vegetables. The shift helped to increase the output of non-cereal food items.[19]

Diversification has been occurring in India since Phase 1, however, it became more prominent in the 1980s (but waned in the 1990s). There is little agreement on how much of this was due to the government efforts and how much transpired because of changing economic conditions. It would be fair to argue for oilseed that the shift from coarse cereals to oilseed in rain-fed areas was aided by (i) a protective trade environment; (ii) favourable price policy; and (iii) the connecting of the Technology Mission on Oilseeds (see Hazra 2001). At the same time diversification was not merely attributable to greater area under high-value commodities; the improvements in yield also would have been generated by government-aided supply and technology-related factors.

Table 4 shows the improvements in both production and yield for the crop sector. There were significant improvements for livestock in the 1980s — the value of the livestock sector in total agricultural output value increased from about 18 percent in the triennium ending (TE) 1980 to 1981 to 23 percent in TE 1990 to 1991 (although it remained stagnant at that level by TE 1997 to 1998 (see Joshi *et al.* 2003). Almost 70 percent of the livestock sector's production (in value terms) is accounted for by the milk and products subsector; the role of "Operation Flood" cannot be understated (Box 1).

Table 4. Compounded annual rates of growth of production and yield

	1980–81 to 1989–90 (production)	1980–81 to 1989–90 (yield)	1990–91 to 1999–2000 (production)	1990–91 to 1999–2000 (yield)
Non-foodgrain	3.77	2.31	2.78	1.04
Foodgrain	2.85	2.74	1.94	1.52
Pulses	1.52	1.61	0.61	0.96
Oilseed	5.20	2.43	2.13	1.25
Cotton	2.80	4.10	1.73	-0.61
Sugar cane	2.70	1.24	2.78	0.95
Tobacco	-1.05	1.79	1.05	-0.23

Source: Deshpande *et al.* (2004).

Box 1. Operation Flood

"Operation Flood" was launched by the National Dairy Development Board in 1970. In the first phase (1970–1980) major milk-producing areas were linked with the four metropolitan cities of Delhi, Mumbai, Calcutta and Chennai. This was expanded during Phase 2 (1981–1985) to cover 290 urban markets. The third phase (1985–1996) saw a further expansion in marketing coverage, but more importantly also included greater emphasis on R&D in animal health and animal nutrition. An Integrated Dairy Development Program was launched in hilly and less-advanced areas in 1992 to 1993 to enhance production, procurement and marketing of milk, and to generate employment opportunities in those areas. By 2001 about 170 cooperative milk unions, operating in over 285 of India's 593 districts and covering nearly 96 000 village level societies and nearly 10.7 million individual producers were procuring an average of 16.5 million litres of milk every day.

The model works on a three-tier cooperative structure with professional staff involved in all operational activities. The three-tier structure rests on: (a) the Village Dairy Cooperative Society, (b) the District Cooperative Milk Producers' Union and (c) the State Federation. Individual milk producers form the Village Dairy Cooperative Society (DCS). Any producer can become a DCS member by buying a share and committing to sell milk only to the society. At the end of each year, a portion of the DCS profits is used to pay each member a patronage bonus based on the quantity of milk poured. The Milk Producers' Union is owned by the dairy cooperative societies. The union buys all the societies' milk, then processes and markets fluid milk and products. Most unions also provide a range of inputs and services to DCSs and their members: feed, veterinary care and artificial insemination to sustain the growth of milk production and the cooperatives' business. Union staff train and provide consulting services to support DCS leaders and staff. The cooperative milk producers' unions in a state form a State Federation, which is responsible for marketing the fluid milk and products of member unions. Some federations also manufacture feed and support other union activities.

The value of the fisheries subsector swelled by about 50 percent during the 1990s, although as a share of the total it declined from 1.3 to 1.0 percent of the total agriculture sector value during the period. There were significant and coordinated government efforts to increase fish production. The central government's outlays towards the fishery sector as a share of the total agriculture sector outlays were more than doubled from 2 to 3 percent in the 1970s to about 5.5 percent in the 1980s and 1990s. Production and development programmes were instituted in both marine and inland areas. Farmers' development agencies were established both for fresh and brackish water areas. These programmes included technology upgrading components, encouragement and involvement of the private sector in activities such as seed, feed and other inputs and also creation of suitable infrastructure for storage, transport, marketing and credit. By 1998/1999 more than 50 seed hatcheries at the national level had been established, fishery industrial estates had been created and 30 minor fishing harbours and 130 fish-landing centres had evolved.

Diversification in favour of high-value commodities is considered by some to have only partly benefited through government efforts. Both econometric and GIS-based studies also suggest that the presence of infrastructure aided diversification. Rao *et al.* (2004) found that in their sample, the areas close to large urban centres (and as a result with better connectivity to urban centres) could diversify more to high-value commodities. They concluded that urbanization is a strong demand driver for high-value commodities. In an earlier econometric study, Joshi *et al.* (2003) came to a similar conclusion — that diversification into high-value commodities was demand driven, unlike the supply driven Green Revolution.

Between 1990–1991 and 1998–1999, the annual average increase in yields was only 1.79 percent and 1.31 percent for wheat and rice, respectively. Despite the successes of the Green Revolution, there continue to be concerns with agricultural performance during Phase 3, the present phase of globalization and diversification, initiated in the 1990s, and some macro issues emerge.[20]

The first macro point is the one already alluded to indirectly. Compared to the 1980s, there was deceleration of agricultural growth in the 1990s. This is evident from Table 4 and cuts across all crops and both production and yields. The quality of the system for collecting agricultural statistics[21] and the extent of deceleration can be debated, but the conclusion that growth in the crop sector decelerated in the 1990s is fairly obvious. In any case, deficiencies in the quality of statistics are constant factors and cannot explain the deceleration. Indeed, growth in non-food and non-crop output was also faster in the 1980s than in the 1990s and growth in animal husbandry, poultry, dairy, horticulture and fisheries also slowed down. This deceleration happened despite the reversal of historical discrimination against agriculture. In the 1990s, the terms of trade moved in favour of agriculture and this was independent of the terms of trade measures used (Misra 2004).[22] There were several reasons for this reversal of trend. There were higher prices for rice and wheat through support/procurement policies and prices of other crops also increased. There is a positive correlation between procurement prices, open market prices and higher prices in the PDS (public distribution system). Simultaneously, because protection granted to manufacturing declined, the relative prices of manufactured products also declined. *A priori*, one should therefore have expected a positive supply response and increased capital accumulation.

However farm profitability declined in the 1990s (Sen and Bhatia 2004; Alagh 2004). Not all farmers had access to higher support prices for rice, wheat or sugar cane, there was a deceleration in yields and real input prices also increased, thanks to prices for fertilizers, power and diesel that were closer to market-determined prices. Higher cereal prices also contributed to increases in wage costs.

Consequent to per capita income growth, NSS data show changes in consumption patterns, with a decline in consumption of cereals in both rural and urban India, despite cereals still being important in the food basket. There has been a shift from consumption of coarse cereals to rice and wheat and also a shift towards consumption of fruit and vegetables and even fish and eggs. Table 5 shows some of these changes. Consumption patterns are changing, even for the bottom 30 percent of the population and the shares of non-cereal food (fruit and vegetables) and non-food items have been increasing in consumption baskets (Mahendra *et al.* 2004). Increased cereal prices and lower rural incomes may have depressed demand for both cereal and non-cereal food, but there is no denying that preferences are also changing.

Table 5. Per capita consumption

Commodity	1955–56	1975–76	1990–91	1997–98
Foodgrain[23] (kg/year)	155.6	158.5	180.6	179.3
Edible oils and vanaspati[†] (kg/year)	3.2	4.2	6.5	8.2
Sugar (kg/year)	5.0	6.2	12.5	14.1
Textiles (cotton equivalent, m/year	14.4	17.6	24.8	28.0
Tea (kg/year)	0.36	0.45	0.61	0.64
Milk (l/year)	4.7	4.6	6.3	7.2
Eggs (no./year)	5.3	15.5	26.0	31.0

[†] Vegetable oil.

Source: Alagh (2004).

2.6 The reason for deceleration

Why did deceleration occur? More importantly, why did deceleration occur when better technologies were more readily available? In answering this question, it is important to distinguish between generic problems that continue to constrain agriculture and issues that became constraints in the reform decade of the 1990s. The former constitutes part of the agricultural cum rural reform agenda, the latter is more specific. First, one confronts a diminishing returns argument, with total factor productivity declining, as opposed to an argument based on increases in input costs or a slower increase in output prices. This argument is usually applied to Punjab, Haryana and the western parts of Uttar Pradesh where agriculture has become overcapitalized. In these traditional Green Revolution areas, there are also questions about unsustainable practices like excessive use of water[24] and imbalanced use of fertilizers.[25] Land has become degraded. These are traditional arguments associated with the Green Revolution and concern reduction in soil fertility, excessive use of fertilizers and imbalance of nutrient content in the soil, problems related to biomass availability, genetic erosion, waterlogging and salinization, depletion of groundwater tables, imbalances in nutrient availability because of changes in cropping patterns and contamination of waterbodies and soil by pesticides and fertilizers (Shiva 1991). Then there is the issue related to lowering of farm profitability in the 1990s. While these are important topics, they are not very convincing in explaining the 1990s deceleration, unless one plugs in a regional dimension. In the 1980s, availability of power, irrigation and infrastructure helped the spread of the Green Revolution to the Eastern Region, particularly for paddy rice. Owing to power shortages, among other factors, this osmosis was less evident in the 1990s.

Another explanation for the 1990s deceleration is reduced public investments, especially in irrigation; this is directly reflected in the reduced share of capital formation in agriculture in the overall GDP (Table 6).[26] Moreover, in the 1990s, the quality of public sector agricultural research, technology development and extension services deteriorated.[27]

Table 6. Gross capital formation in agriculture at 1993–1994 prices

Year	Public (%)	Private (%)	Investment as % of GDP
1990–91	29.6	70.4	1.92
1995–96	30.9	69.1	1.57
1996–97	28.9	71.1	1.51
1997–98	25.0	75.0	1.43
1998–99	26.0	74.0	1.26
1999–2000	24.4	75.6	1.37
2000–01	23.2	76.8	1.28
2001–02	28.9	71.1	1.24
2002–03	23.9	76.1	1.27
2003–04	25.6	74.4	1.31

Source: Economic Survey, GOI (2004–2005).

While public investments in agriculture have declined, especially investments in research, private investments have not been able to compensate for the decline in public sector investments. Thus the burden of fiscal reform has been borne by agricultural investments, especially at the state level, including expenditure on R&D.[28] More specifically, expenditure on research stagnated, while that on extension declined. The state withdrew from spending on agriculture, without establishing alternative institutional mechanisms. State governments lack resources, a problem that was aggravated in the 1990s, and adversely affected the development of agricultural infrastructure.

This can be juxtaposed with the failure of risk mitigation instruments to develop and general regulatory failure. There were no coordinated policies or crop adjustment programmes to enable the move from rice and wheat towards pulses, oilseed or other crops. Diversification led to risk and uncertainty and in the absence of institutions, this was difficult to handle. Within public sector institutions, there was deterioration in management and monitoring norms. Hence, there were instances of adulterated fertilizers and seeds that were substandard. Whether extension departments of state governments are the best agencies for quality checks and inspections of inputs like fertilizers, insecticides, pesticides, feed and seeds is debatable. However, the quality of these extension services deteriorated in the 1990s.

While only tangentially related to the slowdown of the 1990s, there is the question of the form public investments in agriculture should take. The Steering Group on Agriculture and Allied Sectors (SGAAS) does not question this, but the Approach Paper to the Tenth Five Year Plan (APTFYP) does, "The policy approach to agriculture, particularly in the 1990s, has been to secure increased production through subsidies in inputs such as power, water and fertilizer, and by increasing the minimum support price rather than through building new capital assets in irrigation, power and rural infrastructure. This strategy has run into serious difficulties." The statement further identifies that the deterioration in state finances and the financial non-viability of the State Electricity Boards have meant that crowding out has occurred in public agricultural investment/expenditures for:

- roads,
- irrigation,
- expenditure on technological upgrading,
- maintenance of canals and roads,
- expansion of power supply to rural areas not covered,
- improvement in quality of rural power.

Moreover the combination of dependence on subsurface water and free/subsidized power is not only environmentally harmful but has also led to:

- excessive use of water that produced waterlogging in many areas,
- falling water tables.

At the same time, there is no evidence of any improvement in income distribution. Last, it is also increasingly being noticed that despite the best intensions of the policy there is a significant imbalance between usage of N, P and K fertilizers. Moreover, financial constraints are increasing both for the state governments and their State Electricity Boards (SEBs).

These problems are particularly severe in the poorer states. The equity, efficiency and sustainability of this approach are questionable. The subsidies have grown in size and are now financially unsustainable. Power continues to be supplied free for farmers in many states and is otherwise highly subsidized given the high cost of production of SEBs. According to one estimate (Srivastava et al. 2003) energy subsidies (of which power is one component) accounted for about 10 percent of all the subsidies in the late 1990s. This figure is likely to increase subsequently.

Moreover, the small and marginal farmers have been less able to access credit despite the existence of a large rural credit system. Poor land records are endemic across rural India. Also much of the agriculture sector is in the unorganized segment. But the financial system is largely in the organized sector and requires credible land ownership records, systematic record keeping and formal contracts. This has contributed to a situation where the bulk of the small and marginal farmers cannot access formal credit institutions. In the 1990s, availability of credit for large farmers may have risen, but declined for small farmers. Moreover, although 18 percent of priority sector lending is supposed to be for agriculture, agriculture's share in net bank credit has been more like 12 percent.[29]

In summary, there is unarguable stagnation in Indian agriculture and more so in the foodgrain sector. This is due to a combination of factors ranging from overdependence on the government in some areas/sectors, falling ability of the various government entities to subsidize and/or directly provide various inputs and services and overuse of resources. The "mission mode" that was so successful in tackling the problems of low production cannot be a vehicle to take on this set of problems. This requires efficient functioning of the price mechanism, smooth transactions between the various stakeholders, the alignment of incentives at the microlevel and fine-tuning of technology to the needs of the farmer. There are arguments for and against the current system of minimum support price (MSP) and subsidized inputs.

3. Future expectations

3.1 Overview

Because of deceleration in the 1990s, expanding population and rapid economic growth, food security concerns have been raised. Food security at the national level need not be equated with 100 percent self-sufficiency in foodgrain production. Adequate foreign exchange reserves should instead be the issue. The mindset is largely a reflection of the food import scare India confronted before the Green Revolution. Future demand projections are contingent on assumptions made about population, per capita income growth, the time frame and hunger removal. The time frame tends to be 2020. Population projections for 2020 vary with 1.315 billion being closer to the mark now (Dyson 2000).

Consider the basic trends first. With economic growth, population increases and changing age distributions, food requirements will be higher. How they match up with expected production given current trends, and what implications this has for international markets are discussed later.

3.2 Population

India's population in 2001 was 1.02 billion according to the Census of India, making it the second most populous country in the world after China (with a population of 1.28 billion). It has been estimated that in the next 15 years, the population will increase by about 23 percent to 1.24 billion persons. But estimates vary, some being as high as 1.4 billion. High growth rates can be ascribed to death rates being lower than birth rates. Between 2001 and 2010, almost 150 million more people need to be provided with adequate nutrition and between 2010 and 2015, another 83 million people need to be covered (Figure 2). Most GOI estimates do not go beyond 2015, but trends till 2020 are not likely to be any different.

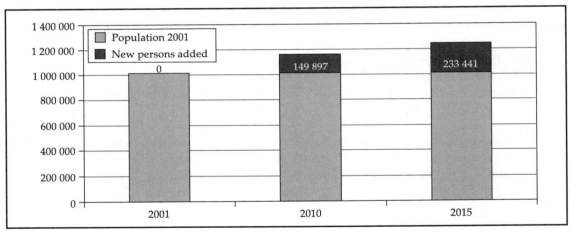

Source: GOI (1996).

Figure 2. Population 2001–2015 (figures in '000s)

3.3 Incomes and expenditures

According to India's national accounts, total GDP in 2003 to 2004 was about US$600 billion (per capita GDP of US$540). Of this, personal disposable income was in the range of US$512 billion and 24.6 percent of this income was directed into savings by the household sector. During the postliberalization decade, from 1993–1994 to 2003–2004 the average annualized growth rate of India's GDP has been around 6.2 percent and this has been accelerating in the early 2000s. Table 7 records the growth rates of some of the key indicators of national accounts of India.

Table 7. Growth of macroeconomic variables

National accounts of India, 2003–2004	Annualized growth rate between 1993–94 and 2003–04
GDP	6.18
National income	6.41
Net national disposable income	6.55
Private income	6.73
Personal income	6.59
Personal disposable income	6.57
Domestic saving for household sector	9.77
Wholesale price index	5.82

Source: GOI (2003–2004b).

As discussed earlier, poverty has declined significantly, and is expected to continue to fall. The poverty line is defined by the GOI as the cost of a package of commodities (about 80 percent food items and 20 percent other essentials such as clothing) that can provide about 2 400 calories and 2 100 calories to an average Indian citizen living in rural and urban areas, respectively. The HCR (head count ratio) in India had fallen to about 26 percent in 1999 to 2000 from 39 percent in 1987 to 1988. Our own estimates are that if the GDP growth is sustained, it will fall to about 14 percent by 2010 and then to 8 percent by 2015 (Figure 3). These are not very different from other estimates discussed earlier. Two further points need to be mentioned in this connection. First, income distributions are typically log normal and as the thick part of the distribution passes through the poverty line, it is possible for sharp reductions in HCRs to occur. Second, when the Indian poverty line evolved in India in the early 1960s, the presumption was that health and education would be merit goods, if not public goods. In either event, they would be provided by the government and need not be ingredients in private consumption expenditure. Hence, these are not included in defining or computing the poverty line. The 1990s, however, witnessed a switch from public expenditure to private expenditure in both health and education. It is thus possible that the Indian poverty line might be redefined at some time in the future. Notwithstanding this possibility, the proposition about decline in HCRs, assuming an unchanged poverty line, remains valid.

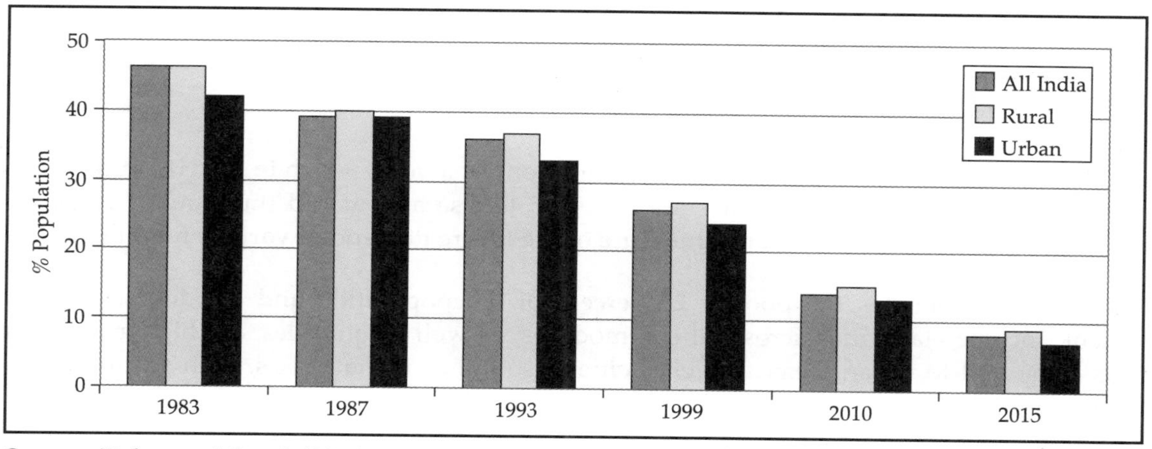

Source: Dubey and Crook (2001) and authors' estimates for 2010 and 2015.

Figure 3. Poverty levels

Both rural and urban areas have a very similar poverty scenario. However, India has a long way to go before the whole population has the means to consume the minimum required calories per day. During 1999 to 2000, more than one-fourth of India's population was below the poverty line and this amounted to about 260 million people at that time. If the rapid rate decline in poverty after 1991 were to continue, not only the percentage, but also the actual number of people below the poverty line is expected to be lower. The net impact on the demand for greater nutrition is obvious.

3.4 The changing food basket

As incomes, and as a consequence expenditures, increase, not only are expenditures on food and agricultural commodities as a whole likely to increase, but the consumption basket characteristics are also likely to change. In both rural and urban areas, dairy products, meat, fruit and vegetables are likely to have a greater share of the additional demand being generated.

This is the standard picture across different countries, and is also reflected in the differing elasticities observed by various studies both for India as well as other countries. The income elasticities for five different income groups (quintiles 1–5) in urban and rural areas of India are shown in Table 8.

Table 8. Income elasticities across quintiles

	Q1	Q2	Q3	Q4	Q5
Rural					
Wheat	0.50	0.49	0.48	0.48	0.47
Rice	0.72	0.47	0.31	0.12	-0.21
Maize	-0.63	-0.51	-0.42	-0.33	-0.17
Milk and products	2.35	1.96	1.70	1.40	0.88
Eggs	2.44	2.17	1.98	1.77	1.39
Chicken	1.35	1.32	1.30	1.28	1.25
Other meat	1.35	1.32	1.30	1.28	1.25
Urban					
Wheat	0.32	0.25	0.19	0.13	0.04
Rice	0.39	0.22	0.09	-0.05	-0.29
Maize	-0.60	-0.63	-0.65	-0.67	-0.71
Milk and products	1.64	1.38	1.19	0.97	0.61
Eggs	1.72	1.56	1.44	1.29	1.06
Chicken	0.48	0.45	0.43	0.41	0.37
Other meat	0.48	0.45	0.43	0.41	0.37

Source: Mohanty *et al.* (1998).

The food requirement is dependent on the consumption behaviour, which in turn is a direct outcome of income. With development, incomes are expected to rise and would thus impact consumption behaviour. The income elasticities are a measure of the future demand of various food items.

Quintile one (Q1) denotes the poorest 20 percent of the population and Q5 denotes the richest 20 percent. Income elasticities across all commodities, as well as quintiles, are higher for the rural areas as compared to urban areas. The elasticities also fall as income rises, both within urban and rural quintiles.

Wheat shows an elasticity of 0.50 and 0.32 for rural and urban areas respectively, in Q1. However, the elasticity decreases to 0.47 and 0.04 for the same areas in the case of Q5. Similarly, the income elasticity of rice in rural areas drops from 0.72 to a negative 0.21 as we move up from Q1 to Q5. A similar pattern is observed in the urban areas as well.

The elasticities of milk and milk products, along with eggs, show very high values of greater than 1 for the lower quintiles, implying that the proportionate change in consumption demand is greater than the proportionate change in income. However, these elasticities also follow the general decreasing trend as we ascend to higher income groups. Elasticities for chicken and other meat are lower than those of milk and eggs. For rural areas, income elasticities for meat are greater than 1 across all income groups (1.25 for Q5), while they are less than 1 for all income groups falling in urban areas. Meat eating is common across India, however a significant share of the population is vegetarian. Even among those who consume meat, at certain times of the year a largely vegetarian diet is followed. Consequently, the income elasticities of meat products may not be as high as in other countries (Table 9).

Table 9. Sensitivity to prices — own price elasticities

	Very poor	Moderately poor	Non-poor, lower	Non-poor, high	All
Rural					
Cereals	-0.7	-0.3	-0.2	-0.1	-0.3
Milk	-1.1	-1.1	-1.1	-0.8	-1.0
Edible oils	-0.7	-0.6	-0.6	-0.6	-0.6
Meat	-0.9	-0.7	-0.8	-0.6	-0.7
Sugar	-0.7	-0.7	-0.8	-0.6	-0.7
Pulses	-2.4	-2.6	-1.2	-1.2	-1.3
Fruit & vegetables	-1.0	-0.7	-0.5	-0.6	-0.6
Other food	-1.4	-0.4	-0.6	-1.0	-0.8
Urban					
Cereals	-0.5	-0.1	-0.1	-0.1	-0.1
Milk	-1.4	-1.0	-0.9	-0.6	-0.6
Edible oils	-0.7	-0.5	-0.4	-0.3	-0.4
Meat	-1.3	-0.8	-0.7	-0.5	-0.5
Sugar	-0.7	-0.4	-0.3	-0.2	-0.3
Pulses	-1.0	-0.9	-0.9	-0.9	-0.9
Fruit & vegetables	-1.1	-1.1	-0.9	-0.6	-0.7
Other food	-0.9	-0.9	-1.2	-0.8	-0.9

Source: Dev *et al.* (2004).

In both rural and urban areas, the own price elasticity declines in absolute terms as we move from the very poor to the non-poor section of the population. For cereals in rural areas, elasticity declines from 0.7 to 0.1, while it changes from 0.5 to 0.1 for the urban areas. Milk, edible oils and meat show similar trends in both urban and rural areas, although demand for milk shows a higher sensitivity to price changes. Price elasticity of demand for sugar in rural areas increases marginally from 0.7 to 0.8, before declining to 0.6 for the non-poor. In urban areas, however, the elasticity shows a gradual decline as we move to higher income groups.

As shown in Table 9, the demand for pulses is extremely sensitive to price changes in rural areas, with the elasticity being as high as 2.4 for the very poor in rural areas, but falls to 1.2 for the non-poor. For the non-poor section in urban areas too, the price elasticity is 0.9.

3.5 Consumption of agricultural products

Others have estimated the growth in food consumption and most have similar insights. Milk and milk products will see the largest increase up to 2020. Fruit and vegetables, sugar and meat and fish consumption will also increase significantly. The reasons are obvious in light of the previous discussion. Income increases matched by the high income responsiveness of these commodities will be the driving force. Among cereals, the highest percentage growth will be in wheat, followed by rice. Coarse grains are not likely to grow as much.

The demand for rice is projected to grow from 78.3 million tonnes/year in 2000 to 118.9 million tonnes/year in 2020, showing a compounded annual growth rate of 2.1 percent. The main factor driving this demand will be the increase in population. Wheat demand rises from 54.2 million tonnes in 2000 to 72.1 and 92.4 million tonnes in 2010 and 2020 respectively, with a growth rate of 2.7 percent. The responsible factors will be the rising population and positive income elasticity for wheat. The demand for other cereals will grow by 0.9 percent, primarily on account of change in preferences as incomes grow. On the whole, consumption demand for all cereals will show a growth of 76 million tonnes from 2000 to 2020 at the rate of 2.1 percent, which is marginally higher than the projected growth rate of the population (Tables 10 and 11).

Table 10. Consumption estimates (million tonnes/year)

Commodity	2000	2005	2010	2015	2020
Rice	78.3	88.1	98.0	108.5	118.9
Wheat	54.2	63.1	72.1	82.2	92.4
Other cereals	13.1	13.6	14.1	14.8	15.6
All cereals	145.1	163.1	181.1	201.1	221.1
Pulses	10.6	12.6	14.6	17.1	19.5
Foodgrain	155.6	175.7	195.7	218.2	240.6
Milk & milk products	64.2	85.3	106.4	136.1	165.8
Edible oils	5.3	6.5	7.7	9.3	10.9
Meat & fish	4.7	6.0	7.3	9.0	10.8
Sugar & *gur*[†]	11.5	14.3	17.2	21.2	25.1

[†] Jaggery (unrefined sugar).
Source: Radhakrishna and Reddy (2002).

Table 11. Growth in consumption

Commodity	CARG (2000–2020), %	Increase between 2000–2020 (million tonnes)
Rice	2.10	40.7
Wheat	2.70	38.2
Other cereals	0.90	2.5
All cereals	2.10	76.0
Pulses	3.10	9.0
Foodgrain	2.20	85.0
Milk & milk products	4.90	101.7
Edible oils	3.70	5.7
Meat & fish	4.30	6.1
Sugar & *gur*	4.00	13.6

Source: Radhakrishna and Reddy (2002).

Demand for food items such as milk products, meat and fruit is expected to grow at much higher levels of 3 to 5 percent in the next few years. This is a natural result of growth in incomes following economic development. The estimated demand for foodgrain in 2020 is 240.6 million tonnes/year, growing from 155.6 tonnes/year in 2000 at the rate of 2.2 percent *per annum*. The income effect will manifest itself to raise the demand for milk and milk products to 166 tonnes, edible oils to 11 tonnes, meat and fish to 11 tonnes and sugar and *gur* (jaggery) to 25 tonnes/year (Tables 10 and 11).

3.6 Production of agricultural commodities

India has one of the largest land masses of any country of the world, and a high proportion of its land mass is arable. Although most of the land depends upon the monsoons for irrigation, irrigated areas have been increasing and comprise about 40 percent of the gross cropped area. However, yields in India are among the lowest in the world, and therefore there is significant scope for increases in the coming future.

A yield comparison across countries (see Appendix 1: Figure A1.1, Figure A1.2 and Figure A1.3) shows how India's crop production fares *vis à vis* international benchmarks. India's figures are contrasted with crop yields in the United States, China and an average for the world. While these can be compared for a number of different crops, the results are remarkably similar, with a few exceptions. For cereals, coarse grains and pulses, both the United States and China are well above the world average. India has extremely low yields, even by developing country standards. For oil crops and primary fibre crops as well, India has yield levels below the United States, China and aggregate world levels. Across different product segments, a similar picture emerges.

While the static picture of India's crop production is not encouraging, the indicators for the future provide grounds for optimism. The potential improvements made possible by improvements in technology, organizational expertise and policy redirection have lifted the yield levels of many of India's crops. From 1961 to 2004, commodities with the largest increases in yield were wheat, maize and jute, and rice to a lesser extent. Pulses, oil crops and primary fibre crops have had muted increases in yield.

On an even more cautionary note, in the last ten years, improvements in yield have plateaued for Green Revolution heavyweights like wheat and cereals (Figure 4). From 2001 to 2004, several crops even experienced an absolute decline in their yields.

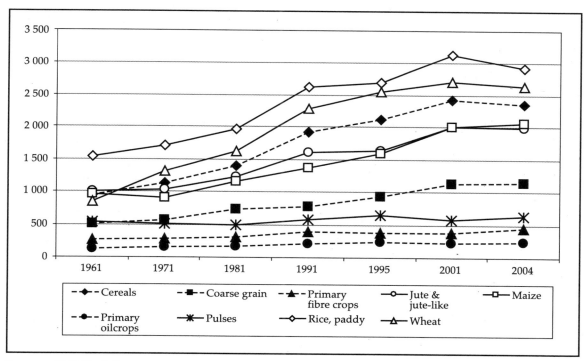

Source: FAO Statistics.

Figure 4. Trend in yield of major crops (kg/ha)

Given these indications, prospects for the future of Indian agriculture production are mixed. While yield levels seem to have plateaued, they are still significantly below competitive levels for most crops. While countries at the peak of the agricultural technology curve must pour funds into R&D to invent new ways to increase production, countries on the other side of the curve stand to benefit from implementing those methods that have already been pioneered. Catching up is always easier and for this reason alone, India should be able to realize fast and significant gains in the near future. The directions to be followed are quite clear and are discussed in other sections.

3.7 Price competitiveness

Currently, there are some estimates of price competitiveness, the results often being functions of whether an importable or an exportable hypothesis assumption is used and whether one uses the nominal protection coefficient (NPC), the effective protection coefficient (EPC), the effective subsidy coefficient (ESC)[30] or the domestic resource cost (DRC). A widely referred to study by Bhalla (2004) revealed that:

- Most crops except oilseed, some coarse cereals and sugar are internationally competitive;

- More crops would be competitive if developed countries withdrew domestic support to agriculture;

- However, import competitiveness becomes reduced over time because:

    - Successive price hikes have led to very high prices for many agricultural commodities. For example major crops such as rice and wheat became non-competitive during recent years because of a fall in their international price combined with a major increase in their domestic price owing to increase in MSP.
    - Productivity growth has decelerated, moreover production efficiency is being affected by lack of implementation of technological innovations.
    - A major thrust is needed in infrastructure investment in general and investment in science and technology in particular for India to maintain and enhance its competitiveness.

3.8 Production, consumption and surpluses

The GTAP model has been used to predict India's trade with the rest of the world including India's own production and consumption. The quantitative assumptions behind the model are given in Table 12.

Table 12. Assumptions: the growth rate of exogenous variables of India in four stages (per year %)

	2001–2005	2006–2010	2011–2015	2015–2020
GDP	6.73	7.00	7.50	8.00
Population	1.80	1.70	1.60	1.50
Cultivated land area				
– net	0.00	0.00	0.00	0.00
– gross	0.50	0.75	1.00	1.00
Labour supply	2.70	2.71	2.08	1.73
– unskilled labour	2.46	2.48	1.85	1.58
– skilled labour	7.24	6.40	5.32	3.63
Capital stock	6.46	6.67	6.92	7.20

Source: Author estimates.

For greater details on the GTAP model and related assumptions see Appendix 2.[31]

India's GDP is expected to grow at more than 7 percent for much of the period under consideration. Moreover, the growth rate is expected to increase for the coming decade. As population growth has been falling owing to falling birth rates for the past two decades, the growth in labour supply would decline over the next decade and a half. Irrigated area is expected to grow, although not too significantly, as further increases will require significant public investments that show no signs of accelerating. Private efforts are likely to be the main driving force behind the 1 percent annual increase in irrigated area. Skilled and highly educated labour is expected to rise much faster than unskilled labour; this reflects the latest improvements in the educational achievements of a large segment of the population. The capital stock would have to grow rapidly as well, and is expected to increase as labour supply growth tapers off to sustain the high growth rates of 8 percent.

These GDP forecasts need to be qualified. The GDP forecasts given in Table 12, with acceleration from 6.73 to 8 percent are actually a worst-case scenario, although one must mention that the BRIC (Brazil, Russia, India, China) report, generated by Goldman Sachs, involves real GDP growth of slightly less than 6 percent (Wilson and Purushothaman 2003).[32] A more likely scenario is GDP growth of 7.5 percent, accelerating to 8.5 percent and a third scenario would involve 7.5 percent accelerating to 9 percent.[33] Long-term GDP forecasts are rare. In the short term, the Tenth Five Year Plan (2002 2007) talks about 8 percent real GDP growth during the Plan, while the National Common Minimum Programme (NCMP) of the UPA government considers 7 to 8 percent.

Although long-term projections are rare, when they are made, most experts expect real GDP growth of 7 to 8 percent for India in the period leading up to 2020. Notwithstanding reservations about the speed of economic reforms, consequent to debates about liberalization in a democratic policy, these estimates of 6, 7 or 8 percent are probably underestimates, even if one ignores the exchange rate aspect. There are different ways to argue this out and all of these trends reinforce one another. Looking forward to 2015, an average savings rate of 30 percent is certainly plausible given the current rate of 28.1 percent rising. Foreign capital inflows are also increasing. There is no reason why the average investment rate should not therefore be 32 percent. The present incremental capital/output ratio (ICOR) is around 4 (though estimates vary between 3.5 and 4.6). Whatever the figure, there is no reason why this should increase significantly in the near future. Indeed, with reforms, competition and resultant efficiency improvements, the ICOR should decline. But even with an ICOR of 4, there is growth of 8 percent.

It is obvious that these quantitative forecasts have not considered the possibilities of future environmental degradation, unforeseen changes in economic and trade policy and of course technological changes. The discussions in the previous sections underscore the importance of enabling reforms. However, given these assumptions and those outlined in Appendix 2, the GTAP model predicts consumption and production characteristics as shown in Table 13.

The growth in rice is going to be in the order of 1 percent *per annum* till 2010, for both production and consumption. For wheat however, the rise in incomes is going to create a marginally higher growth in consumption than expected production increases. For both oilseed and processed foods, consumption increases will outstrip production increases. Given current conditions and trends, similarly, for forestry products, as well as other foods, consumption increases are going to be far higher than likely production increases.

Overall, the patterns are quite unambiguous. Although production levels are likely to increase significantly, they are not going to be able to match the increases in consumption, at current and expected overall economic growth.

This does not imply a fall in export earnings, as overall expected price increases due to the opening of international markets, as well as reduction of subsidies will tend to have a positive impact on

Table 13. Likely production and consumption in 2020

	US$ million 2001		US$ million 2020		CARG*	
	Production 2001	Consumption 2001	Production 2020	Consumption 2020	Production 2001–20, %	Consumption 2001–20, %
Rice	26 804	26 038	32 514	31 649	1.02	1.03
Wheat	14 418	14 001	21 216	21 050	2.05	2.17
Coarse grains	4 259	4 233	6 537	6 499	2.28	2.28
Oilseed	9 434	10 564	17 780	22 582	3.39	4.08
Sugar	13 968	13 740	35 085	35 001	4.97	5.04
Plant-based fibre	4 792	5 344	9 873	11 937	3.88	4.32
Other crops	128 360	127 444	45 441	47 279	-5.32	-5.09
Cattle and meat	4 670	4 397	4 290	3 915	-0.45	-0.61
Other agro products	8 173	8 604	22 961	27 431	5.59	6.29
Milk	29 577	29 513	60 510	60 624	3.84	3.86
Fish	5 212	5 197	16 656	16 641	6.31	6.32
Other food	17 234	15 153	43 120	40 923	4.95	5.37
Forestry	4 865	5 347	15 808	18 333	6.40	6.70

* CARG: compounded annual rate of growth.
Source: Estimates using the GTAP model.

prices. This is regardless of the temporary impasse at WTO on agricultural liberalization, which hopefully, will be temporary. The net export earnings for rice, wheat, sugar and other grains are given in Figure 5a, while Figure 5b illustrates export earnings for cattle, animal products, etc.

India is likely to maintain the status of an exporting country for rice and wheat. However for oilseed, India is likely to be a significant importing country in another decade and a half. It will also remain as a marginal exporter of sugar and coarse grains.

Despite being an exporter of jute and cotton, India will be a net importer of plant-based fibre. Moreover, it will also start to become a net importer of other horticultural crops. Although overall milk production is expected to increase rapidly, consumption increases will prevent India from becoming a large dairy product exporter. Cattle and red meat exports are likely to increase, although other animal products, such as leather, are likely to see a net increase in imports.

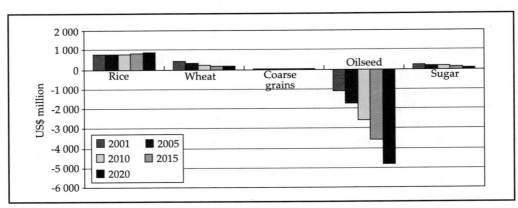

Source: GTAP estimations.

Figure 5a. Export/import earnings for selected agricultural commodities

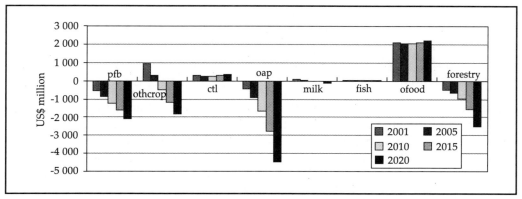

Pfb: plant-based fibre; Othcrop: other crops; Ctl: bovine cattle, sheep and goats, horses; Oap: animal products (not else classified, nec); Ofood: other food.

Source: GTAP estimations.

Figure 5b. Export/import earnings for selected agricultural commodities

3.9 Expectations for India

Overall, India will remain a marginal exporter of wheat, coarse grains, sugar, cattle and red meat, fish and other foods. However, it will become a significant importer of oilseed, forestry products, other animal products and plant fibre. For products such as plant fibre and animal products, its position as a net exporter of manufactured items will be facilitated by larger imports of raw materials. For the other segments, rising domestic consumption not matched by domestic supply increases, will be the driving principle.

Table 14. Net export share of world export in value terms (%)

	2001	2005	2010	2015	2020
Rice	10.0	9.7	9.8	10.2	10.8
Wheat	2.6	1.9	1.4	1.1	1.0
Coarse grains	0.2	0.2	0.2	0.2	0.2
Oilseed	-3.3	-5.0	-7.2	-9.8	-12.8
Sugar	2.7	2.2	1.8	1.3	0.9
Plant-based fibre	-6.6	-9.4	-12.6	-15.5	-18.1
Other crops	1.1	0.3	-0.6	-1.3	-2.1
Cattle and meat	1.0	0.9	1.0	1.2	1.7
Other agricultural products	-0.9	-1.8	-3.2	-5.3	-8.4
Milk	0.2	0.1	0.0	-0.1	-0.3
Fish	0.2	0.2	0.1	0.1	0.2
Other food	1.1	1.1	1.1	1.2	1.3
Forestry	-4.9	-6.1	-8.2	-11.1	-14.6

Source: Estimations from GTAP.

Forestry products are likely to be a significant import item, the bulk being related to wood. Industrial and furniture requirements are the important components that will drive forestry product shortfalls. Although India has large forest cover, commercial forestry is insignificant and is unlikely to expand in a big way given its current environmental protection laws. The statistics for forestry products have large gaps (much more than is usual for India). According to some FAO estimates, production in India for industrial roundwood has been falling (it was about 1.6 billion m^3 in 2000), while fuelwood has stagnated at about 2.9 million m^3 (FAO 2002). Pulp and matchwood have also been showing a negative trend. On the whole, it is expected that India will be substituting imports for domestic production more and more in the near future.

The overall position is quite unambiguous. For Indian policy-makers, the most worrying aspects are stagnating yields. This in itself is not surprising, given the low investments in agriculture, as well as the constraints on agricultural trade. If India is to become a significant exporter of other agricultural products apart from rice, emphasis will have to be placed on improving yields. Investments in rural areas are therefore essential.

How would these estimates change if growth assumptions were different? India would continue to be a large importer of forestry products whether economic growth is 6 or 8 percent. Although the quantum may differ. Similarly, its position as a significant textile and garment producer may require it to import plant-based fibre, in spite of plus or minus 1 percent variation in growth. (What the numbers in this case are more sensitive too is the productivity assumption. Yields are currently quite low in large parts of India and the introduction of new varieties, BT cotton being one example, may lead to a rapid increase in cotton production in coming years.) India's low production of oilseed and high requirements will also drive its oilseed imports. But this needs to be qualified. Given its land area, it is conceivable that productivity enhancements could lead to a lower shortfall in oilseed and pulses. However, current trends indicate this to be a remote possibility. Now rice remains. Compared to the past, rice is not a preferred cereal; income elasticity measures also indicate that at the middle and upper income levels, the parameters are lower. In other words, estimates of rice surpluses are not as sensitive to economic growth assumptions.

How would these surpluses affect India's trade partners? This requires an examination of which countries could potentially be India's major trade partners in agricultural commodities.

4. The agenda for reform

One way to categorize the reform agenda could be in terms of objectives: (a) protection of natural resources, (b) rise in productivity, (c) encouragement for value-added agriculture and (d) disseminating the benefits of agricultural growth for overall rural development. However as many of the necessary actions span these objectives, the requirements can be grouped under: (i) land, (ii) water, (iii) credit, (iv) markets, (v) diversification and (vi) technology.

Numerous reports and studies within various organs of the government have identified the critical issues that need to be addressed. However, it will take some years for the political establishment to tackle many of them even if there is a consensus on the issue.

4.1 Land

The arguments in the Approach Paper to the Tenth Five Year Plan (APTFYP) are almost generic. Both in agriculture and in forestry, uncultivated land must be brought into productive use. This requires a proper land-use policy, including tenurial reforms. Leasing and sharecropping of uncultivated agricultural land needs to be regularized. (Chadha *et al.* 2004).

- There is unequal access to land and this adversely affects farmers at the bottom of the farm size hierarchy. Despite land redistribution attempts, the land base of marginal and near-landless farmers has not improved much over time; land redistribution gains having been restricted mostly to middle levels of the peasantry. Currently, however, land redistribution does not appear to be on the agenda of any political entity.

- Fragmentation of holdings has led to reduced economies of scale, low allocative efficiency and low investments and mechanization. In many cases, this leads to subsistence farming. One should review the policy on land availability and ideally, repeal land ceiling acts.[34] Consolidation of landholdings is important to exploit economies of scale, as has happened in Punjab. Though land rights become complicated because of rights and subrights, it is possible to perform the consolidation on the basis of primary rights and legalize leasing of land. Some states are in the process of improving their land records systems and this is expected to gather

28

momentum in coming years. While it might not address fragmentation directly, it would at the very least enable functioning of land markets and enable mutually beneficial land transactions.

- There is underutilization of available agricultural land. If land is limited, there must be land-augmenting or land-saving technologies. Agricultural holdings of socially disadvantaged groups like "scheduled castes" and "scheduled tribes" also exhibit greater underutilization of land, particularly in states such as Bihar, Uttar Pradesh, Gujarat, Assam and Kerala and this may be due to the poor quality of land. The solution lies in the development of appropriate technologies and provision of support services to enable the small and disadvantaged farmer to utilize this resource.

- There is increasing land degradation because of natural and human-induced factors.[35] Much land has become unusable owing to land degradation, salinization or waterlogging. There is no transparent policy to make this land available to agro-industry. *Panchayats* (village local bodies) can be used to identify unusable, saline or waterlogged land, which can be reclaimed through joint cooperatives of landless farmers and agro-industry for cultivation, afforestation and plantation crops. With greater powers and funds being devolved to the *Panchayats*, it is expected that the local communities will be better motivated to take up these tasks collectively. Moreover there are some measures for growing biofuel-yielding plants that are gathering momentum.

- Notwithstanding official bans on leasing in and leasing out of land, tenancy continues *de facto*, although the form has changed from sharecropping to fixed rent tenancy. Given economies of scale in production, this suggests a conversion of the *de facto* practice to *de jure* legal changes, so that there are incentives to invest in land and land can also act as collateral. However, these changes are likely to be highly sensitive politically and unlikely to be changed in the near future.

Somewhat in the same vein, provisions are needed for contract farming, with explicit clauses on contract enforcement and dispute resolution.

4.2 Water

Of the total agricultural land, only 35 to 40 percent is irrigated and agriculture is therefore still dependent on monsoons. Moreover, during the 1990s[36], the area under canal irrigation declined, despite an increase in expenditure on major and medium irrigation projects (Raju *et al.* 2004). Simultaneously, there was also a decline in the use of tank irrigation; an increasing source of irrigation has been groundwater irrigation, mostly owned and managed by farmers.

There are several issues connected with irrigation and water usage: (a) water conservation and appropriate pricing of water; (b) diversion of water from surplus basins to deficit basins[37]; (c) decline of traditional water management structures and institutions; (d) disparity in the spread of irrigation across regions; (e) absence of sufficient attention to the software of irrigation systems, rules and procedures, allocation and distribution of water and relationships between users and the bureaucracy; (f) inequity in groundwater usage and the absence of legal frameworks and enforcement mechanisms to check overexploitation; (g) insufficient usage of drip and sprinkler irrigation; and (h) declining user management and participation in irrigation systems (Raju *et al.* 2004). Nor should one forget that parts of India are still characterized by rain-fed agriculture, such as parts of Andhra Pradesh, Karnataka, Maharashtra, Madhya Pradesh and Rajasthan, producing coarse cereals and oilseed (Rao 2004). These drought-prone areas often witness farmer trauma and institutional and policy support for dryland agriculture is weak or non-existent.

The solutions are well-known: community-based water conservation measures, revamping of traditional water-harvesting mechanisms, greater investments in maintenance of irrigation systems and appropriate pricing of electricity for agricultural purposes.

Water will emerge as a serious consideration over the next few years, and it is likely that many, if not most, of the above solutions will have to be put in place.

4.3 Credit

The objective of the Agricultural Credit Policy in India since Independence has been gradual replacement of moneylenders by cooperatives and lowering of interest rates. Until banks were nationalized, cooperative institutions were the only source of institutional credit in rural areas. Since nationalization, scheduled commercial banks and regional rural banks (RRBs) have also been part of the formal credit system. As percentage of agricultural GDP, institutional credit to agriculture increased from 2.56 percent in 1970–1971 to 7.11 percent in 1980–1981 to 12.14 percent in 2000–2001, although studies do suggest asymmetries in distribution of credit across farm size and across regions. But small farmers continue to resort to informal lenders (despite the success of *Kisan* credit cards, see Box 2), as the current system of institutional credit to farmers suffers from non-farmer friendly practices, delays in credit delivery and collateral problems. This forces farmers to resort to non-institutional sources of credit at high rates of interest. There should be a shift in attention from the cost of credit to availability of credit.

Box 2. *Kisan* credit card

One of the major challenges in the sector has been ensuring the provision of timely and adequate credit to the farmers. An innovative strategy conceived in 1999 by the GOI created the *Kisan* credit cards through which farmers could avail short-term loans for crops from banks. The scheme was initiated in consultation with the Reserve Bank of India and NABARD (National Bank for Agricultural and Rural Development) and by the end of November 2005, 55.6 million cards were issued to eligible farmers all over India. All cooperative banks, scheduled commercial banks and regional rural banks were given annual targets and their progress was monitored at every step by NABARD.

The *Kisan* credit card is essentially a type of revolving cash credit facility with withdrawals and repayments to meet the production credit needs, cultivation expenses and the contingency expenses of the farmers. Recently, banks have also extended credit towards working capital requirements for other activities such as cattle breeding and poultry farming through this scheme. Each farmer is given a passbook and is sanctioned a credit limit, which can be modified depending on his performance and repayment record, thereby maintaining a working relationship between him and the bank. While the limit of credit depends on the basis of operational landholding, cropping pattern and scale of operations, the full year's credit requirement of the borrower is taken care of and each card is valid for three years. With minimum paper work and simplification of documentation for withdrawal of funds from the bank, not only has availability of credit been made easier but the system has also been made straightforward to operate and farmers have been given sufficient freedom to decide how to use their credit. The card also carries insurance cover at a nominal premium.

The implementation of the scheme has resulted in an increase in the flow of credit to the agriculture sector and a substantial reduction in borrowing from the informal sector for short-term needs. The programme has benefited both farmers and bankers as there has been a significant saving in time and cost of credit delivery, reduction in transaction costs, better recoveries and reduction in the workload of bank branches. However, the sanctioning of lower credit limits, low awareness levels about insurance features and the tendency to treat the card as a term loan facility rather than as a cash credit facility still remain areas of concern.

Banks have now begun taking advantage of the popularity of the cards by enhancing the features of the card — making the card ATM-compatible, issuing chip-based smart cards which will contain embedded information pertaining to land records, limit sanctioned, amount withdrawn against bank account, etc. With near-universal coverage, the *Kisan* credit card has met all its objectives and is on its way to becoming a powerful tool in consolidating the banker–farmer relationship.

There are a number of strands in the reform package:

- First, improvements in the supply of credit by simplifying loan application and documentation procedures, easing collateral requirements and recapitalizing regional rural banks (RRBs) and cooperative banks.[38]

- Second, there are issues in reforming cooperatives and freeing them from government intervention (Datta 2004).

- Third, there are questions of stimulating demand for credit by pushing the formation of self-help groups (SHGs) and NGO involvement (Deshpande *et al.* 2004), especially in the context of microcredit. There is a government policy to link SHGs with banks and up to December 2004, 1.28 million SHGs have been linked with banks (GOI 2004–2005).[39]

- Fourth, the agricultural credit issue cannot be delinked from insurance. There is poor protection for farmers because the current Comprehensive Crop Insurance Scheme is too complicated; it does not cover all crops and has a complex system for loss assessment.

- A simplified crop insurance scheme should have farmer friendly administration, cover all crops, cover farmers who do not take loans, charge actuarial rates and provide subsidies for small and marginal farmers. In all fairness, one should point out that this is easier said than done.

4.4 Markets

In much of the agricultural reform agenda, there is questioning of what has historically believed to have been the government's role in pushing agricultural development. At a generic level, these government policies include agrarian reforms; the broad objective of what was called self-sufficiency in foodgrain production; a price-support policy; government interventions in production and distribution of agricultural products, inputs and services; technology generation and dissemination; and promotion of cooperatives (Thimmaiah and Rajan 2004). For instance, the self-sufficiency in foodgrain production objective led to a system of price-support purchases through the FCI (Food Corporation of India) and subsidized distribution through the PDS.[40] This price-support system for rice and wheat created incentives in favour of rice and wheat, and favoured states that had such surpluses — Punjab, Haryana, the western parts of Uttar Pradesh and Andhra Pradesh. Quite often, the MSPs were increased far more than what the CACP (Commission on Agricultural Costs and Prices) had recommended. The FCI procured both for buffer stocks and the PDS and, in both cases, inefficiencies in FCI procurement have been documented. It is being suggested that while the FCI might continue to procure for buffer stock purposes, for the PDS, procurement should be thrown open to state governments, the private and the cooperative sector.

Nor has the PDS worked well. The APTFYP comments on the targeted PDS, in an attempt to reform the PDS: "There is 36 percent diversion of wheat, 31 percent diversion of rice and 23 percent diversion of sugar from the system at the national level. .... Due to poor off-take by the states and even poorer actual lifting by the BPL families, the scheme has not made any impact on the nutrition levels in [some] states."[41] The Expenditure Reform Commission's (ERC) *Report on Food Subsidy* (July 2000) is a devastating critique of the PDS, highlighting FCI inefficiencies as well as the pro-urban bias of the PDS. The reform agenda therefore encompasses a revamp of the PDS system as well and some states have now begun to experiment with a system of food stamps.

In addition to procurement and PDS, the APMC Acts and the Essential Commodities Act (ECA) are perceived to be unnecessary impediments towards developing a national and common market for agricultural products. Government policies on agricultural marketing have covered regulation of marketing practices, creation of infrastructure, price support, promotion of cooperative organizations, technology transfer, input supply and credit delivery (Acharya 2004). The following trends are evident:

(a)   Marketed surplus per farm rose.[42]

(b)   Marketing charges payable by farmers were dropped, standardized, or liability shifted to buyers.

(c)   More and more reliable information was made available to farmers.

(d)   Better storage facilities and quicker means of transportation became available.

(e)   The trend of village sales declined and market sales increased.

(f)   Price-support programmes helped farmers reduce price risks.

(g)   In some areas, there was an increase in cooperative or group marketing by farmers.[43]

There are 7 161 regulated markets, mostly primary wholesale markets and the number has increased over time (Acharya 2004). Through APMC Acts, marketing boards have often accumulated substantial resources, based on fees that range between 0.5 and 2 percent of the value of produce transacted. These market development funds were supposed to be ploughed back into the development of infrastructure and other services. Whether this has indeed happened, is doubtful.[44] In many states, state governments alone are allowed to set up markets for agricultural commodities. Such monopolistic practices prevent the development of efficient and transparent agricultural marketing and the use of preharvest and postharvest technologies, or the setting up and enforcement of quality standards (Table 15).

Table 15. Number of regulated markets

Year	No. of regulated markets	Regulated markets as % of wholesale assembling markets
End 1945	146	2.00
End 1950	286	3.92
March 1956	470	6.44
March 1961	715	9.80
March 1966	1 012	13.88
March 1974	1 777	24.37
March 1976	3 528	48.38
March 1980	4 446	60.96
March 1985	5 695	78.09
March 1990	6 217	85.25
March 1995	6 836	93.73
March 2001	7 161	98.19

Source: Acharya (2004).

The food chain in India has several intermediaries from the farmer to the consumer. It is estimated that 20 percent of the food produced in India is wasted[45]. Less than 2 percent of fruit and vegetables is processed and wastage is estimated at 25 percent of total production. While private traders are allowed to trade in foodgrain, the APMC regulations create much complication in trade in agricultural commodities.

However, it is now generally agreed that both the APMC and ECA will not remain in force for long in most states. Contract farming will be allowed, and there will be greater flexibility for the farmers and traders to transact freely. However, for these reformed systems to work, the dispute resolution mechanism will need to be strengthened.

The APTFYP also makes the point that such reforms are resource neutral, that is, they do not require significant additional public resources. Success in reducing the layers of intermediation with or without the use of information technology, can allow producers to obtain better prices, without the final consumer having to pay higher prices. It also spills over into better extension services and even credit and insurance.[46]

There are too many statutes and orders and these have not been rationalized or harmonized. Nine different ministries are concerned with food processing and there are 22 related Acts and Orders. Laws to enforce food standards should be unified and rationalized. Simultaneously, enforcement must be strengthened.[47] Indian standards must be aligned with international standards such as CODEX.[48]

In India, experience has proven that a reform is first undertaken in one aspect, which then introduces a need to reform other constraining laws and regulations and institute other policy changes. These are subsequently taken up by policy-makers. In the context of agriculture, once the APMC and ECA are repealed, and intermediation is explicitly recognized as an important component, other facilitative reforms would also be addressed. However, because agriculture is a state concern it is likely that these changes will be slower than in other sectors.

At the same time newer technologies are facilitating the flow of other aspects related to marketing and information to farmers; moreover they are cost effective. Owing to the open economy, liberalization, greater ease in setting up and operating domestic firms, rapidly growing demand, improvement in infrastructure and government subsidies, many different privately backed activities are occurring across India. Private corporations for instance are providing easy access to relevant information for the farmers through the Internet. The *ITC e-Choupal* (Box 3) and the Digital *Mandi* (Box 4) are two examples. Another important feature is related to transparent auctioning systems — the NDDB's horticulture initiative in Karnataka (Box 5) is an example.

Box 3. ITC *e-Choupal*

Indian Tobacco Company (ITC) is one of India's largest private corporations that initially started with the manufacturing of tobacco products but has since diversified into many different activities ranging from hotels to food products. ITC's International Business Division conceived *e-Choupal*, i.e. village Internet kiosks managed by farmers themselves. The kiosks enable the agricultural community to access ready information in their local language on the weather and market prices; disseminate knowledge on scientific farm practices and risk management; facilitate the sale of farm inputs (now with embedded knowledge); and purchase farm produce (decision-making is now information-based). Real-time information and customized knowledge provided by *e-Choupal* help farmers to make decisions, align their farm output with market demand and secure quality and productivity. As a direct marketing channel, virtually linked to the *mandi* system for price discovery, *e-Choupal* eliminates intermediation and multiple nodes and therefore significantly reduces transaction costs. While the farmers benefit through enhanced farm productivity and higher farm-gate prices, ITC benefits from the lower net cost of procurement (despite offering better prices to the farmer) because costs in the supply chain that do not add value have been eliminated.

Launched in June 2000, *e-Choupal*, has already become the largest initiative among all Internet-based interventions in rural India. Today it reaches out to more than 3.5 million farmers growing a range of crops in over 31 000 villages through 5 200 kiosks across six states (Madhya Pradesh, Karnataka, Andhra Pradesh, Uttar Pradesh, Maharashtra and Rajasthan).

Box 4. Digital *Mandi*

Launched in 2004, in Uttar Pradesh, Digital *Mandi* is an electronic trading platform for agricultural commodities developed by the Indian Institute of Technology, Kanpur, in association with Media Labs Asia. It uses the info-*thela* which is a mobile unit for providing and exchanging electronic information.

This is a user-friendly Web-based portal. The farmer can log in when the info-*thela* is accessible. The registered farmers can access the latest local and global information on weather, scientific farming practices, crop information, expert advice, latest statistics, online trading, as well as market prices at the village level through this bilingual facility. The portal also provides links to relevant Web sites and allows farmers to join discussion fora where they can share their experiences. It offers farmers information on enhancing farm productivity by using better technology, improving farm produce prices and cutting transaction costs. There is a proposal to involve banking and para-banking institutions, to provide networking facilities and include merchants and brokers.

Digital *Mandi's* five-point programme to serve the agricultural community of India:

- To exchange knowledge of farming practices
- Accurate information for optimizing operations
- Pricing information that enables lower input prices
- Higher yields for outputs
- A user-friendly approach

The ultimate goal is to provide market information for farmers living in remote areas so they can sow their crops at the right time and sell harvests at a good price.

Box 5. NDDB initiative — efficient terminal markets for horticultural produce

Horticultural produce has been contributing nearly 29 percent of the GDP in agriculture from just 8.5 percent of the area sown; there are critical issues in maximizing the output from this sector. For instance, postharvest handling of fruit and vegetables accounts for 20 to 30 percent of losses at different stages of storage, grading, packing, transport and marketing.

In 2003, the Karnataka Government invited the National Dairy Development Board (NDDB) to set up a network for fruit and vegetable markets. The NDDB launched a sophisticated auction market, the Safal Fruit and Vegetable Auction Market, for handling fresh fruit, vegetables and flowers near Bangalore at the cost of Rs1.5 billion. Backward linkages were set up with farmers' associations and collection centres for channelling the produce into the market while forward linkages were established through retail stores.

The auction market covers more than 200 farmers' associations with 50 000 growers spread across the four states of Karnataka, Andhra Pradesh, Tamil Nadu and Maharashtra. These associations are informal cooperatives and a member must grow a minimum of one tonne of produce on his farm. The NDDB gives essential support by training the farmers and providing inputs for production. Cleaning, sorting and grading the produce are emphasized before sending it to the collection centres set up at various sites in these four states. Since inadequate infrastructure has led to increase in damage and wastage, cold storage facilities have been provided for the growers. The NDDB has built quality facilities for this purpose and has the first imported ripening chambers for bananas in India. While a market fee of 4 percent is charged, the state government cess has been waived for the produce traded through the auction terminals. The auctions are conducted in a transparent manner and information about prices is disseminated throughout the system.

This system allows farmers to plan their production and provides a common platform for buyers and growers to negotiate better rates. By setting up an efficient terminal market for horticultural produce, the NDDB has stimulated productivity, raised quality standards, reduced losses and ensured consumer access to an increasing supply of fresh produce at reasonable prices.

One of the reasons for the success of this programme has been the strong government commitment to open parallel markets, despite protests from the vested interests of middlemen in the *mandis* (government-regulated markets). Such initiatives are crucial if the National Horticultural Mission is to achieve its target of doubling output in India to 300 million tonnes by 2011.

4.5 Diversification

A broader point that is being made through this reform agenda is encouraging diversification. Although not always articulated clearly, diversification will obviously be encouraged through greater private sector participation, removal of policy distortions (such as unnecessarily high procurement prices for foodgrain),[49] scrapping of legal hurdles, development of risk management institutions and a refocusing of public sector driven research. As diversification automatically implies exposure to additional risk, there must be risk and disaster management, or reduction instruments. This spills over into issues connected with insurance, transaction costs associated with futures' markets and management of exogenous shocks connected to natural disasters.[50] Such diversification can include (but is not limited to) dairy, poultry, fisheries and agroforestry. The latter two are discussed hereunder.

4.5.1 Fisheries

With remarkable growth of 800 percent since the 1950s, the fisheries sector has contributed handsomely to overall agricultural growth numbers. Fish production has thus grown at a faster pace than foodgrain, but the manner of its growth leaves much to be desired. This is because most of the growth has come from the expansion of fish culture in inland waters, but little from oceans and rivers. The result is that the readily available potential for developing the marine catch is not being utilized. The annual output of marine fisheries has therefore been stagnant at less than 3 million tonnes for over five years. In 1960, the production of inland fisheries was just over one-fourth (280 000 tonnes) of the marine output (880 000 tonnes). By 1999/2000, inland output caught up with marine output, with both reporting an almost identical catch of about 2.8 million tonnes each. The inland catch has risen since then. States where fish consumption is low, such as Punjab, Haryana and Uttar Pradesh, and even a water-scarce state like Rajasthan, have also taken to aquaculture in a big way. Rajasthan, which is mostly desert, had over 14 000 tonnes of locally raised fish for consumption.

As pointed out by the parliamentary standing committee on agriculture, the overall business has suffered from neglect. Fish harvesting is still largely done by non-motorized traditional boats. There is a shortage of mechanized boats, modern communication systems and fishing gear as well. The infrastructure for landing and berthing of fishing vessels as well as postharvest preservation, packing, processing and refrigerated storage and transportation is in a derelict state. Ice plants and facilities for drying and dehydration of fish are not available in most places. Much of India's vast exclusive economic zone remains virtually untapped. But coastal areas are being overexploited, causing a steady depletion of fishing and a decline in the fish catch. Year after year, the funds earmarked for fisheries development are not spent. In the current Five Year Plan period, of the total allocation of Rs7.5 billion, only Rs2.6 billion has been spent in the first three years. Clearly, a new policy is needed to encourage private investment in deep-sea fishing vessels and the postharvest infrastructure.

The east coast only accounts for about 30 percent of the total marine catch, although it has a much longer coastline. This situation has been ongoing since the late 1970s. Consequently, fishing families on the east coast are more impoverished relatively. The NSS data also indicate that most fisherfolk are undernourished, being highly deficient in both calorie and protein intake. The west coast, too, seems to be headed in a similar direction, as reflected in the progressive reduction in the average size of fish caught in the past few years. At the same time the zone beyond 50-metre depth remains underexploited owing to policy constraints.

In inland aquaculture problems are also emerging. The mushrooming of shrimp aquaculture farms in the vicinity of the coasts, for instance, caused much sea and groundwater pollution. The Supreme Court had to order their closure in 1996.

Policy intervention is needed, for example, to reduce boat density in the overexploited sea zones and encourage fishing activity beyond 50-metre depth. A new prioritization of technologies for every type of market participant must be the first step, backed by appropriate incentives. But emphasis must continue on efforts to increase scale. This requires a new foreign direct investment (FDI) policy, a new financing policy and a suitable tax regime to encourage processing companies that face formidable hurdles such as complicated exporting procedures, high shipping costs, severe competition among exporters, frequent revisions of quality standards by importers, irregular supply of power and raw materials, hygiene issues and lack of arrangements for speedier transportation of highly perishable produce.

As a further refinement, the states could be grouped into three categories — traditional fishing states that have a relatively higher fisheries productivity (Orissa and West Bengal), non-traditional fisheries states that have performed well (Andhra Pradesh and Punjab) and states with untapped fisheries potential (Bihar, Karnataka, Tamil Nadu and Madhya Pradesh). Different strategies are needed for each of these groups to facilitate sustainable high growth in fisheries.

Above all, it is necessary to clarify whether the issue will be viewed from a livelihood or a major business perspective. The two are almost mutually exclusive and until this friction is reduced, the current multipronged strategy, like all multipronged strategies (because they have multiple objectives) will only result in suboptimal solutions.

4.5.2 Agroforestry

Increasing amounts of land are being degraded while demands for timber, fuelwood and grass for fodder are increasing. The central issue in agroforestry, therefore, is to restore degraded lands. Agrisilviculture, agrihorticulture and silvipasture are some of the terms used for describing the processes and methods through which this can be done. These are essentially ecofriendly practices that permit gainful exploitation of land to meet the fuel, fodder and timber needs of the population without impairing land productivity. Agrisilviculture refers to the system of growing multipurpose trees along with agricultural crops. When trees are grown with grass, shrubs and other vegetation that can serve as animal feed, this becomes a silvipastoral system. When some fruit trees are grown with crops, this is called agrihorticulture. The need for these practices has arisen because of rapidly declining local fodder and fuel resources in rural areas, besides, of course, the growing ecological imbalances due to acceleration in denudation of natural vegetative cover and consequential deterioration in soil health.

The newly launched Greening India project to extend forest cover to 33 percent in all the states by 2012 is the first step in this direction. It is novel in several respects. Unlike previous programmes that sought to achieve afforestation, reforestation or wasteland development, this project has land and people as its theme, and poverty alleviation through the generation of income from land as its goal. The situation-specific land and environment upgrading activities will be carried out with the participation of local communities. The trees to be planted in a particular area are to be selected with their market and value-added potential in view. The target area is 107 million ha of degraded land, including 64 million ha categorized as wasteland.

But there is no guarantee of success. Earlier efforts have failed. The National Wasteland Development Board (NWDB), established in 1985 to carry out the equally imposing task of reclaiming over 2 million ha of wasteland every year through reforestation and afforestation, is a case in point. The most significant issue is access to land. Much of the degraded land belongs to forest departments, *panchayats* or private individuals. They do not willingly allow any outside agency to work on their land for fear of losing control. There may be a case here for invoking what in the United States is called the "power of eminent domain" which permits the state to take over land for the greater public good. Funding must also be arranged beforehand, rather than on a pay-as-you-go manner. The existing national wasteland development programme, conceived for developing 88.5 million ha by the end of the 13th Five Year Plan, has estimated that Rs730 billion will be needed.

Biofuels also need to be pursued. This can be done by identifying the most suitable vegetation. These include *jatropha* and *pongamia*. *Jatropha* has emerged as the preferred species. It has a high oil content of over 30 percent and the plant, being a bush, is easy to manage. It begins bearing seed in only four years. Several states are proceeding with large-scale planting on land not suitable for commercial crops (Box 6).

Box 6. Biofuel — an alternative approach to wasteland management

Biofuel plantations of *jatropha* and *pongamia* have attracted various states in India and there are strong complementary relationships being set up between the governments, private sector companies, NGOs and the *panchayats* in villages. In Tamil Nadu for example, Ahimsa, an NGO, has initiated contract farming of *jatropha* on 34 000 acres in the state. The Southern Railway's Locomotive Works in Perambur uses *jatropha* in fairly large quantities: two passenger trains and three diesel shuttle passenger services are run on 5 percent *jatropha*-blended diesel; 20 department road vehicles on 20 percent blend; and a passenger vehicle on 100 percent biofuel.

The Uttaranchal Bio-fuel Board planted *jatropha* on 10 000 ha in 2005; in Chhattisgarh, 80 million saplings of *jatropha* have been planted; Andhra Pradesh plans to plant *jatropha* on 16 000 ha and 33 million *pongamia* saplings in the state; and Karnataka has planted 20 million *pongamia* saplings. In Andhra Pradesh, the Integrated Tribal Development Agency has introduced about 100 Self-Help Groups in tribal areas to raise *pongamia* nurseries, which provide employment and help to meet the large-scale demand for *pongamia* saplings.

On the processing side, several large private sector companies are in the process of setting up biodiesel plants: D1 Mohan Oils Ltd has been supported by the State Bank of India to initiate contract farming of *jatropha* on 40 000 ha in Tamil Nadu and will be establishing an 8 000 tonnes/year capacity refinery in Chennai to produce biodiesel.

Although these experiments are at the nascent stage, much is expected from them. Collaboration between the government, private sector, civil society and university research centres is expected to develop further in this area.

4.6 Technology development and access

4.6.1 Development

India spends 0.26 percent of the agricultural GDP on research and 90 percent of expenditure on R&D comes from the public sector (Alam 2004). However, R&D has paid little attention to crops grown under dryland conditions. Agricultural research and extension services need rehabilitation, with a focus on subsistence crops and dryland agriculture. *Krishi Vigyan Kendras* (KVKs) need to be further integrated with state and district level extension mechanisms and selected agricultural universities and research laboratories need to focus research on high-yielding hybrid coarse grains, pulses and items for mass consumption.[51]

The Protection of Plant Varieties and Farmers' Rights Act (2001) seeks to protect the rights of farmers, breeders and researchers. Issues such as the compulsory licensing of rights and preventing the import of varieties by incorporating the Genetic Use Restriction Technology (GURT), which makes it obligatory for farmers to depend on companies for seeds, are some of its more discussed features. It provides rights to farmers to use the seeds from their own crops for planting the next crop. Further, there are provisions for benefit sharing with farmers and a penalty for marketing spurious propagation material. The act came about after almost a decade of debate on the relative rights of farmers, breeders and developers. However, the success of illegal varieties of BT cotton illustrates the poor capacity of the government to enforce intellectual property rights. The structure now exists, and an efficient enforcement mechanism needs to be created.

This supplements the issue of upgrading facilities and expertise in ICAR (Indian Council of Agricultural Research) and state agricultural universities with full attention to the needs of the industry, with adequate funding linked to outcomes. However, there is a difference between developing technology and disseminating it. In emphasizing the former, one should not lose sight of the latter. During the last decade, the agricultural extension mechanisms of state governments have been considerably weakened.

4.6.2 Access

The discussions in the previous sections also reveal an important lesson. Improvements in yield necessarily require better technologies. However proper mechanisms for making technology accessible to a wide spectrum of potential users are essential for benefits to be realized. In the case of India, the success of the Green Revolution was based on precisely this aspect. However, as further spread was limited due to the inability of the government to develop and disseminate newer technologies and complementary inputs over a larger geographical area, sets of commodities and classes of farmers, significant yield improvements have not continued.

Moreover, once a particular technology delivery regime is initiated, it takes steady and sustained efforts (especially in democratic and multi-tiered governments) to switch to a new delivery regime. Production scenarios are therefore difficult to predict and are to a large extent dependent upon the government's ability to facilitate appropriate technology, input and service delivery mechanisms.

The decentralized system, with many small and large private entities that are cropping up across India, is a good way of ensuring that appropriate technology is developed and disseminated. In this regard it is essential that minimal regulation is applied to the activities of these merging private entities, while at the same time ensuring fair and quick dispute resolution.

4.7 Taxation

Should agriculture be exempted from direct (income) and indirect (excise) taxes?[52] Regarding the latter, there has been a partial move towards a VAT (value-added tax) since 1 April 2005. The move being partial because only unification of state-level sales tax is being contemplated at the moment and other domestic indirect taxes remain. However, the principles of standardization and harmonization and removal of discretion are violated if there are special VAT rates for agricultural products. This is not to say that agriculture is not taxed. Apart from the *mandi* tax which is a tax imposed on the farmer at the point of sale in the regulated market, other taxes such as development cess (as in Punjab) and taxes on property transactions (stamp duties) are imposed across the country.

5. Current efforts for agricultural and rural development

India's UPA government, at the union or central level, came to power in 2004 and the UPA's National Common Minimum Programme (NCMP) forms the foundation of economic policy. The NCMP is as much a political document, as it is an economic one. Many of the statements are echoed across the political spectrum and are not likely to be opposed. There has been a growing consensus on many of the economic aspects of India — decentralization within the government, the growing role of the private sector and the importance of a social security net are some examples. The importance of water conservation and rainfall harvesting and other environmental issues is also echoed across the political spectrum. The importance of rural infrastructure is also universally agreed. Rural credit is becoming easier to provide via increased private sector involvement, the roles of NGOs and microcredit institutions.

5.1 The current agenda

Several antipoverty and employment generation schemes already exist in rural areas, often through centrally sponsored schemes (CSSs). Through the Planning Commission, an attempt is under way to rationalize these CSSs. For example, under the Department of Agriculture and Cooperation, assorted schemes on agricultural statistics may be merged. So will technology missions on oilseed, pulses and maize with technology missions on cotton and horticulture in the northeast being retained as separate programmes. There will be independent CSSs on on-farm water management, agriculture census and macromanagement. In addition, there are CSSs through the Department of Animal Husbandry and Dairying, Ministry of Environment and Forests, Ministry of Land Resources and Ministry of Rural Development.[53]

The NCMP of the UPA Government states, "All centrally sponsored schemes except in national priority areas like family planning will be transferred to States." Otherwise, there is the concept of devolving CSSs downwards to *panchayati raj* institutions (PRIs) and linking CSS releases to states only when states transfer funds, functionaries and financial resources to PRIs.

A National Food for Work Programme (NFWP) was launched in 2004 in 150 less-advanced districts. Subsequently, 167 were identified under the *Rashtriya Sama Vikas Yojana* (RSVY), with terrorism-affected districts being added to districts identified on the basis of economic criteria. Both the NFWP and RSVY identifications have now been superceded by identification of 200 less-advanced districts, undertaken by the Planning Commission, although the list is not available in the public domain yet.

This identification became necessary because of a Backward Regions Grant Fund (BRGF) and the National Rural Employment Guarantee Act (NREGA). The NREGA, in place since 1 February 2006 in 200 districts, provides that state governments will offer 100 days of unskilled manual work every year to every poor household in rural areas whose adult members volunteer for such work, at minimum wage rates. The 100-day ceiling applies to households and not to individuals. Existing CSSs, including the NFWP, will be subsumed under the NREGA. If states fail to provide jobs, there is an unemployment insurance component. There are also legislative plans for introducing social security for unorganized sector workers, including agricultural workers, and minimum protective legislation for agricultural workers.

Agricultural issues cannot be delinked from broader rural development issues. As was mentioned earlier, centrally sponsored schemes exist for rural roads (*Pradhan Mantri Gram Sadak Yojana*), rural housing (*Indira Awas Yojana*) and rural electrification and drinking water (*Pradhan Mantri Gramodaya Yojana*).[54] Yet data show a lack of physical and social infrastructure in rural areas.[55]

The first two phases of the National Highway Development Programme (NHDP) have been reasonably successful and have improved road connectivity. Phase I involves the Golden Quadrangle and links the four metropolises of Delhi, Mumbai, Chennai and Kolkata. Phase II involves a North–South and East–West corridor. Since January 2005, Phases III and IV have been added to the NHDP, to improve connectivity in places not located on the upgraded networks of Phases I and II. More importantly, the PMGSY (*Pradhan Mantri Gram Sadak Yojana*) is being revamped; it has not performed very well in states like West Bengal, Uttar Pradesh, Bihar, Madhya Pradesh, Jharkhand, Assam and Chhattisgarh.

There is now an attempt to push rural infrastructure through clusters, although most clusters have an autonomous origin and are rarely induced, emerging around local skill or natural resource bases. At a conceptual level, there are three kinds of clusters that one can visualize: relatively modern, small firm-dominated industrial clusters that often tend to be located in relatively urban areas; artisan and rural industry-based clusters; and clusters that are based on the agricultural economy. The latter two, particularly the last, tend to be natural resource based. Most policy interventions have focused on the first of the three, rather than the last two. Earlier attempts at cluster formation have not always been successful, as they often tended to be ad hoc and piecemeal. The present PURA (Provision of Urban Amenities in Rural Areas) scheme is more integrated, at least in intention, and builds on different kinds of connectivity: physical connectivity through roads and power, electronic connectivity through village Internet kiosks, knowledge connectivity through education and flowing on from them, economic or market connectivity through access to markets. PURA manifests itself through the *Bharat Nirman* idea, focusing on rural infrastructure. It has six components of irrigation, roads, water supply, housing, rural electrification and rural telecommunications connectivity, with target dates for completion in 2009. The government is also establishing a food processing SEZ (special economic zone) in Kakkancherry in Kerala.

The government has forwarded an Integrated Food Processing Act to parliament to pass and the ECA has been amended repeatedly. Around 200 orders issued by the state governments under the ECA are likely to expire in 2006, unless the states make cases for their continuation and the GOI approves/agrees to the proposals. This is a very positive development. Contract farming, as it is equated with corporate farming, is extremely controversial.

The Food Safety and Standards Bill (2005) has been also placed before parliament; it consolidates eight laws governing the food sector and establishes the Food Safety and Standards Authority (FSSA) to regulate the sector. The FSSA will be aided by several scientific panels and a central advisory committee to lay down standards for food safety. These standards will include specifications for ingredients, contaminants, pesticide residue, biological hazards and labels.

As Table 16 illustrates, several states have amended their APMC Acts, to allow direct marketing, contract farming and establishment of private markets in the private or cooperative sectors.

There seems to be a conscious shift from an agricultural to a rural development policy, with a focus on rural infrastructure like roads, electricity and water (drinking and irrigation). For agriculture proper, the mid-term appraisal of the Tenth Plan flags certain issues (GOI 2005b):

1. Rejuvenation of support systems in extension, credit and delivery systems for inputs like seeds, fertilizers and veterinary services.

2. Investments in irrigation/water management.

3. Appropriate pricing of water.

4. Mega-irrigation projects.

5. Watershed development.

6. Agricultural research.

7. PDS (public distribution system) pricing.

Table 16. Progress in amending APMC Acts (as of January 2006)

State/UT	Whether direct marketing allowed	Whether contract farming allowed	Whether private markets in private/cooperative sectors allowed	Whether APMC Act amended
Andaman & Nicobar	Yes	Yes	Yes	APMC Act, drafting of new law not ongoing
Andhra Pradesh	Yes	Yes	Yes	Through ordinance
Arunachal	No	No	–	No
Assam	No	No	–	No
Bihar	No	No	–	No
Dadra & Nagar Haveli	Yes	Yes	Yes	No APMC Act
Daman & Diu	Yes	Yes	Yes	No APMC Act
Delhi	Yes	No	No	Partial
Goa	Yes	Yes	–	No
Gujarat	No	Yes	No	Drafting stages
Haryana	Yes	No	No	Drafting stage
Himachal Pradesh	Yes	Yes	Yes	Yes
Jammu and Kashmir	No	No	–	No
Jharkhand	No	No	–	No
Karnataka	Yes	Yes	No	Drafting stage
Kerala	Yes	Yes	Yes	No APMC Act
Lakshadweep	Yes	Yes	Yes	No APMC Act
Madhya Pradesh	Yes	Yes	Yes	Yes
Maharashtra	No	No	Yes	Drafting stage
Manipur	Yes	Yes	Yes	No APMC Act
Meghalaya	Yes	Yes	–	No
Mizoram	Yes	Yes	–	No
Nagaland	Yes	Yes	Yes	Yes
Orissa	No	No	–	No
Punjab	Yes	Yes	Yes	Yes
Rajasthan	Yes	Yes	No	Partial
Sikkim	Yes	Yes	Yes	Yes
Tamil Nadu	Yes	Yes	Yes	No prohibition in APMC Act
Tripura	Yes	Yes	–	No
Uttar Pradesh	No	No	–	No
Uttaranchal	No	No	–	No
West Bengal	No	No	–	No

Source: GOI (2006).

8.   Fertilizer pricing.

9.   National Horticulture Mission.

10.   Agricultural marketing and contract farming.

11.   Amendment of the ECA.

12.   An integrated food-processing law.

13.   Promotion of participatory natural resource management.

14.   Promotion of biodiesel.

The broad directions are quite clear — a host of measures related to water conservation, management, availability and accessibility are being addressed. Some support is related to pricing of output, charges for inputs, some legal reform as well as people's participation in environment and resource management. This, combined with the devolution of greater powers to rural local bodies and the powers accorded to the common man through the Right to Information Act, can help ensure that adequate accountability is imposed on the bureaucracy.

5.2 Constraints

The critical constraining aspects are three-fold and will require deft political maneuvering to push through. First, many of these policy measures will require large sums to be generated through other (non-agricultural) revenue means. It is not clear how this will be possible. Second, poor control and monitoring abilities of many state governments limit their ability to implement such large-scale programmes effectively. These abilities will take some time to build up. An example is the collapse of the extension programmes and delivery systems. Without significant administrative reforms within the government, neither is their privatization feasible in the next few years, nor is their rejuvenation likely across many if not most states of the country. Third, if reforms have not matched up to actual expectations, there is a reason. Constitutionally, most agriculture-related areas are state government subjects and it is difficult for the centre to provide incentives for such reforms. The central government will need to put in a significant amount of effort if it wants a nationally coordinated approach.

5.3 The private sector

Despite constraints, the policy regime is increasingly moving towards the greater role of private entities; economic policies in general have been moving towards the larger role of the private sector, private–public partnerships, the increasing role of communities, self-help groups and non-profit organizations for delivering critical inputs and services. Following constitutional amendments in the early 1990s, *Panchayats* have been given greater powers. State-level finance commissions have been established to oversee the devolution of funds to these bodies. It is now generally agreed that the Agricultural Produce Marketing Act that limited transactions between buyers and sellers except through *mandis* will be changed to allow for contract farming. Over the next few years, it is also expected that the laws and rules limiting internal trade in agricultural commodities will be changed to enable greater choice for the farmer.

The government is finally tackling the building of rural roads, the objective being to connect all of the roughly 600 000 villages to each other and with cities via all-weather surface roads.

At the same time developments on the IT front have enabled the setting up of Internet kiosks on a mass scale throughout rural India. Basic primary education for everyone has become a thrust area and it is only a matter of a few years when literacy will be universal, at least among young adults. India already boasts some of the cheapest cellular phone tariffs, and services for Internet and cellular communication are emerging. Private entities are marrying the advantages of Internet infrastructure and distributional networks to provide purchase, retail, information and knowledge delivery under one umbrella.

Meanwhile private sector banks are increasingly becoming aggressive lenders in the rural domain as well. Insurance firms are targeting agricultural markets more and more. Private seed companies have sprung up across the country and with some changes in the IPR regime are expected to become significant players. Moreover, after many years, the private sector has emerged as an investor in building and running quality agricultural warehousing facilities across India.

But all of the above components are recent changes; they hold great promise but currently are at a nascent stage of development. More importantly carry-overs from the past continue, and currently it is difficult to see reforms in the following areas:

- Electricity for farmers is quite cheap or free, a result of competition between various political parties;

- Investments in irrigation facilities, tanks and ponds are not rising to the levels required. State government funding is constrained;

- Water tables are falling rapidly throughout western and northwestern India, primarily due to extraction of water for agriculture;

- Central and state governments are increasingly unable to find the resources to maintain the existing infrastructure (canals for example) or to provide traditional services (such as extension services);

- User charges continue to be absent or insignificant so even basic running costs need to be subsidized for most services through the public exchequer;

- Large sections of the electorate believe that whatever the government provides should be subsidized.

In other words, the private sector will be constrained as well owing to externalities, expectations due to past policies and lack of public funds for critical public infrastructure.

6. International trade: multilateral, bilateral trade and potential impact

6.1 Multilateral issues

Although agricultural reform issues are primarily an internal or domestic matter, it is impossible to escape from the WTO (World Trade Organization). In this section, we therefore turn to the international angle.

There was no attempt to liberalize agriculture and integrate it into the General Agreement on Tariffs and Trade (GATT) framework before the Uruguay Round (1986–1994).[56] Hence, agricultural liberalization proposed in the Uruguay Round and set out in the Agreement on Agriculture (AOA) is at best a beginning and is no more than imperfect and incomplete liberalization. There are three pillars to the liberalization proposed in the AOA.[57] There are disciplines placed on domestic support, through computation of an aggregate measurement of support (AMS). Once this has been done, there are reduction commitments on the base period for AMS, if the computed AMS is above the threshold.[58] This only leads to a reduction in the base period for AMS, without setting a cap on it. Some policies (Green Box, Blue Box) are also exempted from AMS calculations. Quantitative restrictions (QRs) on imports have to be converted into tariffs and after this tariffication, tariffs have to be reduced.[59] Yet again, there is no cap on tariffs (although there are bindings) and reductions apply to the base period tariff. Nor are tariff rate quotas (TRQs) precluded.[60] For export subsidies on agricultural products, there is a reduction commitment on base period export subsidies, with no cap.[61]

There is sufficient evidence to demonstrate that the promised agricultural liberalization, which accounted for the bulk of the market access liberalization promised in the Uruguay Round, has not happened.[62] Rather perversely, using exemptions, export subsidies on agricultural products in developed countries are higher after the Uruguay Round began to be implemented. The QRs have been converted into artificially high tariff equivalents, referred to as "dirty tariffication". As with industrial products, there are specific duties, high peak tariffs and tariff escalation. The TRQs lead to low tariffs below the threshold, but extremely high tariffs above the threshold. Exemptions have been freely used to violate the spirit of AMS liberalization. The special safeguards clause[63] has been used to hinder market access, not to speak of the SPS agreement.

This is known and agriculture is part of the built-in or mandated agenda of the Uruguay Round. That is, even if there were to be no DDA (Doha Development Agenda), agriculture would have been negotiated. Agricultural liberalization in all its three pillars forms part of the DDA, now formalized in the framework agreement of 31 July 2004. The argument for disciplining distortions in developed countries is fairly simple,[64] although perceptions differ on whether a country is a net exporter or importer of agricultural products. What complicates matters further is the required *quid pro quo* on the part of developing countries and interpretation of the special and differential (S&D) treatment clause.

Shorn of public posturing, the Indian approach to agricultural negotiations exhibits some schizophrenia, with the fear of self-reliance in foodgrain production being destroyed; this is not very easy to dismiss.[65] If one takes the issues item by item, for domestic support, Indian AMS levels are around 7 percent[66], well below the permitted threshold of 10 percent. There is enough slack for increasing domestic support. It is a separate matter that central and state governments are in no fiscal position to increase such support.[67] India has no specific export subsidies on agriculture [68], so the disciplines on export subsidies do not bite either. That leaves tariffs on agriculture, QRs on imports having been phased out.[69] Unlike domestic support and export subsidies, negotiating positions here are probably more than public posturing, compounded by the fact that domestic agricultural reform has not happened[70] and agriculture was in trouble in the second half of the 1990s. In addition, in the absence of reforms that facilitate diversification, agriculture has been equated with foodgrain production and foodgrain policy. There are also differences in perceptions among the Commerce Ministry, Agriculture Ministry and Food and Civil Supplies Ministry.[71]

The argument for liberalizing agriculture in developed countries is a reasonably simple one, regardless of whether it materializes or not. The point about restricting an import surge in certain segments is also reasonably easy to understand, pending long-run adjustments. Edible oils, milk and milk products, fruits and vegetables, rubber, cotton and silk, tea and coffee and alcoholic beverages figure in the list of sensitive products identified and tracked by the Commerce Ministry. Of these, edible oils and milk and milk products are the most important. Having said this, does India need the present high levels of bindings in agriculture? Almost certainly not. For the most part, tariffs of the order of 20 to 25 percent should be suitable, not to speak of exemptions through special products and temporary deviations through special safeguard mechanisms.[72]

6.2 South Asian Free Trade Area (SAFTA) and agriculture

India has its own plethora of regional trade agreements (RTAs). FTAs (free trade agreements) are covered by Article XXIV of GATT, although India's RTAs are notified under a 1979 enabling clause that requires less trade to be liberalized than through Article XXIV. For a long time, India's RTAs were limited to the Bangkok Agreement and SAARC. But India has several more now. This plethora of FTAs and CEPAs (Comprehensive Economic Partnership Agreements) originated with the NDA government. But it continues under the UPA Government, with a perceptible switch from FTAs to CEPAs.

There are signed FTAs or PTAs (Preferential Trade Agreements) with Sri Lanka, Thailand, Bhutan, MERCOSUR (*Mercado Común del Sur* or Southern Common Market), Afghanistan, SAFTA and the Bay of Bengal Initiative (formerly BIMSTEC), apart from the Bangkok Agreement, and those with Bangladesh, ASEAN and Southern African Customs Union are under negotiation. China and Australia have not been settled yet. There is a CEPA with Singapore, Sri Lanka and Mauritius are in advanced stages, and Japan, Pakistan, Malaysia, Indonesia, Israel, Chile, Republic of Korea and Australia are possible. To the extent that these initiatives represent liberalization, they are welcome. However, multilateral liberalization is preferable to discretionary regional liberalization, even if negotiating the latter is easier.

There are three layers to India's RTAs. First, there is the multilateral, so to speak, SAPTA or SAFTA. Second, there is the subregional BIMSTEC and BBIN (Bangladesh, Bhutan, India, Nepal) quadrilateral growth initiative. Third, we have the purely bilateral agreements with Bhutan, Nepal, Sri Lanka and Bangladesh.

Intra South Asian Association for Regional Cooperation (SAARC) trade as a percentage of total SAARC trade is estimated at around 4 percent. There is an obvious problem in citing such figures, as a significant part of intra SAARC trade is informal trade or is routed through third countries.[73] It is sometimes argued that such trade, including third country trade, is almost as large as formal trade. Therefore, formal trade figures represent half of what trade figures actually are. Over time, all SAARC members have liberalized their economies and become more open and the trade/GDP ratios have consequently increased. However, for present purposes, one needs to note that intra SAARC trade as a percentage of total trade turnover is much higher for countries like Bangladesh, Bhutan, Maldives and Nepal, than for a country like India.[74]

SAARC's share in India's trade is low. In 2004 and 2005, exports to the SAARC region were US$4.300 billion, representing 5.4 percent of total exports. Imports from the SAARC region were US$0.905 billion, representing 0.85 percent of total imports.[75] If one goes back to 1990 and 1991, exports to the SAARC region as a percentage of total exports were 2.9 percent and imports from the SAARC region as a percentage of total imports were 0.55 percent. The SAARC shares have increased, but not spectacularly.

There are innumerable studies on the potential for greater inter SAARC trade. Most studies focus on gains from SAFTA, as opposed to bilateral trade potentials, and there are issues connected with modeling, estimating trade diversion *vis à vis* trade creation, computing static gains apropos dynamic gains and so forth. What do the studies show? (Strategic Foresight Group, 2005):

- First, complete elimination of tariffs will increase intraregional trade by 1.6 times the existing levels. The volume of intra SAARC trade will increase from the present figure of US$5 billion to around 14 billion in 2015. As overall trade also increases, this does not necessarily represent an increase in the ratio of inter SAARC trade to total trade by SAARC members.

- Second, dynamic gains are 25 percent more than static gains.

- Third, smaller member countries tend to gain relatively more than larger ones. The latter is stated as an empirical argument, but it is a theoretical one as well, and is borne out by the experiences of other FTAs elsewhere in the world.

How much of a constraint are tariffs to increasing trade? In the GATT/WTO system, there are tariff bindings and tariff reduction commitments on bound rates. India has bound 73.8 percent for tariff lines, 100 percent for agricultural products and 69.8 percent for non-agricultural products (WTO 2005). The simple average of tariff bindings is 49.8 percent, 114.5 percent for agricultural products and 34.3 percent for non-agricultural products.

The Indian tariff structure can indeed be faulted. First, notwithstanding the tendency towards a monotonic decline, there are differences across sectors, the difference between agricultural and manufactured products being an obvious case. In principle, any such differentiation distorts resource allocation and there is no reason why agricultural tariff rates should be higher than non-agricultural ones. While this is a valid point to make, every country in the world is equally culpable. And the plethora of FTAs within the South Asia region and outside it, invariably exclude agriculture from liberalization commitments. Second, other than the agriculture/manufactured dichotomy, there is arbitrary variation across sectors, compounded by occasional use of specific duties. Such discretion distorts effective rates of protection across sectors, other than encouraging lobbying. Conceptually, every economist ought to argue that there should be a single uniform tariff, invariant across sectors. But, in practice, every country implements tariff escalation, with low tariffs for raw materials, higher tariffs for intermediates and highest tariffs for finished products. Because it is not immediately apparent what a finished product is, discretion sets in. Tariff escalation in India may deter value-added exports from other countries in the South Asia region, just as tariff escalation in the United States deters value-added exports from India.

There is a unilateral Indian reform attempt at tariff reduction that is independent of multilateral negotiations and commitments. Indeed, GATT's role in reducing global tariffs may have been important in the first few rounds of multilateral trade negotiations (MTNs). But in the post-Uruguay Round (1986–1994) scenario, it will be difficult to establish GATT's role in reducing tariffs, except in the case of countries that acceded to WTO as new members. Most tariff reductions have been unilateral, or driven by structural adjustment packages and this partly explains the bridge between bound rates and applied ones. Accordingly, there is a unilateral Indian tariff reform agenda. This is articulated in different places, but the most commonly cited one is the Vijay Kelkar Task Force on Indirect Taxes (GOI 2002c). For manufactured products, this has the following timeline for 2006 to 2007: 5 percent for basic raw materials like coal, ores, concentrates and xylenes, 8 percent for intermediate goods used for future manufacture, 10 percent for finished goods that are not consumer durables and 20 percent for consumer durables. But agriculture in such unilateral reform blueprints continues to be treated differently.

Next consider informal trade. Other than the existence of porous borders that are impossible to police, why does informal trade take place? Other than trade and domestic policy distortions, the reason is higher transaction costs (procedural costs) in formal trade, as opposed to informal trade. A desire to avoid not just import duties, but also domestic indirect taxes, may also be a contributory factor. The avoidance of a domestic indirect taxes objective will remain. But despite what has been hitherto said for the medium term, if there is a trade liberalization agenda, spliced with a trade facilitation agenda, one can probably expect informal trade to switch to formal channels. Although tariff elimination may not be sufficient, there seems to be a case for reducing agricultural tariffs unilaterally and regionally, regardless of what happens to multilateral negotiations.

6.3 India's trade in agricultural commodities and potential impact

Between 10 and 13 percent of the Indian export basket of goods (excluding services) comes from the agriculture sector. In absolute terms, such exports are around US$7 billion a year. Tea, coffee, rice, wheat, sugar and molasses, tobacco, spices, cashew nuts, oilmeal, fresh fruit and vegetables, meat and meat preparations and marine products[76] figure prominently in this export basket.[77] Table 17 gives details of India's exports of agricultural and allied products in 2003 and 2004. India's interests in agricultural exports are often described as peripheral. To some extent this is true, especially if contrasted with manufacturing or services. However, India's export shares in global exports are large for items like tea, coffee, tobacco, spices, sugar, rice and fish and preparations. And, contingent on domestic reforms, there is enormous potential in meat and preparations, fruit and vegetables and processed foods. Imports of agricultural products account for between 4.5 and 5.5 percent of India's imports of goods (excluding services) and pulses, cashew nuts, other fruits and nuts and edible oils account for the bulk of such imports. The absolute import figure is between US$2 and 3 billion a year.

46

Table 17. India's exports of agricultural products, 2003–2004
(US$ million)

Commodity	Exports	Share (%) in world exports, 2002
Fish and preparations	1 329	2.6
Rice	1 025	18.1
Oil cakes	729	0.9
Fruit, vegetables & pulses	513	1.1
Meat and preparations	373	0.6
Cashew nuts	370	
Tea and mate	356	12.6
Spices	336	8.5
Miscellaneous processed foods	305	
Sugar & molasses	269	2.4
Tobacco	238	2.1
Coffee	236	2.3
Raw cotton	205	
Total	7 888	

Source: GOI (2004–2005).

The GTAP model predicts an interesting scenario for 2020. This is shown in Table 18.

Table 18. Net export share of world export (%)

	2001	2020
Rice	10.0	10.8
Wheat	2.6	1.0
Coarse grain	0.2	0.2
Oilseed	-3.3	-12.8
Sugar	2.7	0.9
Plant-based fibre	-6.6	-18.1
Other crops	1.1	-2.1
Cattle and meat	1.0	1.7
Other agricultural products	-0.9	-8.4
Milk	0.2	-0.3
Fish	0.2	0.2
Other food	1.1	1.3
Forestry	-4.9	-14.6

Source: GTAP estimations.

Appendix 3 details on a commodity-by-commodity basis the export and import trends in the five-year period from 1997 to 2001 for the commodities for which comparable data exists. The appendix also contains a country-by-country discussion on commodity-wise exports and imports of the major items. Key points are summarized here:

- As India's share in the world market is not likely to change much, India does not appear, prima facie, to pose much of a threat as a competitor to future exporters such as China, Thailand and Viet Nam;

- Overall, India's share of the world wheat pie is insignificant and expected to remain so in net terms;

- India is likely to become an important importer of edible oil and oilseed and countries such as Philippines, Malaysia and Indonesia are likely to benefit;

- India is not likely to be among the major sugar exporters by 2020, an easier export market for Thailand is therefore likely;

- The net result is that by 2020, India is expected to account for an estimated 18 percent of world imports of plant-based fibre. The only large cotton exporter in the geographical vicinity is Australia and Pakistan. Most other countries in the vicinity are themselves significant importers;

- India is unlikely to become a significant world supplier or buyer of meats;

- Although it will be a major consumer and producer of dairy products, India is expected to be an insignificant supplier or buyer of milk products;

- India is likely to remain a marginal exporter of fish products;

- Major opportunities exist for those countries that export forestry products such as wood. Currently only Australia is a significant exporter of these products in the vicinity.

7. Summary and conclusion

The objectives of the study are mainly to understand the dynamics of the agriculture sector within India, how it is likely to emerge in coming years and how other countries, in the vicinity or otherwise can gain from greater interaction with India.

Doubtless there will be high levels of increase in demand for agricultural products. These will be on account of both increases in population and high economic growth. Together they will generate rapid increases in the demand for food products, although of course to varying degrees for different items. At the same time, India is a large producer of most of the commodities that it consumes. Agricultural productivity appears to be stagnating, but this is observable from only a few data points and there is much that could happen to put productivity back on a high growth path.

The success of the Green Revolution provides us with one important insight that the government — even for a country as diverse and heterogeneous as India — can play an important role in putting the agriculture sector on a high growth path. It has done so in the past, with the promotion of technology, massive supply of credit and extension services, timely announcement of a minimum support price and government purchasing, subsidized fertilizer and pesticides as well as increased investments in small irrigation projects. The critical success factor was not just the availability of HYV seeds or subsidized inputs, but the fact that this was done in a coordinated manner.

All this coordination however could not help to disseminate the benefits of the new technologies across all parts of the country, and the Green Revolution has yet to spread to many areas. The reason is that the coordinated approach in a large agroclimatically diverse agricultural economy, governed by a multi-tiered democracy, and having a predominantly free economy, is difficult to sustain. In India it worked best when there was a critical lack of food and foreign exchange, which resulted in heavy dependence on external largesse. Once the crisis was over, coordinated efforts for expanding the reach of services and benefits to newer areas could not be continued.

One of India's significant successes in the past few decades has been the massive reduction in poverty levels at a time when the population was expanding rapidly at about 2 percent *per annum*. Was the Green Revolution responsible for this? The facts are: The greatest increases in productivity occurred in the 1970s and 1980s. The greatest reduction in poverty occurred in the 1980s and 1990s. The 1980s and 1990s were also a period of high economic growth and economic liberalization. The Green Revolution facilitated the availability of agricultural commodities; it also increased incomes for many cultivators who could access the technologies. When the high income growth phase occurred (whether as a result of the Green Revolution, or due to liberalization, or both) poverty levels fell significantly, as even those who did not benefit from the HYV technologies as producers, benefited as consumers. In other words, purely greater production may not have generated the required impact on poverty; it had to be supplemented with greater income growth.

At the same time, the coordinated and government-subsidized "mission-mode" approach may also have affected the emergence of private sector initiatives — whether in the for-profit or non-profit/community cooperation domains. Consequently private sector initiative was scarce. Therefore government efforts could not expand the scope and scale of the Green Revolution beyond a certain set of areas; the private sector also did not take up the initiative.

Although it is too soon to tell, this appears to be changing. With greater openness of the economy, and greater liberalization many different privately backed activities are occurring across India. Most of these have a small spread currently and are widely scattered. However, they have the potential to rapidly generate dynamic changes, as many are bottom-up responses to requirements and appear to be scaleable. Moreover, the government still continues to and will continue to play an important role. Partly as a beneficiary, where its scientific agencies are continuing and accelerating their efforts in the development of newer technologies. It continues to subsidize many, if not most, agricultural inputs, and regulates and controls many activities.

Perhaps inadvertently, the government has also introduced distorted incentives owing to its thrust on rapidly expanding output. Excess extraction of groundwater partly due to subsidized or free electricity or unsuitable cultivation patterns such as sugar cane cultivation in water-scarce areas are some examples. Inaction, slow response or disagreement in the political ranks have also affected the lack of or slowness of reforms in the agriculture sector. Many laws that need to be changed such as the APMC Acts and the Essential Commodities Act continue to remain in force. Contract farming has not been legalized in several states. Lastly, some of the services provided by the government in the past are no longer as effective owing to a multiplicity of factors; poor scale, scope and quality of extension services is one example.

India is unlikely to be in a position to tap global potential should it be opened up. On the flip side, there is no particular reason for India to fear a deluge of agricultural imports. Barring isolated sectors, India is cost competitive in agricultural products. The bindings are also sufficiently high. Therefore, other than edible oils (especially soybean), and odd items like milk powder, chicken legs or sugar, there is no reason to fear large-scale imports. Of course, non-viability of edible oil production has a strong geographical dimension, with significant transition pains.

Reform needs can be summarized as:

- Create infrastructure: for irrigation, for marketing and distribution and for transportation and storage;

- Change laws that will enable the free flow of goods and services;

- Allow for greater flexibility in production and trade;

- Ensure availability of credit by not only increasing penetration by public sector banks, but also moving from cost to accessibility;

- Stop overuse of water and the unsustainable use of land.

What can other countries learn from India's experience? The critical differentiating factor between India and many other countries, in the view of the authors, is not that India has greater population or land mass but that agroclimatically, culturally and economically India is a highly diverse and heterogeneous country. Moreover it has a decentralized system of governance. Hence government coordinated efforts are difficult to manage and sustain. They can lead to great successes for a while but their sustainability is debatable. The alternative option is a system where the government leaves the role of coordination to the price system and limits itself to ensuring price stability and rural development efforts. This is the system that India appears to be moving towards. Whether it works or not, only time will tell.

The GTAP model is a general equilibrium model that has in-built parameter estimates from the world, assumptions drawn from experiences in other countries as well as key growth and elasticity estimates from India. Using past experience and these estimates it predicts that if business as usual occurs, if India sustains the acceleration in economic growth rate (that is widely expected) and population growth follows the trends of the past, the expected productivity increases will largely be consumed domestically, leaving little for exports in most commodity segments. However, this does not mean that India will not be a significant agricultural trader in the future. On the contrary. For many commodities it would continue to be a significant exporter, and will emerge as a significant importer in others. The Indian market would require significant imports of oilseed, plant-based fibre, other agricultural products, forestry products and to a lesser extent milk and its products. Perhaps as importantly, and this the GTAP model cannot predict, India is likely to be engaged in switch trade with many countries in other segments such as fresh fruit and vegetables.

Economic growth and development in India will generate many opportunities within India and for other countries. Export opportunities and the possibility of technology imports are two examples. Although private R&D in the agriculture sector is at a nascent stage, it appears to be a growing sector. The diversity of India's agroclimatic zones and its large highly educated pool of human resources provide many opportunities for developing an array of technologies specific to different conditions and soil types.

Tables

Table A1.1. Growth rates, 1868–1946 (annual trend growth rates in percent)

	Agriculture	NDP	Population	Per capita NDP
1868–98	1.01	0.99	0.40	0.59
1882–98	1.08	1.29	0.51	0.78
1900–46	0.31	0.86	0.87	-0.01

Source: Roy (2000).

Table A1.2. Trend growth rates of crop output, acreage and yield for British India 1891–1946 (% *per annum*)

	Growth in output	Growth in acreage	Growth in yield per acre	Growth and stagnation in yield per acre in selected periods		
				1891–1916	1916–21	1921–46
All crops	0.37	0.40	0.01	0.47	-0.36	-0.02
Foodgrain	0.11	0.31	-0.18	0.29	-0.63	-0.40
Non-foodgrain	1.31	0.42	0.67	0.81	0.34	1.16

Source: Roy (2000).

Table A1.3. Indicators of rural unemployment (% of labour force)

Year	UPS	UPSS	CWS	CDS
1977–78	3.26	1.54	3.74	7.70
1983	1.91	1.13	3.88	7.94
1987–88	3.07	1.98	4.19	5.25
1993–94	1.80	1.20	3.00	5.63
1999-2000	1.96	1.43	3.19	7.21

Source: Employment and Unemployment Situation in India (2001); National Sample Survey Organization, Report No. 458, Ministry of Statistics and Programme Implementation, Government of India, New Delhi.

Table A1.4. Green Revolution trends in yields (kg/ha)

	1961	1971	1981	1991
Cereals	9 473	11 361	13 988	19 263
Coarse grain	5 129	5 679	7 382	7 755
Primary fibre crops	2 638	2 809	3 108	4 013
Jute & jute-like	10 091	10 262	12 206	16 104
Maize	9 567	8 999	11 622	13 763
Primary oilcrops	1 319	1 612	1 752	2 116
Pulses	5 401	5 141	4 874	5 784
Rice, paddy	15 419	17 110	19 623	26 271
Wheat	8 507	13 066	16 299	22 814
Sugar cane	455 868	483 243	578 444	653 949
Vegetables & melons	66 449	75 338	85 001	102 728
Fruit excl. melons, total	86 320	88 990	92 596	100 551

Source: FAO Statistics, various years.

Table A1.5. Crops and major states that grow them

Crop	States
Rice	Andhra Pradesh, Assam, Bihar, Chhattisgarh, Jammu & Kashmir, Madhya Pradesh, Orissa, Punjab, Tamil Nadu, Uttar Pradesh, West Bengal
Wheat	Bihar, Gujarat, Haryana, Himachal Pradesh, Jammu & Kashmir, Madhya Pradesh, Punjab, Rajasthan, Uttar Pradesh
Bajra[†]	Gujarat, Haryana, Maharashtra, Rajasthan, Uttar Pradesh
Barley	Bihar, Haryana, Himachal Pradesh, Punjab, Rajasthan, Uttar Pradesh
Maize	Andhra Pradesh, Bihar, Gujarat, Himachal Pradesh, Jammu & Kashmir, Karnataka, Madhya Pradesh, Rajasthan, Uttar Pradesh
Ragi[†]	Andhra Pradesh, Bihar, Karnataka, Maharashtra, Orissa, Tamil Nadu
Small millets	Himachal Pradesh, Jammu & Kashmir, Karnataka, Madhya Pradesh, Tamil Nadu
Jowar[†]	Andhra Pradesh, Karnataka, Madhya Pradesh, Maharashtra, Tamil Nadu
Gram	Haryana, Madhya Pradesh, Maharashtra, Rajasthan, Uttar Pradesh
Tur[†]	Andhra Pradesh, Gujarat, Madhya Pradesh, Karnataka, Maharashtra, Orissa, Tamil Nadu, Uttar Pradesh
Groundnut	Andhra Pradesh, Gujarat, Karnataka, Maharashtra, Tamil Nadu
Linseed	Bihar, Madhya Pradesh, Maharashtra, Uttar Pradesh
Rape and mustard	Assam, Gujarat, Haryana, Jammu and Kashmir, Madhya Pradesh, Rajasthan, Uttar Pradesh, West Bengal
Safflower	Karnataka, Maharashtra
Sesame	Andhra Pradesh, Gujarat, Karnataka, Maharashtra, Rajasthan, Tamil Nadu, Uttar Pradesh, West Bengal
Sunflower	Andhra Pradesh, Karnataka, Maharashtra, Punjab
Sugar cane	Andhra Pradesh, Haryana, Karnataka, Maharashtra, Punjab, Tamil Nadu, Uttar Pradesh
Tobacco	Andhra Pradesh, Bihar, Gujarat, Karnataka, Tamil Nadu
Cotton	Andhra Pradesh, Gujarat, Haryana, Karnataka, Maharashtra, Punjab, Tamil Nadu
Jute	Assam, Bihar, West Bengal
Tea	Assam, Kerala, Tamil Nadu, West Bengal
Cardamom	Karnataka, Kerala, Tamil Nadu
Pepper	Kerala
Rubber	Kerala, Tamil Nadu
Arecanut	Assam, Karnataka, Kerala
Coconut	Andhra Pradesh, Karnataka, Kerala, Tamil Nadu
Onions	Andhra Pradesh, Assam, Bihar, Gujarat, Karnataka, Maharashtra, Orissa, Tamil Nadu
Potatoes	Assam, Bihar, Himachal Pradesh, Punjab, Uttar Pradesh, West Bengal
Soybean	Andhra Pradesh, Karnataka, Madhya Pradesh, Maharashtra, Rajasthan

[†] *Bajra* – millet; *ragi* – finger millet; – *jowar* – *Sorghum vulgare*; *tur* – pigeon peas or red gram.

Source: www.agricoop.nic.in

Table A1.6. Production of major crops (million units)

	Unit	1960–61	1970–71	1980–81	1990–91	2000–01	2003–04*
Foodgrain	Tonnes	82.0	108.4	129.6	176.4	196.8	212.0
Cereals	Tonnes	69.3	96.6	119.0	162.1	185.7	196.8
Pulses	Tonnes	12.7	11.8	10.6	14.3	11.0	15.2
Rice	Tonnes	34.6	42.2	53.6	74.3	85.0	87.0
Wheat	Tonnes	11.0	23.8	36.3	55.1	69.7	72.1
Jowar	Tonnes	9.8	8.1	10.4	11.7	7.5	7.3
Maize	Tonnes	4.1	7.5	7.0	9.0	12.0	14.7
Bajra	Tonnes	3.3	8.0	5.3	6.9	6.8	11.8
Gram	Tonnes	6.3	5.2	4.3	5.4	3.9	5.8
Tur	Tonnes	2.1	1.9	2.0	2.4	2.2	2.4
Oilseed**	Tonnes	7.0	9.6	9.4	18.6	18.4	25.1
Groundnut	Tonnes	4.8	6.1	5.0	7.5	6.4	8.3
Rapeseed and mustard	Tonnes	1.4	2.0	2.3	5.2	4.2	5.8
Sugar cane	Tonnes	110.0	126.4	154.2	241.0	296.0	236.2
Cotton	Bales@	5.6	4.8	7.0	9.8	9.5	13.8
Jute and mesta	Bales+	5.3	6.2	8.2	9.2	10.5	11.2
Jute	Bales+	4.1	4.9	6.5	7.9	9.3	10.3
Mesta[†]	Bales+	1.1	1.3	1.7	1.3	1.2	0.9
Plantation crops							
Tea	Tonnes	0.3	0.4	0.6	0.7	0.8	0.8
Coffee	Tonnes	Neg.	0.1	0.1	0.2	0.3	0.3
Rubber	Tonnes	Neg.	0.1	0.2	0.3	0.6	0.7
Potato	Tonnes	2.7	4.8	9.7	15.2	22.5	NA

[†] Vegetable-based fibre plants more commonly known as roselle.

NA: Not available. * Provisional ** Include groundnut, rapeseed & mustard, sesame, linseed, castorseed, nigerseed, safflower, sunflower and soybean. @ Bale of 170 kg + bale of 180 kg. Neg. Negligible sources: 1) Directorate of Economics & Statistics, Department of Agriculture & Cooperation. 2) Ministry of Commerce & Industry.

Figures

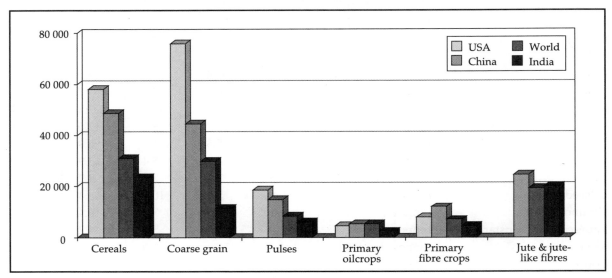

Source: FAO Statistics.
Note: Data are 3-yr average (2001–2003).

Figure A1.1. Comparison of yield for different crops across countries (kg/ha)

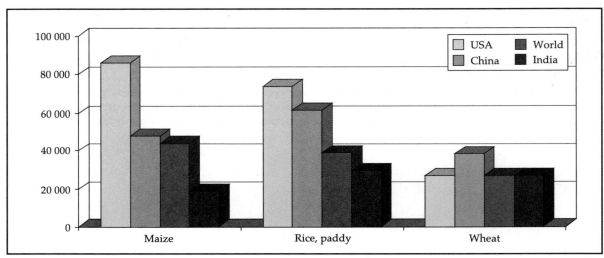

Source: FAO Statistics.
Note: Data are 3-yr average (2001–2003).

Figure A1.2. Comparison of yield for different crops across countries (kg/ha)

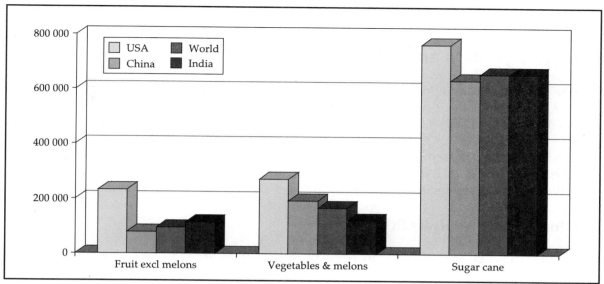

Source: FAO Statistics.
Note: Data are 3-yr average (2001–2003).

Figure A1.3. Comparison of yield for different crops across countries (kg/ha)

Methodology, data and assumptions

This note borrows from the information prepared by Jikun Huang and Jun Yang of the Center for Chinese Agricultural Policy, Chinese Academy of Sciences for the GTAP forecasts. The GTAP forecasts for India were also conducted by the same authors and we would like to acknowledge their efforts.

The main analytical tool used in this study is a model of global trade, which is based on the Global Trade Analysis Project (GTAP). In this appendix, after a brief introduction of the model, the assumptions on macroeconomic development such as GDP and population growths are summarized.

The Global Trade Analysis Project

The well-known GTAP has been used to assess the implications of India and China's rapid economic growth for agriculture and food security in both these countries and the rest of world. The GTAP is a multiregion, multisector computable general equilibrium model, with perfect competition and constant returns to scale. The model is fully described in Hertel (1997). It has been used to generate projections of policy impacts in the future (Arndt *et al.* 1996; Hertel *et al.* 1999; van Tongeren and Huang 2004).

In the GTAP model, each country or region is depicted within the same structural model. The consumer side is represented by the country or regional household to which the income of factors, tariff revenues and taxes is assigned. The country or regional household allocates its income to three expenditure categories: private household expenditures, government expenditures and savings. For the consumption of the private household, the non-homothetic Constant Difference of Elasticities (CDE) function is applied. Firms combine intermediate inputs and primary factors, i.e. land, labour (skilled and unskilled) and capital. Intermediate inputs are composites of domestic and foreign components, and the foreign component is differentiated by region of origin (Armington assumption). On factor markets, the model assumes full employment, with labour and capital being fully mobile within regions, but immobile internationally. Labour and capital remuneration rates are endogenously determined at equilibrium. For crop production, farmers make decisions on land allocation. Land is assumed to be imperfectly mobile between alternative crops, and hence endogenous land rent differentials should be taken into account. Each country or region is equipped with one country regional household that distributes income across savings and consumption expenditures to maximize its utility.

The GTAP model includes two global institutions. All transport between regions is carried out by the international transport sector. The trading costs reflect the transaction costs involved in international trade, as well as the physical activity of transportation itself. Using transport inputs from all regions the international transport sector minimizes its costs under the Cobb–Douglas technology. The second global institution is the global bank, which takes the savings from all regions and purchases investment goods in all regions depending on the expected rates of return. The global bank guarantees that global savings are equal to global investments.

The GTAP model does not have an exchange rate variable. However, by choosing as a numeraire index of global factor prices, each region's change of factor prices relative to the numeraire directly reflects a change in the purchasing power of the region's factor incomes on the world market. This can be directly interpreted as a change in the real exchange rate. The welfare changes are measured by the equivalent variation, which can be computed from each region's household expenditure function.

Taxes and other policy measures are represented as *ad valorem* tax equivalents. These create wedges between the undistorted prices and the policy-inclusive prices. Production taxes are placed on intermediate or primary inputs, or on output. Trade policy instruments include applied most-favoured nation tariffs, antidumping duties, countervailing duties, export quotas and other trade restrictions. Additional internal taxes can be placed on domestic or imported intermediate inputs, and may be applied at differential rates that discriminate against imports. Taxes could be also placed on exports and on primary factor income. Finally, where relevant taxes are placed on final consumption, they can be applied differentially to consumption of domestic and imported goods.

The GDP can be treated either endogenously or exogenously in simulations. Normally, the GDP is treated as an endogenous variable when analysing the impacts of trade liberalization or other policy shocks (e.g. technology changes, resource endowment changes and fiscal or financial policy changes). However, the GDP also can be treated as an exogenous variable when one uses the GTAP to analyse the impacts of overall economic growth on the performance of individual sectors, trade and others. In this case, technology variables become endogenous if capital investment is exogenous, or capital investment becomes endogenous if technological change is exogenous.

The GTAP database contains detailed bilateral trade, transport and protection data characterizing economic linkages among regions, linked with individual country input–output databases which account for intersectoral linkages among the 57 sectors in each of the 87 regions. The database provides quite detailed classification on agriculture, with 14 primary agriculture sectors and seven agricultural processing sectors. All monetary values of the data are in US$ million and the base year for the version (Version 6) used in this study is 2001. For the purposes of this study, the GTAP database has been aggregated into 14 regions and 18 sectors.

Assumptions: the baseline scenario

Initial GDP growth. For initial assumptions on GDP growth over the next 20 years (2001–2020) for all countries except China and India, we adopted the World Bank's projections. The World Bank's projection on global and regional GDP growths has been widely used in many similar studies (e.g. Walmsley *et al.* 2000; van Tongeren and Huang 2004). Meantime, we also incorporate the economic growth prospects of Asia with information from *Economic outlook* (ADB 2002). The assumptions on annual growth of GDP for 2001 to 2020 are based on the prospects of China's economic growth. Initial GDP growths for all countries are used to calibrate the implicit assumptions of technology changes (e.g. total factor productivity [TFP]) embodied in these initial GDP growths given the input–output tables in individual countries or regions. After the embodied TFP growths are estimated and used as exogenous assumptions in the model, the GDP is treated as endogenous in the final analysis. For India, the assumptions are found in the main text and are also provided hereunder.

Population and labour. Population data for 2001 to 2020 for all countries except for India and China are from the United Nations' population projection. China's population projection is from a recent study by IIASA (Toth *et al.* 2003).

Natural resource endowments. No effort has been made to develop a comprehensive database on natural resource endowments. In this study, we directly adopted those assumptions that were in a recent LEI–CCAP study (van Tongeren and Huang 2004). They assume that the annual growth rate of natural resource endowment will be 0.3 percent for all countries.

Physical capital. Assumptions of physical capital growth are from Walmsley *et al.* (2000) and van Tongeren and Huang (2004) although there are several methods to keep the capital endogenously based on the static model (Francois *et al.* 1996; Walmsley, 1998). However, it usually assumes the initial and final results are stable states and the return rates of capital in the beginning and the final stage equally. Therefore it is not suitable to simulate a short time span (five years) in our simulations. Moreover such a method also assumes the capital is freely mobile among countries and does not trace the ownership.

Recursive dynamic simulation. The baseline is constructed through the recursive dynamic approach. We implement the simulation through four steps (2001–2005, 2006–2010, 2011–2015 and 2016–2020) to reflect the change of endowment in different countries and periods. This procedure has been used in several other studies (Hertel *et al.* 1999; van Tongeren and Huang 2004). Comparing these methods, we keep the long-term trade balance of different countries fixed. The basis for this assumption is that investment must be financed solely from domestic savings and thus capital is not mobile across regions (Walmsley 1998). If we do not trace the ownership and pay the foreign capital inflow back, it will cause large foreign capital inflow via trade deficits. Although it is not perfect as the recent GTAP model, which lets the capital freely mobile among countries and traces the foreign ownership, there is no public version available; it requires the creation of a new accounting database to reflect the foreign capital inflow, which is beyond the scope of this study. On the other hand, under our approach, the equivalent variable (EV) can be directly interpreted as change in welfare.

Trade and other policies. The baseline projection also includes a continuation of existing policies and the effectuation of important policy events related to international trade as they are known to date. The important policy changes are: implementation of the remaining commitments from the GATT–Uruguay Round agreements; China's WTO accession between 2001 and 2005; global phase out of the Multifibre Agreement under the WTO Agreement on Textiles and Clothing (ATC) by January 2005; European Union enlargement with Central and Eastern European Countries (CEECs); and possible trade agreement in Doha negotiations during 2005 to 2010. For the baseline projection, this results in a number of assumptions with regard to import tariffs, tariff rate quotas, production and export subsidies. Because there are still high uncertainties on the results of the current Doha Round negotiation, we assume the possible outcome by simply averaging the offers provided by the United States, European Union and CAIRNS proposals in 2004. Details of these assumptions are adopted from van Tongeren and Huang (2004).

Assumptions for India

Table A2.1. The growth rate of exogenous variables for India in four stages (per year %)

	2001–2005	2006–2010	2011–2015	2015–2020
GDP (gross domestic production)	6.73	7.00	7.50	8.00
Population	1.80	1.70	1.60	1.50
Cultivated land area				
Net	0.00	0.00	0.00	0.00
Gross	0.50	0.75	1.00	1.00
Labour supply	2.70	2.71	2.08	1.73
unskilled labour	2.46	2.48	1.85	1.58
skilled labour	7.24	6.40	5.32	3.63
Capital stock	6.46	6.67	6.92	7.20

Table A2.2. The change in trends of income elasticity in India

	2001	2005	2010	2015	2020
1. Rice	0.29	0.26	0.23	0.21	0.18
2. Wheat	0.29	0.26	0.23	0.21	0.18
3. Coarse grains	0.29	0.26	0.23	0.21	0.18
4. Oilseed	0.66	0.64	0.61	0.59	0.56
5. Sugar	0.77	0.74	0.71	0.68	0.65
6. Plant-based fibre	1.10	1.11	1.13	1.15	1.16
7. Other crops	0.78	0.78	0.77	0.77	0.76
8. Bovine cattle, sheep and goats, horses	0.88	0.85	0.81	0.78	0.74
9. Animal products (nec)	0.88	0.85	0.81	0.78	0.74
10. Milk	1.25	1.20	1.16	1.12	1.07
11. Fish	0.88	0.85	0.81	0.78	0.74
12. Other food	0.66	0.62	0.57	0.53	0.49
13. Forestry	1.10	1.11	1.13	1.15	1.16
14. Oil	1.10	1.11	1.13	1.15	1.16
15. Gas	1.10	1.11	1.13	1.15	1.16
16. Coal	1.10	1.11	1.13	1.15	1.16
17. Minerals	1.10	1.11	1.13	1.15	1.16
18. Textile and leather	1.10	1.11	1.13	1.15	1.16
19. Labour-intensive manufacturing	1.10	1.11	1.13	1.15	1.16
20. Capital intensive manufacturing	1.10	1.11	1.13	1.15	1.16
21. Services	1.10	1.11	1.13	1.15	1.16

Table A2.3. The change in trends of uncompensated own price elasticity in India

	2001	2005	2010	2015	2020
1. Rice	-0.31	-0.22	-0.20	-0.18	-0.16
2. Wheat	-0.31	-0.22	-0.20	-0.18	-0.16
3. Coarse grains	-0.31	-0.22	-0.20	-0.18	-0.16
4. Oilseed	-0.56	-0.44	-0.43	-0.42	-0.41
5. Sugar	-0.63	-0.49	-0.48	-0.46	-0.45
6. Plant-based fibre	-0.95	-0.77	-0.79	-0.80	-0.81
7. Other crops	-0.83	-0.65	-0.64	-0.62	-0.61
8. Bovine cattle, sheep and goats, horses	-0.75	-0.58	-0.57	-0.55	-0.53
9. Animal products (nec)	-0.75	-0.58	-0.57	-0.55	-0.53
10. Milk	-1.01	-0.79	-0.78	-0.76	-0.74
11. Fish	-0.75	-0.58	-0.57	-0.55	-0.53
12. Other food	-1.58	-1.21	-1.16	-1.12	-1.07
13. Forestry	-0.95	-0.77	-0.79	-0.80	-0.81
14. Oil	-0.95	-0.77	-0.79	-0.80	-0.81
15. Gas	-0.95	-0.77	-0.79	-0.80	-0.81
16. Coal	-0.95	-0.77	-0.79	-0.80	-0.81
17. Minerals	-0.95	-0.77	-0.79	-0.80	-0.81
18. Textile and leather	-0.95	-0.77	-0.79	-0.80	-0.81
19. Labour-intensive manufacturing	-0.95	-0.77	-0.79	-0.80	-0.81
20. Capital intensive manufacturing	-0.95	-0.77	-0.79	-0.80	-0.81
21. Services	-0.95	-0.77	-0.79	-0.80	-0.81

References (Appendix 2)

Arndt, C., Hertel, T., Dimaranam, B., Huff, K. & McDougall, R. 1997. China in 2005: implications for the rest of world. *Journal of Economic Integration*, 505–547.

Francois, J.F., MacDonald, B.J. & Nordström, H. 1996. *Trade liberalisation and capital accumulation in the GTAP model.* GTAP Technical Paper No. 7.

Hertel, T.W. & Martin, W. 1999. *Would developing countries gain from inclusion of manufactures in the WTO negotiations?* GTAP working paper, Purdue University.

Hertel, T.W. (ed). 1997. *Global trade analysis: modelling and applications.* Cambridge University Press.

Huang, J., Rozelle, S. & Chang, M. 2004. Tracking distortions in agriculture: China and its accession to the World Trade Organization. *World Bank Economic Review*, 18 (1): 59–84.

Van Tongeren, F. & Huang, J. 2004. *China's food economy in the early 21st century.* Report #6.04.04. The Hague, Agricultural Economics Research Institute (LEI).

Walmsley, T.L., Betina, V.D. & Robert, A.M. 2000. *A base case scenario for the dynamic GTAP model.* West Lafayette, Center for Global Trade Analysis, Purdue University.

Walmsley, T.L. 1998. *Long-run simulations with GTAP: Illustrative results from APEC trade liberalization.* GTAP technical paper No. 9.

India and international trade of agricultural commodities

The gap/surplus between domestic production and consumption is expected to be complemented by trade in agricultural commodities and hence by the world production and consumption trend. Trade in agricultural commodities has suffered significantly from declining prices in the recent past, although this is not expected to be a sustained trend. During the last 40 years, real prices of agricultural commodities, relative to prices of all manufactured goods, have declined significantly, even as nominal prices have risen. Real prices have fluctuated considerably around the long-term downward trend. According to the Commodities and Trade Division of FAO it appears that the balance between supply and demand of agricultural commodities has improved and with it the prospects for higher commodity prices after the sharp and persistent decline during the late 1990s.

In spite of the recent strengthening, agricultural commodity prices generally remain close to historically depressed levels; their longer term decline relative to the prices of manufactured goods continues. The link between rising international prices and the opening of international markets and reduction of subsidies cannot be underemphasized. The estimations given above depend critically on how the international prices play out.

What will happen to international commodity prices?

It has also been argued that prices of agricultural commodities will continue to decline relative to industrial products as technological advances reduce costs and make it possible to expand production at a rate that outstrips both population growth and increases in demand spurred by rising incomes. Prices of some commodities have also been driven lower by oversupply, fuelled by intense global competition in production, reduced transportation costs and new technologies that have increased productivity and introduced synthetic alternatives to some commodities. In some cases, the emergence of major new producers has also affected market balance (for example, Viet Nam in coffee exports between 1985 and 2001). Moreover, export subsidies and subsidies to producers in some developed countries have also depressed world prices for many agricultural products grown in temperate zones, reducing the export earnings of developing countries that export commodities such as cotton, sugar and rice.

However, trade liberalization and technological change have played a part in diminishing price variability by reducing the incidence of supply-side shocks. Trade liberalization has permitted a wider range of countries to participate in world commodity markets, reducing the relative importance of the supply situation in any one country, while technological advances have reduced the vulnerability of some crops to climatic influences. The low price levels reached in recent years have themselves limited the scope for extensive variability, at least downwards.

Although real prices for all agricultural commodities have declined over the past 40 years, the rate of decline has varied from one commodity to another. Some developing countries have managed to take advantage of these trends by shifting production and trade into higher-value sectors. By doing so, they have reduced their dependence on products whose prices have fallen more sharply and remained highly erratic. However, in general, developing countries — being major exporters of agricultural commodities — suffered from decline in terms of trade between agriculture and industry. A decline in the agricultural terms of trade can be counteracted by increases in the quantity produced and exported so as to maintain or increase the real value of export earnings.

In fact, for developing countries as a group, increases in the quantity of agricultural exports have more than offset the effect of declining real export prices, such that the real value of their export earnings has risen by nearly 30 percent in the last two decades (source: FAO). In other words, their "agricultural income terms of trade" have increased.

However, the evolution of the terms of trade varied considerably among less-developed countries (LDCs) and other developing countries. For LDCs, export earnings failed to increase, and rising import prices further eroded their purchasing power.

In this context, the information provided hereunder discusses by various commodities India's position *vis à vis* the rest of the world.

Rice

Rice has become one of India's largest agricultural commodity exports and India is currently among the top three exporters of rice in quantity terms. From 1997 to 2001 India was among the few countries whose exports increased both in quantity and US$ terms. Among the major world importers, Indonesia, Philippines, Papua New Guinea, Malaysia, Islamic Republic of Iran, Nigeria and Saudi Arabia are in India's vicinity, but so are the major exporters — China, Thailand and Viet Nam. However, as India's share in the world market is not likely to change much, India does not appear, prima facie, to pose much of a threat as a competitor to these countries.

From 1997 to 2001, the growth of rice exports in terms of value shows a declining trend. However, in terms of volume it registered a positive value. The export unit price (US$/tonne) declined sharply from US$418 to US$247/tonne. Developing countries are the major suppliers of rice in the world. Major importers according to total import from 1997 to 2001 were Indonesia, Philippines, Papua New Guinea, Islamic Republic of Iran, Nigeria, Saudi Arabia, the Russian Federation and Brazil. The world import growth rate is only 0.84 percent. Rice being a food product is inelastic in nature. The world price is falling but imports are not increasing rapidly. Quite interestingly, the world import unit price is falling but remains higher than the export price. The difference gives an idea of difference between the cif (cost, insurance, freight) and fob (free on board) values or in other words cost of transport, insurance, etc.

India is the third (second in some years) exporter of rice in the world in terms of quantity (1997–2001). India exports maximum semi- or wholly milled rice. India's export share in the world market was around 20 percent on an average between 1997 and 2001 although there are considerable year-to-year fluctuations. Thailand and China are India's main competitors.

Table A3.1. Top ten importers and exporters of rice

Exporters	Qty (mill. tonnes) 5-yr sum	Value CARG (%)	Qty CARG (%)	Importers	Qty (mill. tonnes) 5-yr sum	Value CARG (%)	Qty CARG (%)
World	58.1	-7.5	5.5	World	43.6	-8.2	0.8
Thailand	27.9	-7.5	7.9	Indonesia	7.0	92.6	126.2
China	11.6	5.8	19.3	Papua New Guinea	5.6		
India	**10.6**	**-10.1**	**-13.1**	Philippines	5.2	-9.7	2.8
United States	7.2	-8.0	-1.0	Islamic Republic of Iran	4.2	-3.9	5.1
Australia	2.7	-11.5	-3.5				
Italy	2.6	-8.2	-1.8	Nigeria	4.0	-27.3	82.1
Uruguay	2.1	-10.7	3.2	Saudi Arabia	3.3	-10.1	-0.8
Argentina	1.7	-25.5	-14.1	Malaysia	2.9	-14.3	-6.2
Egypt	1.6	17.0	34.1	Brazil	2.2	-28.2	-17.0
Spain	0.5	-7.9	-3.9	Japan	1.8	-10.0	5.7
				Russian Federation	1.8	-18.5	-1.3

Source: Personal Computer Trade Analysis System (PCTAS), UNCTAD.

Table A3.2. Top ten destinations of India's export of rice*

Qty, tonnes	India's export	Import from world	India's share (%)	Unit value of India's exports (US$/tonne)	Unit value of imports from world (US$/tonne)	Indian unit value as a % of world value
World	152 711	7 404 972	2.06	421.32	319.70	131.79
Saudi Arabia	63 141	763 019	8.28	454.64	479.16	94.88
Bangladesh	31 842	NA	NA	204.89	NA	NA
United Kingdom	11 377	135 277	8.41	591.00	657.64	89.87
Kuwait	9 032	NA	NA	579.72	NA	NA
South Africa	5 860	NA	NA	248.62	NA	NA
UAE	5 644	NA	NA	472.37	NA	NA
United States	3 894	375 132	1.04	764.31	464.50	164.54
France	2 232	196 097	1.14	570.72	770.38	74.08
Nepal	2 163	NA	NA	242.26	NA	NA
Yemen	2 108	NA	NA	347.77	NA	NA

* HS. 10630 semi-milled or wholly milled rice, polished or glazed.

UAE – United Arab Emirates.

Source: Indiatrade, CMIE.

Table A3.3. Rice export and import unit prices, US$/tonne of major exporters

	1997	1998	1999	2000	2001
Export					
World	417.84	348.76	323.61	286.79	246.67
Thailand	396.54	331.83	294.96	277.68	214.37
China	271.61	242.30	234.54	185.26	167.74
India	385.06	302.16	386.59	427.14	NA
United States	421.72	410.43	376.12	355.93	314.80
Import					
World	464.92	392.85	361.55	358.05	319.70
Indonesia	488.49	297.71	267.59	233.45	256.94
Philippines	317.31	296.86	286.29	211.00	188.84
Islamic Republic of Iran	385.23	325.74	318.89	298.46	269.32
Saudi Arabia	NA	641.83	614.44	526.48	479.16

Source: PCTAS, UNCTAD.

India's export growth rate from 1997 to 2001 was -13 percent whereas the world growth rate was 5.5 percent, China's 19 percent and Thailand's 8 percent. India's export unit price is rising whereas the world price is falling. India's major destinations are Saudi Arabia, Bangladesh, the United Kingdom, Kuwait, South Africa, United Arab Emirates and the United States. India's price was almost 30 percent higher than the world price in 2001 when calculated from the importer's side. However, India was able to sell at a cheaper price to the United Kingdom and Saudi Arabia. India is expected to remain as a net exporter of rice and will occupy a significant position as an exporter supplying more than 10 percent of world exports.

Wheat

India is currently a minor exporter of wheat and products. This share is expected to fall further. Though domestic production is likely to increase, the increases in consumption are likely to reduce the potential surpluses. Overall India's share of the world wheat pie is insignificant and expected to remain so in net terms.

Major exporters of wheat in the world are the United States, Canada, France, Argentina, Germany and the United Kingdom. Most countries are experiencing a negative growth rate in terms of values and some also in terms of quantity exported from 1997 to 2001. World growth rate in terms of export values was -6 percent during this time. The United Kingdom is experiencing -23 percent growth in terms of export values and -18 percent in terms of quantity. Argentina (4 percent) and Germany (5 percent) experienced positive growth in terms of quantity. Major wheat importers in the world are Italy, Brazil, Japan, Islamic Republic of Iran and Egypt. World import growth was 1.36 percent from 1997 to 2001. Brazil registered 8 percent growth during this time. Japan and Egypt had negative growth. The export unit price is coming down for most of the major exporting countries.

Table A3.4. Export unit prices, US$/tonne

	1997	1998	1999	2000	2001
United States	164.82	139.74	127.67	123.80	134.23
Canada	168.78	159.69	144.49	135.11	147.11
France	174.26	154.82	133.40	128.17	151.74
Argentina	158.44	128.00	116.85	112.94	122.91
Germany	189.65	179.36	158.41	150.17	145.33
United Kingdom	166.01	143.97	139.28	121.24	130.04

Source: PCTAS, UNCTAD.

Table A3.5. Top ten exporters and importers of wheat

	Qty (mill. tonnes)	Value	Qty		Qty (mill. tonnes)	Value	Qty
Exporters	5-yr sum	CARG (%)	CARG (%)	**Importers**	5-yr sum	CARG (%)	CARG (%)
World		-6.1	NA	World	351.7	-5.0	1.4
USA, PR, USVI*	138.1	-5.1	-0.1	Italy	34.7	-5.4	2.0
Canada	94.3	-9.6	-6.5	Brazil	34.2	-1.6	8.2
France	88.0	-2.8	0.7	Japan	29.5	-6.5	-3.3
Argentina	52.2	-2.0	4.5	Islamic Republic of	28.6	-5.7	2.0
Germany	30.1	-1.5	5.3	Iran			
United Kingdom	16.6	-23.1	-18.2	Egypt	19.2	-5.3	-2.5
Turkey	7.9	-10.6	10.3	Republic of Korea	19.2	-2.8	2.2
Hungary	6.3	-0.5	8.8	Algeria	18.2	-8.4	5.4
Belgium	5.5	-22.6	-25.9	Netherlands	18.2	-0.7	7.6
Russian Federation	5.4	13.9	31.7	Spain	17.3	-1.4	6.9
India	1.2	117.7	165.5	Indonesia	17.3	-12.8	-4.8
				India	**4.7**	**-78.9**	**-81.2**

* USA, PR, USVI (United States, Puerto Rico and US Virgin Islands).
Source: PCTAS, UNCTAD.

India is not a significant exporter. Its export share in the world has not yet reached even 0.5 percent except in 2000 when it touched 0.8 percent. However, India's export is experiencing a high growth rate (165 percent between 1997 and 2000 in terms of quantity). The export unit price of India stood at 112.18 in 2000 which is much lower than major exporters. This also has a declining tendency. Periodically India has also imported wheat. However, there is no significant trend in this. India's import constituted around 1.33 percent of the total world import of wheat from 1997 to 2001. India's import unit price is more or less at par with the world's except in 2000 when it rose to US$253/tonne (US$148 as the world import unit price).

India is projected to be a net exporter of wheat although it will remain an occasional importer in future. This will depend on rise in consumption and production shortages in some years. In another 15 years, India's position as a net exporter will deteriorate owing to the internal demand factor.

Maize

Major exporters of maize are the United States, Argentina, France, China, Hungary and Brazil. The world export growth rate from 1997 to 2001 was 4 percent. Brazil experienced 97 percent growth of export followed by Italy (10 percent), Germany (9 percent) and Hungary (7 percent). China's growth rate was -2.45 percent and for the United States this was 3.38 percent. The United States supplied almost 60 percent of total world export of maize followed by Argentina (14 percent), France (10 percent) and China (8 percent). The world unit price is declining. Major importers of maize in the world are Japan, Republic of Korea, Mexico and Spain. World import growth during this time was 3.84 percent. Canada (30 percent), Mexico (30 percent) and Egypt (16 percent) had higher import growth rates. Perhaps Canada and Mexico took advantage of being members of NAFTA and imported much from the United States (top exporter). India is an insignificant importer (less than 0.1 percent of world imports). However India's import growth was 264 percent from 1997 to 2000. India mainly imports from China (49 percent in 2001) and the United States (43 percent in 2001). India imports at price of US$302/tonne from the United States while its export unit price to the world was around US$103 in 2001.

Table A3.6. World export and import unit prices, US$/tonne

	1997	1998	1999	2000	2001
Export					
World	142.98	126.03	113.85	110.43	111.98
Import					
World	170.74	149.48	134.33	128.66	128.88

Source: PCTAS, UNCTAD.

Table A3.7. Top ten exporters and importers of maize

Exporters	Qty (mill. tonnes) 5-yr sum	Value CARG (%)	Qty CARG (%)	Importers	Qty (mill. tonnes) 5-yr sum	Value CARG (%)	Qty CARG (%)
World	392.4	-2.2	4.0	World	291.8	-3.2	3.8
USA, PR, USVI*	233.4	-2.9	3.4	Japan	81.1	-5.5	0.2
Argentina	53.5	-7.4	-0.1	Republic of Korea	40.8	-7.0	0.6
France	39.6	-2.2	-1.0	Mexico	27.6	18.6	29.6
China	32.3	-7.6	-2.5	Egypt	15.3	9.8	16.3
Hungary	7.8	1.5	7.4	Spain	15.1	-2.3	3.1
Brazil	6.1	72.2	97.0	Malaysia	11.1	-11.2	-4.5
Germany	3.1	-0.4	8.9	Netherlands	10.2	-6.2	1.6
Canada	2.1	-12.1	-10.2	Colombia	9.3	-7.9	0.3
Italy	2.0	6.4	10.5	Canada	8.9	16.0	30.1
Netherlands	1.5	1.0	3.6	United Kingdom	7.4	-7.6	0.7
India				**India**	**0.3**	**184.8**	**264.3**

* USA, PR, USVI (United States, Puerto Rico and US Virgin Islands).
Source: PCTAS, UNCTAD.

Edible oil and oilseed

The major exporters are Malaysia, Indonesia, Argentina, the United States and Germany. In terms of value, the world export growth rate from 1997 to 2001 was -9 percent. In terms of quantity export Malaysia experienced 9 percent, Indonesia 9 percent, the United States -6 percent and Brazil 8 percent growth. However there appears to be a long-term fall in prices. In quantity terms as well as in nominal terms, India is likely to become an even more important player in edible oil and oilseed imports. In its vicinity, Philippines, Malaysia and Indonesia are the largest international suppliers and likely to remain so if the five-year trends are anything to go by. India is likely to become an important trade partner for these countries where edible oils and oilseed are concerned.

The products include crude and refined oil, kernels, seeds of soybean, groundnut, olives, palm, sunflower, cotton, coconut, rapeseed, linseed, maize, castor and sesame seed.

Major exporters are Malaysia, Indonesia, Argentina, the United States and Germany. In terms of value, the world export growth rate during 1997 to 2001 was -9 percent. In terms of export quantity, Malaysia experienced 9 percent, Indonesia 9 percent, the United States -6 percent and Brazil 8 percent growth. There has been a significant fall in prices. Possibly this has triggered a negative growth in terms of values. Quantity exported increased, prices fell but overall value did not increase. This indicates that products have low elasticity. The import unit price varies significantly from country to country. However, it also has a declining trend in general.

Table A3.8. Top ten exporters and importers of edible oils

Exporters	Qty (mill. tonnes) 5-yr sum	Value CARG (%)	Qty CARG (%)	Importers	Qty (mill. tonnes) 5-yr sum	Value CARG (%)	Qty CARG (%)
World				World			
Malaysia	41.0	-9.0	9.4	**India**	**11.0**	**20.2**	**47.6**
Indonesia	22.0	-11.5	8.8	China	11.0	-21.0	-7.7
Argentina	21.7	-8.8	3.1	USA, PR, USVI	7.8	-7.8	0.5
USA, PR, USVI*	8.8	-13.8	-6.1	Netherlands	7.6	4.2	21.0
Germany	6.5	-7.1	1.1	Germany	6.7	-6.1	6.7
Netherlands	6.3	-8.5	1.8	Italy	5.5	-8.3	6.7
Brazil	6.2	-5.6	8.6	United Kingdom	4.9	-8.0	4.8
Philippines	5.2	-11.3	7.0	Islamic Republic of Iran	4.2	-2.1	13.4
Spain	4.1	-9.2	-1.8				
Canada	3.4	-16.2	-7.6	Malaysia	4.1	4.0	81.3
				France	4.0	-0.5	3.5

* USA, PR, USVI (United States, Puerto Rico and US Virgin Islands).
Source: PCTAS, UNCTAD.

Major importers are India, China, the United States, the Netherlands, Germany and the United Kingdom. Being the major exporter of oilseed, the United States imports specific products like sesame, palm and coconut oil significantly. Malaysia also imports soybean, palm and groundnut products. Between 1997 and 2000 the import growth of India (48 percent) was significant. The Netherlands (21 percent) and Islamic Republic of Iran (13 percent) registered high import growth during 1997 to 2001. India is mainly importing from Malaysia (25 percent), Indonesia (31 percent) and Argentina (28 percent). India was importing almost 32 percent of Malaysia's, 25 percent of Indonesia's and 13 percent of Argentina's world export of edible oil from 1998 to 2002. India is importing on an average lower than or at par with the world average unit price. India is projected to remain as a major importer of oilseed in the future. Import demand is expected to rise by almost 300 percent by 2020.

Table A3.9. Export and import unit prices, US$/tonne

	1997	1998	1999	2000	2001
Export					
Malaysia	546.40	634.14	406.38	320.07	262.11
Indonesia	520.39	521.61	393.74	303.60	227.71
Argentina	561.75	644.92	447.71	339.89	343.32
United States	604.35	665.95	565.66	476.14	428.69
Import					
India	583.00	692.74	440.13	315.30	NA
China	547.42	631.54	528.24	371.30	293.46
Netherlands	604.47	641.85	550.83	407.35	332.13
Germany	697.65	733.13	709.56	515.81	418.67

Source: PCTAS, UNCTAD.

According to FAO, in the last few years, prices of oilseed have improved steadily from the low levels recorded in 1999 to 2000 and producers have responded with a robust increase in production. The increase in prices was triggered mainly by sustained growth in demand that outstripped the expansion in supplies. With demand firm and stocks at relatively low levels, both global output and prices for oil-crop products are expected to continue to rise in the short term.

Sugar

The major exporters of sugar in terms of quantity were Brazil, Cuba, France, Thailand, Germany, Colombia and India between 1998 and 2002. Most of the other exporters experienced negative growth. Brazil was supplying more than 25 percent and India 4.45 percent of world exports in 2002. However rapid economic growth is likely to increase domestic requirements. India therefore is not likely to be among the major exporters by 2020. As many of the large importers, namely, Republic of Korea, Malaysia, China and Japan are in Asia, easier export opportunities are in store for Thailand. Provided other countries do not emerge as sugar exporters.

Major exporters of sugar in terms of quantity were Brazil, Cuba, France, Thailand, Germany, Colombia and India between 1998 and 2002. Brazil's export growth rate during this period was 13 percent and India's 180 percent. Most of the other exporters experienced negative growth. Brazil supplied more than 25 percent and India 4.45 percent of world exports in 2002. The sugar price has been volatile. In 2002, export unit prices for some countries increased. Major importers in the world are the Russian Federation, Malaysia, Republic of Korea, Japan, the United Kingdom, China and Indonesia. From 1998 to 2002, Malaysia's import registered growth of 90 percent. China is also registering high import growth of 16 percent.

India's major export destinations are Sri Lanka (14 percent of total exports during 1998 to 2002), Malaysia (13 percent), Bangladesh (11.5 percent) and Indonesia (10 percent). India's sugar exports are projected to have many variations and the net exporter's position will deteriorate in future which will be mainly attributable to rise in internal demand and decline in productivity.

Table A3.10. Top ten exporters and importers of sugar

Exporters	Qty (mill. tonnes) 5-yr sum	Value CARG (%)	Qty CARG (%)	Importers	Qty (mill. tonnes) 5-yr sum	Value CARG (%)	Qty CARG (%)
World		-1.0	NA	World		-2.5	NA
Brazil	51.9	2.2	12.5	Russian Federation	25.7	-6.9	3.7
Malawi	40.2			Malaysia	20.2	-0.4	89.2
France	15.0	-4.0	-1.9	Republic of Korea	11.3	-5.0	1.4
Thailand	13.7			United Kingdom	11.2	-4.2	1.5
Germany	9.6	-5.6	-3.9	Japan	9.5	-6.8	-1.7
Cuba	9.0			Canada	8.9	-2.6	2.7
Guatemala	7.6	-7.3	-0.4	Indonesia	7.8	-11.5	0.6
Colombia	5.9	-7.3	1.2	Belgium	6.5	2.0	7.3
Belgium	5.8	3.4	6.1	China	6.4	13.1	15.6
South Africa	4.7			Germany	5.8	2.7	7.1
India	**4.5**	**142.4**	**179.8**				

Source: PCTAS, UNCTAD.

Table A3.11. Sugar — export and import unit prices US$/tonne

	1998	1999	2000	2001	2002
Export					
Brazil	231.95	157.82	184.22	203.92	157.98
France	469.42	454.89	401.55	379.35	430.06
Thailand	NA	148.99	134.73	163.18	NA
India	366.00	88.54	151.79	227.95	206.14
Cuba	NA	150.80	134.61	227.75	NA
Import					
Russian Federation	299.16	194.74	161.17	226.20	194.07
Malaysia	265.53	132.80	219.86	136.53	20.40
Republic of Korea	205.33	158.19	156.75	186.14	158.15
United Kingdom	486.99	439.82	395.33	371.67	387.24

Source: PCTAS, UNCTAD.

Vegetables and fruit

Major exporters of fruit and vegetables are Spain (15 percent of world exports), the United States (12 percent), the Netherlands (9 percent), Mexico (8 percent), Italy (7 percent) and France (6 percent). The world average growth rate of exports from 1997 to 2001 was only 0.38 percent. Mexico registered 8.5 percent and Chile 5 percent growth. Most of the other top exporters experienced a negative growth rate. India supplied around 1.5 percent of world exports and registered a growth of 7.30 percent from 1997 to 2001. India is projected to remain as a net exporter of fruit and vegetables.

Top importers from 1997 to 2001 were Germany (around 15 percent of world import), the United States (15 percent), the United Kingdom (9 percent), Japan (8 percent) and France (9 percent). India's import share was close to 1 percent but the import growth rate was negative from 1997 to 2000.

Table A3.12. Top ten exporters and importers of fruit and vegetables

Exporters	Value in bill. US$	Share of world	CARG (%)	Importers	Value in bill. US$	Share of world	CARG (%)
World	205.8	100.0	0.4	Sum reporters	246.8	100.0	-0.1
Spain	31.1	15.1	-1.4	Germany	39.0	15.8	-5.4
USA, PR, USVI*	26.1	12.7	-0.2	USA, PR, USVI*	36.4	14.8	6.4
Netherlands	19.7	9.6	-0.4	United Kingdom	24.0	9.7	-1.4
Mexico	14.3	7.0	8.5	Japan	20.1	8.1	0.2
Italy	13.8	6.7	-1.2	France	19.8	8.0	3.2
France	13.4	6.5	2.6	Netherlands	13.2	5.3	-2.5
China	10.0	4.9	2.5	Canada	12.0	4.9	3.2
Belgium	8.4	4.1	-4.6	Italy	10.2	4.1	-0.2
Turkey	7.9	3.8	-3.3	Belgium	7.2	2.9	-3.7
Chile	6.3	3.0	4.7	Spain	6.6	2.7	5.1
India	**3.2**	**1.5**	**7.3**	**India**	**2.3**	**0.9**	**-10.4**

* USA, PR, USVI (United States, Puerto Rico and US Virgin Islands).
Source: PCTAS, UNCTAD.

Fish

Although India has a large coastline, and a significant population dependent on fishing, it accounts for a small percentage of world fish and products exports. This share is not likely to change much. Aquaculture has not really taken off in India to the extent that is possible. Much of the fish "production" continues to be non-mechanized; processing and canning plants are absent, cold storage and transport facilities are also poor. Although India is likely to remain a net exporter of fish products, it is going to remain a marginal player. Inasmuch as fish consumption is likely to double in East Asia in the next few decades, the markets are present for India to benefit from (FAO 2002a).

Major exporters of fish are Norway (10 percent of world exports), the United States (8 percent), Canada (7 percent), Thailand (7 percent) and China (6.5 percent). World export growth from 1997 to

Table A3.13. Top ten exporters and importers of fish

Exporters	Value in bill. US$	Share of world	CARG (%)	Importers	Value in bill. US$	Share of world	CARG (%)
World	158.6	100.0	1.3	World	209.9	132.3	2.0
Norway	16.2	10.2	0.0	Japan	59.8	37.7	-3.4
USA, PR, USVI*	12.0	7.6	3.7	USA, PR, USVI*	38.5	24.3	5.1
Canada	11.0	6.9	4.8	Spain	16.3	10.3	5.6
Thailand	10.9	6.8	-3.5	France	12.8	8.1	5.4
China	10.4	6.6	8.2	Italy	10.7	6.8	1.6
Denmark	8.0	5.0	-1.1	Germany	8.8	5.5	0.9
Indonesia	7.4	4.7	-1.8	Hong Kong S.A.R.	8.2	5.2	-3.9
Spain	6.5	4.1	4.5	United Kingdom	6.2	3.9	4.9
Chile	6.0	3.8	9.2	Republic of Korea	5.1	3.2	14.2
Netherlands	5.2	3.2	3.9	Canada	4.9	3.1	5.8
India	**4.8**	**3.0**	**3.9**				

* USA, PR, USVI (United States, Puerto Rico and US Virgin Islands).
Source: PCTAS, UNCTAD.

2001 was only 1.29 percent. Chile (9 percent), China (8 percent) and Canada (5 percent) had relatively high growth. India supplied around 3 percent with a growth of 4 percent from 1997 to 2000. Major importers in the world are Japan (28 percent), the United States (18 percent), Spain (8 percent) and France (6 percent). World import growth during 1997 to 2001 was only 2 percent. However, Japan experienced a negative growth (-3 percent) whereas Republic of Korea had 14 percent import growth. India is not an importer of fish. However, it is expected that in another 15 years India will increase its fish import significantly. However, the country will remain a net exporter but the share will be insignificant.

Meat (including cattle)

India is currently an insignificant exporter of poultry, pork, beef, lamb, goat meat and mutton, having slightly less than 1 percent of the world market. Although production is likely to increase significantly, India is unlikely to become a significant world supplier of this category of commodities.

Poultry

Major exporters in terms of quantity were the United States (40 percent), Brazil (13 percent), France (11 percent), the Netherlands (11 percent), China (5 percent) and Thailand (4 percent) during 1997 to 2001. India's exports are not significant being less than 0.005 percent of world export. The world export growth rate is 6.6 percent. Among the major players Brazil (18 percent), Thailand (21 percent) and Germany (13 percent) had high export growth. Export unit price generally had a declining tendency with a rise in 2001. Major importers in terms of quantity are Hong Kong Special Administrative Region (19 percent), the Russian Federation (16 percent), Japan (10 percent), China (10 percent) and Germany (8 percent). India is not an importer. World import growth during 1997 to 2001 was 6.6 percent. Among the top importers China (36 percent), Mexico (10 percent) and France (8 percent) registered high growth.

Table A3.14. Top ten exporters and importers of poultry

Exporters	Qty (mill. tonnes) 5-yr sum	Value CARG (%)	Qty CARG (%)	Importers	Qty (mill. tonnes) 5-yr sum	Value CARG (%)	Qty CARG (%)
World	33.2	1.5	6.7	World	26.4	0.4	6.7
USA, PR, USVI*	13.2	-1.7	4.8	Hong Kong S.A.R.	5.1	-3.7	3.1
Brazil	4.4	11.0	18.3	Russian Federation	4.3	-1.9	4.8
France	3.7	-2.2	-3.6	China	2.8	35.9	35.5
Netherlands	3.5	2.0	10.9	Japan	2.7	-3.8	1.2
China	1.8	-0.7	5.6	Germany	2.0	-6.1	-2.5
Thailand	1.3	11.7	20.6	Mexico	1.6	5.2	10.4
United Kingdom	1.0	-7.9	-1.0	United Kingdom	1.4	3.7	5.4
Belgium	0.9	16.1	10.5	Saudi Arabia	1.2	3.3	9.0
Germany	0.6	5.2	12.8	Netherlands	0.8	-2.1	6.6
Denmark	0.6	2.8	4.7	France	0.7	5.3	8.9
India							

* USA, PR, USVI (United States, Puerto Rico and US Virgin Islands).
Source: PCTAS, UNCTAD.

Pork

Major exporters in terms of quantity are Denmark (21 percent), the Netherlands (18 percent), the United States (10 percent) and Canada (9 percent). World growth of quantity exported was 6.23 percent during 1997 to 2001. Among the major exporters Spain (17 percent), Germany (27 percent), Canada (16 percent) and the United States (10 percent) had substantially high export growth rate. Periodically India also exports in the world market. From 1997 the export unit price declined but rose again 2001. Major importers in terms of quantity are Germany (15 percent), Italy (14 percent), Japan (11 percent), the United Kingdom (8 percent), the Russian Federation (8 percent) and Mexico (5 percent). India is not an importer of pork. The world import growth rate was 8 percent during 1997 to 2001. Among the major importing countries Mexico (25 percent), the United States (14 percent), Greece (43 percent), Hong Kong Special Administrative Region (9 percent) and the United Kingdom (9 percent) had higher import growth rates.

Table A3.15. Top ten exporters and importers of pork

Exporters	Qty (mill. tonnes) 5-yr sum	Value CARG (%)	Qty CARG (%)	Importers	Qty (mill. tonnes) 5-yr sum	Value CARG (%)	Qty CARG (%)
World	26.6	1.5	6.2	World	28.4	1.4	7.8
Denmark	5.7	-0.3	4.3	Germany	4.3	-11.7	-6.7
Netherlands	4.8	-3.5	1.3	Italy	3.8	-0.2	6.0
USA, PR, USVI*	2.6	6.5	10.2	Japan	3.0	5.8	8.3
Canada	2.3	10.7	15.8	United Kingdom	2.3	2.6	8.5
France	2.2	0.1	0.7	Russian Federation	2.1	-11.3	-0.5
Germany	2.0	17.2	27.0	France	1.9	0.3	0.5
Belgium	1.8	18.9	7.6	Hong Kong S.A.R.	1.6	3.0	9.2
Spain	1.6	12.1	17.4	Mexico	1.5	29.1	25.4
Belgium-Luxembourg	1.1			USA, PR, USVI*	1.4	11.4	14.1
United Kingdom	1.1	-35.9	-32.7	Greece	1.4	4.2	42.8
India							

* USA, PR, USVI (United States, Puerto Rico and US Virgin Islands).
Source: PCTAS, UNCTAD.

Beef

Major exporters in terms of quantity are the United States (20 percent), Australia (18 percent), Germany (8 percent), Canada (8 percent), New Zealand (6 percent) and Brazil (4 percent). India also exports 3 percent on an average. But in 2001 its export figure declined to a very insignificant level. India's major export destinations are Malaysia (around 35 percent), Philippines (30 percent), United Arab Emirates (8 percent) and Armenia (10 percent). World export growth is -1.08 percent. Among the major exporters, Brazil (61 percent), Canada (10 percent) and India (18 percent) had a positive growth rate whereas France (-21 percent), Ireland (-11 percent) and New Zealand (-23 percent) had a negative growth rate. The export price is more or less constant with slight variations. However, at the country level variations are greater. Quite interestingly, India's export unit price is significantly lower than the world average. India's low export volume may be because of product quality and lack of SPS compatibility in developed country markets.

Table A3.16. Top ten exporters and importers of beef

Exporters	Qty (mill. tonnes) 5-yr sum	Value CARG (%)	Qty CARG (%)	Importers	Qty (mill. tonnes) 5-yr sum	Value CARG (%)	Qty CARG (%)
World	27.0	-1.5	-1.1	World	26.3	-0.7	1.3
USA, PR, USVI*	5.5	1.6	3.9	USA, PR, USVI*	4.5	14.6	7.7
Australia	5.0	6.1	3.3	Japan	3.9	-0.3	0.9
Germany	2.2	-3.3	4.6	Russian Federation	2.8	-12.2	-8.8
Canada	2.0	18.1	10.5	Mexico	1.9	25.8	21.8
Ireland	1.9	-9.8	-10.8	Italy	1.9	-12.2	-6.7
Netherlands	1.8	-13.0	-9.6	France	1.5	-5.7	-4.0
New Zealand	1.6	0.1	-23.5	Canada	1.0	3.5	5.3
France	1.5	-18.7	-20.8	Republic of Korea	0.9	3.7	4.9
Brazil	0.9	39.4	61.2	Greece	0.8	-21.6	0.4
Argentina	0.8	-33.2	-28.3	Germany	0.8	-20.9	-16.6
India	0.8	15.9	17.8				

* USA, PR, USVI (United States, Puerto Rico and US Virgin Islands).
Source: PCTAS, UNCTAD.

In terms of quantity, major importers are the United States (17 percent), the Russian Federation (15 percent), Japan (11 percent), Mexico (7 percent) and Greece (3 percent). World import growth rate during 1997 to 2001 was 1.31 percent. Among the major importing countries, Mexico (22 percent) and the United States (8 percent) had high growth rate and Germany (-17 percent), the Russian Federation (-9 percent) and Italy (-7 percent) had negative growth rate. Import unit prices increased in some countries but decreased in others. Overall the world import unit price remains constant with a slight dip in 2001.

Table A3.17. Beef — export and import unit prices, US$/tonne

	1997	1998	1999	2000	2001
Export					
World	2 557.44	2 583.35	2 572.53	2 535.85	2 515.14
United States	3 029.07	2 729.08	2 867.39	2 835.27	2 759.33
India	1 113.20	1 066.93	1 012.57	1 061.30	NA
Import					
World	2 681.09	2 679.37	2 678.59	2 601.25	2 478.87
USA, PR, USVI*	2 077.51	2 094.60	2 299.53	2 461.71	2 656.33
Russian Federation	1 197.20	1 149.38	1 024.76	1 137.64	1 029.90

* USA, PR, USVI (United States, Puerto Rico and US Virgin Islands).
Source: PCTAS, UNCTAD.

Other meats

This includes lamb, mutton and goat meat. Major exporters during 1997 to 2001 were New Zealand (34 percent), Australia (32 percent) and the United Kingdom (9 percent). India is not an exporter. In terms of quantity, world export growth rate during 1997 to 2001 was -5.47 percent. New Zealand (-21 percent) and the United Kingdom (-25 percent) had a negative growth rate. Australia registered a positive growth rate of 6 percent. The world export unit price has increased. For New Zealand it was a significant rise. In terms of quantity, major importers are France (25 percent), the United Kingdom (17 percent), the United States (7 percent), Saudi Arabia (6 percent) and Mexico (6 percent). The world import growth rate in terms of quantity was only 0.75 percent during 1997 to 2001. Mexico (23 percent) and the United States (15 percent) registered a high growth rate among top importers during this time. Other countries have a negative growth rate.

Table A3.18. Top ten exporters and importers of other meat (not including beef/poultry)

Exporters	Qty (mill. tonnes)	Value	Qty	Importers	Qty (mill. tonnes)	Value	Qty
		CARG (%)	CARG (%)			CARG (%)	CARG (%)
World	4.8	-1.5	-5.5	World	3.7	-0.8	0.7
New Zealand	1.7	-2.6	-20.7	France	0.9	-1.1	-4.6
Australia	1.5	4.6	5.8	United Kingdom	0.6	-9.6	-6.1
United Kingdom	0.4	-26.6	-25.1	USA, PR, USVI*	0.3	12.8	14.7
Ireland	0.3	8.1	9.4	Mexico	0.2	20.8	22.7
Argentina	0.2	-4.9	-3.8	Saudi Arabia	0.2	-7.4	-5.6
Belgium	0.1	7.7	4.5	Italy	0.2	3.2	4.3
Spain	0.1	7.2	6.7	Germany	0.2	-1.9	-0.5
USA, PR, USVI*	0.1	-0.7	0.4	Japan	0.2	-8.7	-7.8
Uruguay	0.1	-3.8	-5.8	Belgium	0.2	0.9	-0.9
Belgium-Luxembourg	0.1			Belgium-Luxembourg	0.1		

* USA, PR, USVI (United States, Puerto Rico and US Virgin Islands).
Source: PCTAS, UNCTAD.

According to FAO, the international market for meat continues to be disrupted by animal disease outbreaks. During the first half of 2004, approximately one-third of global meat exports was affected by outbreaks of avian flu or by identified cases of bovine spongiform encephalopathy (BSE). Import bans on poultry and beef from disease-affected countries are leading to higher prices for products originating from disease-free zones. Constrained export supplies of meat are also pushing up prices for other animal protein products. The rise in prices is perhaps due to supply shortages in the global market.

Plant-based fibre

Though India exports raw cotton and jute, it is a net importer of plant-based fibre. The large exports of cotton garments are important. Moreover, all indications are that India is going to become an even more important exporter of cotton garments. The net result is that by 2020, India will account for an estimated 18 percent of the world's imports. The only large cotton exporter in the geographical vicinity is Australia, with all other Asian countries (barring Pakistan) being large importers.

Milk and milk products

Milk and milk products are likely to be among the most rapidly increasing consumption items given their high income elasticities across the income spectrum. This is likely to overpower domestic production increases. The country is therefore likely to become a net importer of milk and products. However, it will be a marginal importer accounting for barely 0.3 percent of the world market.

Forestry

It is estimated that about half of the forest area worldwide can be used for wood supply. But wood is only one component; food products such as spices, nuts, ornamental plants, some animal products, bark, medicinal plants, organic chemicals (including those for industrial uses) are others. However wood and products remain the largest import items currently and are likely to form the bulk of the imports in the future. As the bulk of the exporting countries are in the western hemisphere and Australia, opportunities for East and Southeast Asia are expected to exist but are unlikely to be exploited.

Bibliography

Acharya, S.S. 2004. Agricultural marketing. *State of the Indian Farmer*, Vol. 17. Ministry of Agriculture and Academic Foundation.

Ahluwalia, M.S. Undated. *India's economic performance, policies and prospects*, Planning Commission, Government of India. (mimeo)

Alagh, Y.K. 2004. An overview. *State of the Indian Farmer*, Vol. 1. Ministry of Agriculture and Academic Foundation.

Alam, G. 2004. Technology generation and IPR issues. *State of the Indian Farmer*, Vol. 5. Ministry of Agriculture and Academic Foundation.

Anwarul, H. (ed.). 2002. *WTO agreement and Indian agriculture*. Social Science Press and ICRIER.

Bhalla, G.S. 2004. Globalization and Indian agriculture. *State of the Indian farmer*, Vol. 19. Ministry of Agriculture and Academic Foundation.

Blyn, G. 1966. *Agricultural trends in India, 1891–1947: Output, availability, and productivity*. Philadelphia, University of Pennsylvania Press.

Chadha. G.K., Sen, S. & Sharma, H.R. 2004. Land resources. *State of the Indian Farmer*, Vol. 2. Ministry of Agriculture and Academic Foundation.

Chidambaram, P. 2005. *US-India economic relations and the evolving world economy*. 2005 Trumbull Lecture. Yale University.

Datta, S.K. 2004. Cooperatives in agriculture. *State of the Indian Farmer*, Vol. 24. Ministry of Agriculture and Academic Foundation.

De Soto, H. 2000. *Mystery of capital, why capitalism triumphs in the west and fails everywhere else*. Basic Books.

Deshpande, R.S., Bhende, M.J., Thippaiah P. & Vivekananda, M. 2004. Crops and cultivation. *State of the Indian Farmer*, Vol. 9. Ministry of Agriculture and Academic Foundation.

Deshpande, R.S., Rajasekhar, D., Apte, P. & Sathe, D. 2004. NGOs and farmers' movements. *State of the Indian Farmer*, Vol. 23. Ministry of Agriculture and Academic Foundation.

Dev, M.S., Ravi, C., Viswanathan, B. Gulati, A. & Ramachander, S. 2004. *Economic liberalisation, targeted programmes and household food security: A case study of India*. MTID Discussion Paper No. 68. International Food Policy Research Institute.

Dyson, T. 2000. India's demographic and food prospects: State level analysis. *Economic and Political Weekly*, 30 (46).

Joshi, P.K., Gulati, A., Birthal, P.S. & Tewari, L. 2003. *Agriculture diversification in South Asia: patterns, determinants, and policy implications*. MSSD Discussion Paper No. 57. International Food Policy Research Institute

Food and Agriculture Organization (FAO). 2002a. *World agriculture towards 2015/2020*. Rome.

Food and Agriculture Organization (FAO). 2002b. Forest products statistics in South and Southeast Asia.

Government of India (GOI). 1996. *Population projections for India and states 1996–2016*, Ministry of Home Affairs. Registrar General of India.

Government of India (GOI). 2000a. *Report of the task force to study the cooperative credit system and suggest measures for its strengthening*. Ministry of Finance. Academic Foundation.

Government of India (GOI). April 2000b. *Report on food and agro industries management (RFAIM)*. Council on Trade and Industry.

Government of India (GOI). 2001a. Approach paper to the Tenth Five Year Plan (APTFYP). Planning Commission.

Government of India (GOI). July 2001b. *Report of the task force on employment opportunities.* Planning Commission.

Government of India (GOI). 2001c. *Report of expert committee on strengthening and developing of agricultural marketing.* Forward Markets Commission.

Government of India (GOI). 2001d. *Employment and unemployment situation in India 1999–2000.* National Sample Survey Organization, Report No. 458, Ministry of Statistics and Programme Implementation.

Government of India (GOI). 2002a. *Report of the task force on direct taxes.* Ministry of Finance.

Government of India (GOI). 2002b. *Report of the task force on indirect taxes.* Ministry of Finance.

Government of India (GOI). 2002c. *Report of the task force on indirect taxes.* Ministry of Finance and Company Affairs.

Government of India (GOI). 2003–2004a. *Economic survey.* Ministry of Finance.

Government of India (GOI). 2003–2004b. *National account statistics.* Central Statistical Organisation (CSO).

Government of India (GOI). 2004–2005. *Economic survey.* Ministry of Finance.

Government of India (GOI). 2005a. *Agriculture statistics at a glance 2005.* The Directorate of Economics and Statistics (DES).

Government of India (GOI). June 2005b. *Mid-term appraisal of 10th Five Year Plan* (2002–2007). Planning Commission.

Government of India (GOI). 2006. Agricultural Marketing Information Network Website. Directorate of Marketing and Inspection. Department of Agriculture and Cooperation. (http://agmarknet.nic.in/amrscheme/westbengal.htm)

Gulati, A. & Narayanan, S. 2003. *The subsidy syndrome in Indian agriculture.* New Delhi, Oxford University Press.

Gulati, F. & Dalafi. 2005. *The dragon and the elephant: Agriculture and rural reforms in China and India.* MTID Discussion Paper No. 87; DSGD Discussion Paper No. 22. International Food Policy Research Institute.

Hazra, C.R. 2001. Crop diversification in India. *In* M.K. Papademetriou and F.J. Dent, eds. *Crop diversification in the Asia–Pacific Region.* Rome. Food and Agriculture Organization.

Misra, V.N. 2004. Terms of trade. *State of the Indian Farmer,* Vol. 15. Ministry of Agriculture and Academic Foundation.

Mohanty, S., Alexandratos, N. & Bruinsma, J. 1998. *The long-term food outlook for India.* CARD Technical Report 98-TR 38.

National Council of Applied Economic Research (NCAER). 2001. *Economic and policy reforms in India.* New Delhi.

Radhakrishna, R. & Reddy, V.K. 2002. *Food security and nutrition: Vision 2020.* India Development Report.

Raju, K.V., Narayanamoorthy, A., Gopakumar, G. & Amarnath, H.K. 2004. Water resources. *State of the Indian Farmer,* Vol. 3. Ministry of Agriculture and Academic Foundation.

Ramaswami, B., Ravi, S. & Chopra, S.D. 2004. Risk management. *State of the Indian Farmer,* Vol. 22. Ministry of Agriculture and Academic Foundation.

Rao, V.M. 2004. Rainfed agriculture. *State of the Indian Farmer,* Vol. 10. Ministry of Agriculture and Academic Foundation.

Rao, P.P. Birthal, P.S., Joshi, P.K. & Kar, D. 2004. *Agricultural diversification in India and role of urbanization.* MTID Discussion Paper No. 77. International Food Policy Research Institute.

Research and Information System for the Non-Aligned and Other Developing Countries (RIS). 2002. *South Asia development and cooperation report.*

Research and Information System for the Non-Aligned and Other Developing Countries (RIS). 2004. *South Asia Development and Cooperation Report.*

Reserve Bank of India (RBI). 2005. *Handbook of statistics on the Indian economy*, 2004–2005.

Roy, T. 2000. *The economic history of India 1857–1947.* New Delhi, Oxford University Press.

Sen, A. & Bhatia, M.S. 2004. Cost of cultivation and farm income. *State of the Indian Farmer*, Vol. 14. Ministry of Agriculture and Academic Foundation.

Shiva, V. 1991. *The violence of the green revolution.* Penang, Third World Network.

Singh, M. 27 October 2005. Inaugural address at National KVK Conference. National Agricultural Research Centre, Pusa, New Delhi.

Singh, S. & Sagar, V. 2004. Agricultural credit in India. *State of the Indian Farmer*, Vol. 7. Ministry of Agriculture and Academic Foundation.

Srivastava, D.K., Rao, C.B., Chakraborty, P. & Rangamannar, T.S. 2003. *Budgetary subsidies in India: subsidising social and economic services.* New Delhi. National Institute of Public Finance and Policy.

Strategic Foresight Group. 2005. *The Second Freedom, South Asian Challenge 2005–2025.* Mumbai.

Subbiah, A.R. 2004. Natural disaster management. *State of the Indian Farmer*, Vol. 21. Ministry of Agriculture and Academic Foundation.

Taneja, N., Sarvananthan, M., Karmacharya, B. & Pohit, S. 2005. Informal trade in India, Nepal and Sri Lanka. *In* M. Khan, ed. *Economic development in South Asia.* Tata McGraw Hill.

Thimmaiah, G. & Rajan, K. 2004. Policy and organizational support. *State of the Indian Farmer*, Vol. 26. Ministry of Agriculture and Academic Foundation.

United Nations Conference for Trade and Development (UNCTAD). Various years. *Annual reports.*

United Nations Development Programme (UNDP). 2005. *Human development report 2005.*

Virmani, A. Undated. Unpublished presentation. New Delhi, ICRIER.

Wilson, D. & Purushothaman, R. 2003. *Dreaming with BRICs: The path to 2050.* Global Economics Paper No. 99. Goldman Sachs.

World Bank. World Development Indicators Database.

World Trade Organization (WTO). 2005. *World trade report 2005.* http://www.wto.org/english/res_e/booksp_e/anrep_e/wtr05-tariff_e.pdf.

World Trade Organization (WTO). Various years. *Annual reports.*

Notes

[1] Inaugural Address by Dr Manmohan Singh, National KVK Conference, 27 October 2005, National Agricultural Research Centre, Pusa, New Delhi.

[2] Even at 4 percent annual growth in agriculture and 10 percent growth in non-agricultural sectors the share of agriculture would be around 10 percent.

[3] Strictly speaking, NSS (National Sample Survey) data are on expenditure rather than income.

[4] The decadal rate of population growth from Census 1991 to Census 2001 is 2.14 percent.

[5] The last official figures of 28.1 percent are for 2003–2004.

[6] We are grateful to Jikun Huang and Jun Yang of the Center for Chinese Agricultural Policy, Chinese Academy of Sciences for the GTAP forecasts.

[7] These five-year plans began with the First Five Year Plan, for the period 1951 to 1956. India follows a fiscal year system, from 1 April to 31 March of the succeeding year. There were three deviations from the five year plan trajectory, during three annual plans between 1966 and 1969, an annual plan for 1979–1980 and two annual plans between 1990 and 1992.

[8] These are GNP figures. GDP figures are marginally different, at the first decimal place. The 4.2 percent in 2002–2003 was because of a relatively disastrous agricultural performance and the spectacular 8.5 percent in 2003–2004 was because of the low 2002–2003 base.

[9] More accurately, there is no single national poverty line. The poverty line varies from state to state.

[10] There has been a debate about comparability problems between the NSS surveys of 1993–1994 and 1999–2000. For present purposes, we can ignore this debate. It is sufficient to note that attempted corrections reduce the degree of poverty reduction by a factor of about one-third. However, the remaining two-thirds is also a substantial decline. The new NSS survey for 2004–2005 will enable us to obtain a better picture, when the data eventually become available.

[11] The rural/urban classification is a Census one and does not always reveal the true extent of deprivation. Certain parts of rural India are integrated into the urban mainstream, but other parts are not.

[12] Large NSS surveys are roughly held at five-year intervals. Before 1999/2000, the last one was in 1993–1994.

[13] Computed from the GDP in constant 1993–1994 (and not current) prices figures given in *Economic Survey 2004–2005*.

[14] Computed from CSO (Central Statistical Organization) figures.

[15] Within agriculture, there are different subcomponents — foodgrain (rice, wheat, coarse cereals, pulses), commercial crops (oilseed, cotton, jute and *mesta*, sugar cane), plantation crops (tea, coffee, natural rubber), horticulture and livestock, poultry and fisheries. Most of the policy discussion however tends to focus on crop output, and within that, on foodgrain, especially rice and wheat.

[16] Though these could not be attributed directly to land reforms alone.

[17] 6.51 percent of area cultivated by small and marginal farmers was under oilseed in 1970–1971, increasing to 6.71 percent in 1980–1981 and 9.22 percent in 1990–1991.

[18] Note that though differentiation in cropping strategies and technologies were built in, institutional and delivery mechanisms were largely similar.

[19] We are grateful to an anonymous referee for this comment.

[20] There are several levels at which one can articulate these concerns. For the Tenth Plan (2002–2007), there was the report of the Steering Group on Agriculture and Allied Sectors (SGAAS). This was the *Task Force on Agriculture*, set up in September 2000. Mention should also be made of the Sharad Joshi Task Force, which also had similar points to make.

[21] In particular, the drought of 2002 raised questions about the reliability of agriculture-related statistics, such as production, yields or state-level investments. In addition, the drought raised questions about the quality of early warning systems (or their lack) and monsoon data and methods used to gauge impact of deficient rainfall on crops. There are also questions about the efficacy of disaster management systems, which seem to be predicated on historical famine relief operations.

[22] *Terms of Trade*, V.N. Misra, *State of the Indian Farmer*, Vol. 15, Ministry of Agriculture and Academic Foundation, 2004. In this study, the terms of trade were found to be unfavourable to agriculture between 1952–1953 to 1964–1965, favourable between 1967–1968 to 1977–1978, unfavourable between 1978–1979 and 1990–1991 and quite favourable between 1991–1992 and 1999-2000. Favourable agricultural terms of trade may affect the rural poor adversely, but this is a separate issue.

[23] This is actually a five-year moving average, ending at the year indicated.

[24] Without appropriate water-harvesting techniques, rainwater runs off. Check dams are poorly constructed and the emphasis has been on creating waterbodies on the surface rather than on converting surface flow to subsurface flow.

[25] For fertilizer usage, this seems to be a law of diminishing returns argument. For water, the link with deceleration in the 1990s is less clearly stated. Excessive water usage is encouraged by artificially low prices. Extrapolated, there is the argument that prices are such that environmental costs are not internalized. But was there greater internalization of such costs in the 1990s? Or was there a greater switch to more water-intensive crops?

[26] It must however be noted that the gross capital formation data in agriculture do not include general investment in rural infrastructure for items such as roads, rural electrification, warehousing, etc. Further investment in R&D, development of marketing networks, grading packaging, etc. are also not included here. These are both within the private as well as public sector. For instance initiatives such as Market Development by the Ministry of Agriculture. (We are grateful to an anonymous referee for this point.) All inclusive and comprehensive data on much of these issues for rural areas are not available.

[27] This argument is not explicitly stated in SGAAS, although it figures implicitly. It is explicitly stated in the APTP, Planning Commission, September 2001.

[28] However, the point should also be made that most expenditure (90 percent) is on salaries and very little is spent on actual research.

[29] Revamping cooperatives is an integral element in pushing credit to agriculture. See, *Report of the Task Force to Study the Cooperative Credit System and Suggest Measures for its Strengthening*, August 2000. This is the Jagdish Capoor Committee.

[30] In 1998–1999, aggregate budgetary subsidies of the central and state governments are estimated to be about 13 percent of GDP at market prices, and 85 percent of the combined revenue receipts of the centre and states. Of the total subsidies about 20 percent was for agriculture. In other words agriculture subsidies accounted for about 2.6 percent of India's GDP. See Srivastava *et al.*, March 2003, Budgetary Subsidies in India: Subsidising Social and Economic Services, National Institute of Public Finance and Policy, New Delhi Also, Gulati and Narayanan, The Subsidy Syndrome in Indian Agriculture, 2003, Oxford University Press, New Delhi.

[31] We would like to thank Jikun Huang and Jun Yang of the Center for Chinese Agricultural Policy, Chinese Academy of Sciences for the GTAP forecasts.

[32] "Dreaming With BRICs: The Path to 2050," Dominic Wilson and Roopa Purushothaman, *Global Economics Paper No. 99*, Goldman Sachs. This is actually the first BRIC report. There have been two subsequent ones.

[33] One should mention that Q1 for 2005–2006 has GDP growth of 8.1 percent and most forecasts of growth in 2005–2006 are now around 7.5 percent.

[34] Legitimizing tenancy is a weaker option.

[35] The shift to the watershed approach was a recognition of such environmental problems and the success of such land development programmes varies regionally, with greater success in the west and the south. But watershed development programmes are implemented by too many departments, with conflicting guidelines. Not only is harmonization necessary, project beneficiaries need to participate in decisions taken.

[36] Data are for the period 1990–1991 to 1996–1997.

[37] These inevitably lead to inter-state disputes.

[38] Some of these are addressed by the RBI Advisory Committee on Flow of Credit to Agriculture and Related Activities from the Banking System (chaired by V.S. Vyas), which submitted its report in June 2004. There are also issues of stamp duties on land mortgages and freeing up land markets.

[39] *Economic Survey 2004–2005*. Credit is also extended through Kisan Credit Cards (KCCs) and 43.6 million cards had been issued up to March 2004, the scheme having started in 1998–1999.

[40] Where the consumer pays below the costs of procurement, storage and transportation.

[41] But one should note that because of income increases, there has been a consumption shift to high value products, a point that SGAAS makes.

[42] The overall marketed surplus/output ratio went up from 33.4 percent in 1950–1951 to 64.1 percent in 1999–2000.

[43] For all agricultural commodities, the marketed surplus handled by cooperatives is 10 percent, that by public agencies 10 percent and that by private trade 80 percent.

[44] Punjab and Haryana may be exceptions and Tamil Nadu, Kerala and Gujarat can be added to this list. Out of 7 161 regulated markets, grading facilities are available only in 1 321. Some states, such as Karnataka, have amended APMC Acts.

[45] Acharya gives a figure of 7 percent for foodgrain, 30 percent for fruit and vegetables and 10 percent for spices as being lost before reaching the market.

[46] ITC's *e-Choupal* and *choupal sagar* experiments can be mentioned, but there are other such experiments also.

[47] There are specific recommendations for the Prevention of Food Adulteration (PFA) Act, which we are ignoring.

[48] There is a separate point about India being adequately represented at international bodies that frame such standards. SPS standards may act at NTBs, but in addition, there is no question that Indian standards fall short. For instance, one can mandate that all food-processing units should have GMP/HACCP certification.

[49] In passing, poultry is classified as neither agriculture, nor industry, and thus suffers on both counts.

[50] Droughts and cyclones. Drought-prone areas are Gujarat, Rajasthan, Madhya Pradesh, Maharashtra and parts of Punjab, Haryana, Uttar Pradesh, Karnataka, Tamil Nadu, Andhra Pradesh, Bihar and West Bengal. See, *Risk Management*, Bharat Ramaswami, Shamika Ravi and S.D. Chopra, *State of the Indian Farmer*, Vol. 22, and *Natural Disaster Management*, A.R. Subbiah, *State of the Indian Farmer*, Vol. 21, Ministry of Agriculture and Academic Foundation, 2004.

[51] In publicly funded R&D, there has been an exclusive focus on rice and wheat. But one should also mention that most new areas (such as biotechnology) are in the private sector. Consequently, public–private partnerships rather than the public sector alone, provide the key.

[52] The Kelkar Task Force on Direct Taxes argued for taxation of agricultural income on the grounds of horizontal and vertical equity. That apart, there is a conduit for tax evasion since non-agricultural income is disguised as agricultural income. The proposal was for a tax rental arrangement between the centre and the states under Article 252 of the Constitution, whereby the centre would collect tax on agricultural income and pass it on to the states. See, *Report of the Task Force on Direct Taxes*, Ministry of Finance, December 2002. The Task Force estimated that because of the threshold, 95 percent of farmers would be below the personal income tax net. Political economy has ensured that this taxation proposal is redundant. In the absence of the rural sector being taxed, it is impossible to extend the number of income tax assessees from the present figure of around 30 million.

[53] Within the CSS category, one should specifically mention the Swarnajayanti Gram Swarozgar Yojana (SGSY) for self-employment of the rural poor, the Sampoorna Gramin Rozgar Yojana (SGRY) which is a wage employment scheme, the rural housing scheme known as Indira Awas Yojana (IAY), the National Social Assistance Programme (NSAP) with ingredients of old-age pensions and death benefits and the Annapurna scheme, which provides for subsidized food.

[54] There are many more. APTP says there are more than 200 centrally sponsored schemes (CSSs).

[55] NSS data for the 58th round (July–December 2002) on village facilities is an example, covering five heads of proximity to administrative centres, access to the rest of the economy, physical and social infrastructure, coverage of government support programmes and presence of private initiatives.

[56] From 1 January 1995, the Uruguay Round agreements entered into force and the historical GATT was subsumed under the WTO umbrella.

[57] Two other agreements also have indirect implications for agriculture. First, there is the agreement on TRIPs (trade-related intellectual property rights), with provisions on geographical indications (GIs) and plant and seed varieties. Plant and seed varieties have to be protected through patents, or through a *sui generis* system, which can be weaker in the sense of providing less protection to the patent holder. There is the agreement on SPS measures, which allows standards. There is documentation that SPS standards act as NTBs (non-tariff barriers). Milk, fruit and groundnut exports from India can be mentioned.

[58] The threshold is 5 percent for developed countries and 10 percent for developing countries. LDCs have no commitments in agriculture.

[59] There is a difference between developing and developed countries in terms of the reductions required and in terms of the timeframe over which reductions have to be brought about.

[60] TRQs have low tariffs for imports below a threshold and higher tariffs for imports above that threshold.

[61] There are separate commitments on value and volume of export subsidies.

[62] UNCTAD and WTO Annual Reports are good sources. Depending on the source of the estimate, 90 percent of welfare gains from market access liberalization were supposed to come from agriculture. These are welfare gains rather than trade gains and hence, accrue to consumers in developed countries also, through lower prices. But the export or trade gains to developing countries are not insubstantial.

[63] This is in addition to the regular safeguards clause and is a special feature of the AOA.

[64] The argument is simple. Protectionist pressures in the EU, Japan, Republic of Korea and even the United States, are extremely complex.

[65] The papers in *WTO Agreement and Indian Agriculture*, edited by Anwarul Hoda, Social Science Press and ICRIER, 2002, represent a comprehensive survey.

[66] They vary from year to year though. Also, the text has been kept simple. There are separate reduction commitments for product-specific and non-product-specific support.

[67] The efficiency of present public expenditure on agriculture in the form of input subsidies is an internal reform issue.

[68] Existing export subsidies are not agriculture specific. Introduction of agriculture-specific export subsidies will also run into the fiscal constraint problem.

[69] Implying QRs on balance of payments (Article XVIIIB of GATT) grounds. QRs through Articles XX and XXI of GATT continue.

[70] There is a long list, encompassing public investments, R&D, extension services, credit, insurance, infrastructure, procurement and distribution, input subsidies, contract farming, export and import controls and restrictions on inter-state movements. All of these have been mentioned earlier.

[71] There are also WTO-linked issues connected with fertilizer imports and the viability of domestic fertilizer plants, especially the ones that produce urea.

[72] Though there are other arguments as well…"On the other hand, agricultural trade has not been reformed in true spirit. Despite the framework of commitments in the Uruguay Round, prevalence of high subsidies rendered the trade arena iniquitous for different stakeholders. Secondly, the volatility of prices in the international market had caused border deprotection beyond available tariff levels…Thirdly, different countries have varying concerns, primarily on account of their production profile and trade interests. India's commodity production profile is highly diversified with a very large population dependent on agriculture for its livelihood. In the past few years, the terms of trade in agriculture have already become weak due to differentiate behaviour of prices in the domestic market, which is not as insulated from the rest of the world." We would like to thank an anonymous referee for this argument.

[73] See, *South Asia Development and Cooperation Report*, 2002 and 2004, Research and Information System for the Non-Aligned and Other Developing Countries and Nisha Taneja, Muttukrishna Sarvananthan, Binod Karmacharya and Sanjib Pohit, "Informal Trade in India, Nepal and Sri Lanka," in, Mohsin Khan editor, *Economic Development in South Asia*, Tata McGraw Hill, 2005.

[74] Consider, for instance, the export to GDP ratio, exports meaning exports of goods, as well as services. In 2003, this was 14 percent for Bangladesh, 22 percent for Bhutan, 14 percent for India, 85 percent for Maldives, 17 percent for Nepal, 20 percent for Pakistan and 36 percent for Sri Lanka (UNDP 2005). Conversely, the import (goods plus services) as a ratio of GDP was 20 percent for Bangladesh, 43 percent for Bhutan, 16 percent for India, 66 percent for Maldives, 29 percent for Nepal, 20 percent for Pakistan and 42 percent for Sri Lanka (UNDP 2005).

[75] In 2004–2005, India's aggregate exports were US$79.247 billion and India's aggregate imports were US$107.066 billion (RBI 2004–2005). These are trade figures through the Directorate General of Commercial Intelligence and Statistics (DGCI&S), used by the Ministry of Commerce, and cover merchandise trade alone. They exclude services. In addition, they exclude trade of goods that do not require customs clearance. This is more of an issue for imports than for exports. However, it is unlikely that goods trade not requiring customs clearances ever figures in trade with other SAARC members. It is fair to argue that this import figure is slightly misleading. In 2004–2005, 27.9 percent of India's import basket consisted of crude petroleum and products and these should be excluded to obtain a better idea of SAARC shares. If this is done, imports from the SAARC region as a share of total non-POL (petroleum, oil, lubricants) imports increase to 1.2 percent. India's present cycle of reforms dates to 1991.

[76] However, fish products are not covered by the WTO agreement on agriculture.

[77] There continue to be quantitative restrictions on exports of agricultural products, apart from trade of some products being channeled (canalized) through designated state trading agencies.